Wade-Bridge

Notes on the history of the fifteenth century bridge

Andrew G. Langdon

The Federation of Old Cornwall Societies

Published by

The Federation of Old Cornwall Societies
Wingfield, 5, British Road
St Agnes, Cornwall
TR5 0TX

www.oldcornwall.org

ISBN No. 978 0 902660 45 8

Typeset by the Author

Printed by R Booth Ltd, The Praze, Penryn

To Mum

A Wadebridge girl

Eleanor Joyce (Joy) Langdon

1925-2012

Author's notes

Please note: *When I refer to* **Wadebridge**, *I am talking about the town and when I refer to* **Wade-Bridge**, *I mean the bridge, i.e. 'the bridge at Wade'. When writing about the Reverend Lovibond, I use this spelling of his surname, and only use other variations of spelling if quoting from a particular historical text.*

All references to the arches of the bridge are counted from the eastern or Egloshayle end towards the western or town end, including those that are no longer visible. Today the open arches of the bridge include arch 2 on Egloshayle (eastern) side to 14 on the town or St Breock side, with arches 15, 16 and 17 hidden on the town or western side and arch 1 forming a cellar on the Egloshayle side. The reason for this is that within this work I argue that the bridge would have been built from Egloshayle bank to the St Breock bank.

The content of this book is based on my own views and interpretations and I accept any errors are my own. Notes on the engineering work are based on contemporary newspaper reports and are not necessarily technically accurate.

Foreword

Andrew Langdon is well known in Wadebridge as an athlete, and of late he has acquired a reputation as the foremost authority on Cornish Crosses, on which he has published books covering the whole of Cornwall for which deservedly he was made a Bard of the Cornish Gorseth.

Mr Langdon has turned his attention to his home town of Wadebridge, with particular reference to the bridge itself, a structure used and abused for centuries, yet the town's most precious asset, and one of the most important structures in the county.

In this work Andrew traces with meticulous research, personal knowledge and fascinating insights and accounts, the Wade-Bridge story from its 15th century beginning to the present day, referring to original documents, skilfully intertwining national and local history so bringing the importance of Wadebridge to the fore, even proving the great Cornish historian Charles Henderson in error, in dating the original bridge widening to 1847 instead of some 5 years later. Other accepted references by historians as to the age, length and even the original instigator he shows to be incorrect. He also clearly resolves the issue of river names, viz. Camel and Allen.

With some modesty Andrew says he is no academic, however it is certain that academics will find much to appreciate in this Andrew's latest offering.

This is a very comprehensive history of the bridge which will only be improved by reference to further archives, archaeology and with time.

This work will always be recognised as the definitive history of the bridge, and sets a great standard for all local historians. I have great pleasure in being part of this great work.

Finally Andrew makes a statement, which will long be remembered:-

'John Lovibond is to Wadebridge as Richard Trevithick is to Camborne.'

Councillor Collin Brewer
Cornwall Council

Acknowledgements

I would like to express my sincere gratitude to everyone who has assisted me in producing this book on Wade-Bridge. The gathering of information, documents and photographs has taken many years and I appreciate all the generosity and help which people have given me.

I would also like to thank the Publications Committee of the Federation of Old Cornwall Societies for kindly agreeing to publish this book, and to Anne Knight, Publications Officer for her help in preparing this work for publication.

Many thanks to the members of Wadebridge Old Cornwall Society, past and present. In particular to Margaret and David Bartlett who have given a great deal of their time in reading through and editing early drafts of this work, and encouraging and helping me at every stage. Also to Collin Brewer for generously allowing me to reproduce several photographs from his archive and for kindly agreeing to write a foreword to this work. To Margaret Thompson for allowing me to publish a photograph from the Hilda Hambley collection and for all her help in answering the many questions I have put to her about both the town and the bridge. To May Garland for allowing me to reproduce some of her colour slides of the second widening of the bridge, and to the committee of Wadebridge Old Cornwall Society for allowing me permission to reproduce photographs from the Roy Glasson collection depicting the second widening of the bridge and several other photographs from their archives. Mr Glasson's methodical dating of the photographs has been of great value in ascertaining the sequence of events during 1962-63.

I am indebted to artist Jane Stanley for producing the three wonderful reconstruction paintings to illustrate my chapter on historical accounts. David Thomas gave much time transcribing medieval and Tudor documents for me and Oliver Padel kindly translated and transcribed the Ministers' Accounts document, which refer to John Lovibond and additional documents. Lady Molesworth St Aubyn allowed me access to Pencarrow House on two occasions to take photographs of the paintings of Wade-Bridge and gave permission to use them in this publication. Also to Mr and Mrs Anthony Wills of Trevelver Farm for allowing me permission to reproduce the image of the bridge in their parlour.

I would like to acknowledge the help of the many institutions, libraries and depositories that have granted me permission to publish photographs and documents. These include, Angela Broome of the Courtney Library at the Royal Institution of Cornwall, Kim Cooper and staff of the Cornwall Centre at Redruth, Deborah Tritton and staff of the Cornwall Record Office, Bryn Tapper of Historic Environment, Cornwall Council, Karl Mitchell of Wadebridge Town Council, staff at the National Archives at Kew, the National Portrait Gallery at London, Paul Holden and the National Trust, John Irons of Cornwall Council's bridge department, Wadebridge Museum and David Hooley of English Heritage.

Thanks are also due to the following for providing help, information or photographs: John Armstrong, David Attwell, Eric Berry, the late Beckie Chapman, David Donaldson, Andrew Eddy, Bill Glanville, Jo Goode, the late Hilda Hambley, Derek Hannaford, the late Douglas Harbour, Duncan Harwood, Alex Hooper, Clayton Irons, David Jewell, Terry Knight, Ada Martin, Joanna Mattingly, Philip Mutton, John Neale, Thelma Riddle, Mike Rowe, David Stark, Carole Stark and Leonard Threadgold.

I also would like to acknowledge the use of postcards by local photographer J E Oatey of Wadebridge and Hartmann of London. Every effort has been made to identify the original source of photographs in this book, although some still remain anonymous.

Amongst my family, I thank my brother Adrian for his photographic expertise and for allowing me to publish several of his photographs and my brother Martin for helping to survey the levels of the bridge and causeway. My daughter Nicola helped to read through some of the early drafts of chapters, while my aunt, Mrs Peggy Irons allowed me access to my late uncle Garfield's collection of photographs. Ann Preston-Jones read through and edited this work and put up with my continuing discussions about the 'bridge' story over a number of years. Finally I would like to dedicate this work to my mother who sadly did not live to see it in print.

I have tried to acknowledge everyone who has helped with this book, but I may have accidentally missed someone, and if so I apologise.

Contents

List of plates

List of figures

Preface

When, in 1997, I was asked to give a talk on some aspect of Wadebridge history, I immediately chose our fifteenth century bridge. I had always been fascinated by its legendary history, and as a boy growing up in the town had many opportunities to gaze at the excellent mural in the town hall depicting its construction. Until 1998 I had spent my entire life living in the town, alternating between the parishes of St Breock where I was born and Egloshayle on the other side of the river, and have therefore walked the bridge thousands of times, in all conditions and have observed its many changes.

The town of Wadebridge takes its name from the bridge, which is itself at the heart of the town, uniting the two ecclesiastical parishes of St Breock and Egloshayle, yet to the majority of local people it inspires little or no interest. But ever since my days at primary school I have been able to recite a few facts about the structure:

The bridge was built in the fifteenth century, it was credited to one Reverend Lovibond, it originally had seventeen arches, was widened in both 1852 and 1962 and now has thirteen open arches.

All this information is readily available in nineteenth century parochial histories of the county and also in several local guidebooks, but when I started to research the history of the bridge in more depth, I soon realised that there were many discrepancies.

When was the bridge built? Various dates have been quoted, including both 1468 and 1485, but surely it must have taken several years to build? Who should take the credit for this project? Was it John or Thomas Lovibond who instigated the work? Some publications say John Lovibond while others, including the cast iron plaques on the bridge, state Thomas. If there were 17 arches originally and there are now only 13, where are the missing arches now and when were they filled in? As there were few roads in the fifteenth century, how did the builders transport the thousands of tons of stone to the site of the bridge? Who paid for the building of the bridge? The parishes of St Breock and Egloshayle would surely not have been able to fund such a massive project without a great deal of help! Where did the money come from to pay for the work? Some parochial histories describe the bridge as originally having 17 arches and being 320 feet long. However even today with only 13 arches it is still over 300 feet long. So how long was it when it was originally built? It must have been far more than the 320 feet often quoted. How does this bridge compare with the contemporary estuarine bridges at Bideford, Barnstaple, Exeter and Looe? Is Wade-Bridge longer, shorter, newer or older? Does it have more or less arches? Is it similar in style and construction, or different?

These are some of the questions that began to fascinate me and this book is the result of my research. The book endeavours to question some of the myths and legends appertaining to the bridge, highlight some of the discrepancies in Victorian parochial histories and build a collection of information based, where possible, on primary data from original documents.

Many Wadebridge people will recognize some of the early photographs and illustrations in this work, some of which have been reproduced in several previous publications about the town, however where possible I have tried to provide a fresh interpretation to them, provide an accurate date where possible and glean more information about Wade-Bridge from them.

I am not the first person to write a history of our medieval bridge, and I would like to acknowledge the work of Ronnie Hoyle, Reverend James West, Hilda Hambly, Eric Tatlow, Fred Luke and Peter Tutthill, who have all included information about the bridge, in their publications on the town. Clearly, this book will not be the final word on the history of the bridge, but I hope it will be seen as another piece in the jigsaw of knowledge, which will stimulate further debate and research on both the bridge and the town.

In this book I intend not only to tell the story of the bridge, but also to place it in its historical context, by looking at events within Cornwall and nationally that may have influenced its history. I have also attempted to compare Wade-Bridge with similar long estuarine bridges in Cornwall and Devon, especially those at Bideford, Barnstaple, Exeter and Looe, as well as those in other parts of the country.

This book is divided into an introduction, thirteen chapters, plus a conclusion and appendices, and is loosely set out in a chronological order. The introduction provides general information on early and medieval bridges, fifteenth century Cornwall, some of its best medieval bridges that survive, and their architectural features. Chapter 1 looks at the history and development of the village of Wade, the river Camel and the need for a bridge. Chapter 2 investigates the building of the bridge, the Reverend Lovibond and his legacy, and considers the legend of the 'Bridge on Wool'. Chapter 3 provides detailed information about the original structure and its early benefactors, as well as examining the earliest depictions of the bridge. Chapter 4 explores the approaches to the bridge, the walled causeway and the two pre-Reformation chapels that stood at either end of the bridge. Some of the historical events of the sixteenth and seventeenth centuries associated with the bridge are recorded in Chapter 5. Chapter 6 examines the role of the Bridge Trust, its trustees and the collection of pontage or tolls, while Chapter 7 looks at the need for maintenance and repairs. Chapter 8 assesses the narrowness of the bridge, and the first project to widen it. The impact of the nineteenth century development is considered in Chapter 9. Chapter 10 records travellers' accounts and their impressions of the bridge. It also examines representations of the bridge on early travel maps. Chapter 11 reports on the increased traffic with the introduction of motor vehicles and the associated need to widen the bridge for a second time. It includes a full account of the second widening scheme. Chapter 12 examines the stresses and strains caused by adding a modern structure to a medieval one and the ongoing maintenance that is required. Finally, Chapter 13 looks at the social aspects of the bridge, as a focal point in the town, a promenade and viewing platform for parades, processions and regattas, and how it has contributed so much to the town's social history. The conclusion provides the results of several years of research and offers some fresh ideas and arguments about Wade-Bridge and looks at the bridge in the twenty-first century. Further appendices provide additional data, lists of both primary and secondary sources, accounts of bridge widenings etc.

Introduction

It is not possible to write a history of Wade-Bridge without setting the bridge in its wider historical context, both within medieval Cornwall and the whole country. This introduction attempts to provide a brief overview of bridge construction and development.

There were several important stone bridges in Cornwall prior to the building of Wade-Bridge. However Wade-Bridge is particularly special, being the longest surviving medieval bridge in the county, showing late medieval craftsmanship and engineering at its best.

Early bridges

Evidence for bridges at an early date is fragmentary. Many small streams may have been crossed by a simple plank bridge, but crossings would frequently have been made at fords, or by ferry on wider rivers. The routes of Roman roads, incorporated bridges as needed. Although Harrison[1] has noted that there are hundreds of books and articles about Roman roads in Britain, few contain any detailed references to bridges, fords or ferries. Roman bridges were timber constructions, or possibly stone piers with a timber walkway. Such timber bridges would not have survived for long, although their foundations and stone piers may have become incorporated into later Anglo-Saxon bridges.[2]

Archaeological evidence at London does indicate that there was once a Roman bridge across the Thames. When the old London Bridge was de-constructed in 1832 and the piers removed, oak timbers used as piles are said to have been revealed in the river bed as well as thousands of Roman coins in the silt.[3] Dendrochronology of the timbers dated them between 55 and 60 AD. At Rochester, archaeological evidence suggests that there may also have been a Roman bridge across the Medway from Watling Street. Recently excavations and underwater exploration in 2009 by Time Team at Piercebridge in County Durham, discovered timbers of a Roman bridge, with a radiocarbon date in the first century AD.[4] Although there is no archaeological evidence of a Roman bridge at Exeter over the Exe, the site of the medieval bridge was also a Roman crossing point and it is quite possible that a wooden bridge may have existed in Roman times.

Documentary and Place-name evidence for Cornish bridges

Although there may not be any physical evidence for early bridges in Cornwall, documentary and place-name evidence indicates that some small bridges, possibly wooden rather than stone, existed before the Norman Conquest in Cornwall. In a tenth century charter for St Buryan, a boundary clause refers to *ponsprontirỳon*, the name containing Cornish *pons* + *pronter*, 'priest's bridge', while in another tenth century charter, for Lanow in St Kew, *pont magano* is recorded,

---

[1] Harrison, D, 2007. *The Bridges of Medieval England*, 31.
[2] Harrison, D, 2007. 33.
[3] Pierce, P, 2001. *Old London Bridge: The Story of the Longest Inhabited Bridge in Europe*, 16-17.
[4] Wessex Archaeology, 2010. *Piercebridge,County Durham Archaeological Evaluation and Assessment for Time Team*, ref no. 71506.

'Magano's bridge'.[5]   Today many surviving Cornish place-names containing the element *pons* refer to bridges, or indicate the former site of a bridge. Penpont meaning 'end of the bridge' or 'bridge end'; survives as a place-name at Chapel Amble in St Kew, St Breward and Altarnun, while Penpons or Penponds survives in the parishes of Kenwyn, Camborne, Merther and Madron. Chypons (*chy* + *pons*) 'bridge house', can be found at Marazion, Crowan, Cury, Towednnack, Paul and Sithney; while Ponsmere or Ponsmeur (*pons* + *meur*) meaning 'big or great bridge', is the equivalent of Norman-French Grandpont or Grampound.[6]

Fifteenth century Cornwall

The landscape of medieval Cornwall was one of dispersed settlements, small hamlets and farms with large areas of open downland, all linked by a network of footpaths and tracks.[7] Documentary evidence suggests that there were only three towns in existence at the time of the Norman Conquest, at Bodmin, Launceston and Helston.[8] However by the fifteenth century, with the establishment of additional markets, increasing trade opportunities and the patronage of both feudal and ecclesiastical lords, a network of small towns had been established.[9]   Most of these grew up or were 'planted' on main roads, at river crossings, on the coast or beside estuaries, as water was the main carrier of both communication and transport.

According to Hatcher, Cornwall's economy was firmly based on agriculture, as was much of England, although Cornwall differed in having many other primary industries.[10] By far the most important of these was the tin industry; however the county's diverse economy during the fifteenth century also included fishing, quarrying and secondary industries such as shipping, shipbuilding, and a growing textile production.

Taking place during the fifteenth and early sixteenth centuries in Cornwall, were many building projects, both ecclesiastic and secular. At this time the large majority of parish churches and many chapels were either completely rebuilt or extensively enlarged,[11] with the addition of aisles and bell towers. Many public works were also funded, including the building of bridges, causeways, quays and harbours. For example, in 1437 at Newlyn, papal indulgences were offered to those who contributed to repairing the quay.[12] Henderson considered the fifteenth century to have been the 'golden age' for bridge building.[13]   Neither Elliott-Binns nor Hatcher considered this massive

---

[5] Hooke, D, 1994. *Pre-Conquest Charter-Bounds of Devon and Cornwall*, 22-25, 33-34 and Padel, O J, 1985. *Cornish Place-name Elements*, 190.

[6] Padel, O J, 1985. 166, 180 and 190 and Henderson C G, and Coates, H, 1972 Ed. *Cornish Bridges and Streams*, 35 and 85.

[7] Preston-Jones, A, and Rose, P, 1986. 'Medieval Cornwall', *Cornish Archaeology*, **25**. 135 and 141.

[8] Preston-Jones, A, and Rose, P, 1986. 164-5.

[9] Elliott-Binns, L E, 1955. *Medieval Cornwall*, 196.

[10] Hatcher, J, 1970. *Rural Economy and Society in the Duchy of Cornwall 1300-1500*, 149.

[11] Brown, Miles H, 1964. *The Church in Cornwall*, 37, and Brown, Miles H, 1973. *What to look for in Cornish Churches*, 22.

[12] Mattingly, J, 2009. *Cornwall and the Coast: Mousehole and Newlyn*, 27.

[13] Henderson, C G, and Coates, H, 1972 Ed. 19 .

building boom as an industry in its own right: perhaps as it did not have an end product for export or consumption. However large quantities of stone would have been required for all these building projects, quarrying and stonemasonry would have been crucial industries, not to mention (in the case of churches) glazing, woodcarving and metalworking.

Medieval bridges

Perhaps the earliest stone bridge to be recorded in Cornwall was over the river Lynher: *pontem lapideum* was named as part of the boundary of the manor of Rillaton in the Launceston Cartulary, dated *c*1155-65.[14] This was probably some form of simple stone slab or clapper bridge, although today there is no evidence of where it once straddled the Lynher. Henderson notes that the most primitive looking bridges were usually clam or clapper bridges and many of these are still found in the moorland areas of both Cornwall and Devon, although not all are ancient. [15]

Other than this, the earliest documentary reference to a surviving bridge in Cornwall is of thirteenth century - Lostwithiel in 1280, while another five bridges are recorded during the fourteenth century at Helland over the Camel (1381), Respryn over the Fowey (1300), St Erth over the Hayle (1340) Yeolm over the Ottery (Attery) and Druxton over the Tamar (1370). During the fifteenth century, as well as Wade-Bridge, bridges are recorded at Treverbyn over the Fowey (1412), Ruthern over the river Ruthern (1494), Horse Bridge, Greystone Bridge and New Bridge over the Tamar (1437, 1439 and 1467) with New Bridge over the Lynher in 1478.[16]

Throughout the country as a whole, the medieval period saw many bridges constructed and according to Harrison, this number hardly altered until the eighteenth century when increased traffic required new bridges to be built and others to be widened.[17] In the time of the Civil War they were seen as strategic sites that were always defended and were often the sites of conflict.

The earliest medieval bridges were probably constructed from timber, but by the thirteenth century, stone was the preferred material. Between 1280 and 1300 a timber bridge was constructed over the river Torridge at Bideford in North Devon. Later on between 1460 and 1474 a stone bridge was built over and around the wooden structure. Evidence of these earlier structures has been found in the fabric of bridges during subsequent widening schemes, when timbers are occasionally discovered within the stonework, or sunk in the river-bed below the bridge.[18] A timber recovered from Bideford Bridge is on display at the town's museum. However there is no evidence to suggest that Wadebridge ever had a timber predecessor, before Lovibond's stone bridge.

---

[14] Hull, P L, (ed) 1987. 'The Cartulary of Launceston Priory' *Devon and Cornwall Record Society* NS, **30**, 196 .

[15] Henderon, C G, and Coates, H, 1972 Ed. 27. - According to Henderson, a Clam bridge is a wooden bridge, usually just a tree trunk across a stream or a river, while a Clapper bridge is usually constructed of massive uncut stone piers (usually granite in Cornwall and Devon), with similar flat stones forming the road way across.

[16] Henderson, C G, and Coates, H, 1972 Ed. 32-33.

[17] Harrison, D, 2007. 221.

[18] Whiting, F E, 1997. *The Long Bridge of Bideford - through the centuries*, 5.

Henderson suggests that bridges built of stone were not constructed in Cornwall until the thirteenth century, with Lostwithiel and Respryn perhaps the earliest examples. However both of these consist of only five arches, whereas to span the river Camel at Wadebridge a seventeen arch bridge was required. By the fifteenth century, the knowledge and engineering skills required to build long stone bridges had grown.

Architectural Features

Medieval bridges can be identified by their architectural features: the most obvious being that the arches are normally pointed. Good examples in Cornwall are at Lostwithiel, Respryn and Yeolm Bridge. Nevertheless, a few such as Horse (Hautes) Bridge (c1437) and Greyston Bridge (c1439) across the river Tamar have semi-circular arches, while the Trekelland (Trekellearn) Bridge (c1504) across the river Inney near Lewannick has much flatter four-centred arches reflecting its sixteenth century origin. The four arched Trewornan Bridge over the river Amble on the road from Wadebridge to St Minver, was built in the late eighteenth century, but with pointed arches in the style of a medieval bridge.

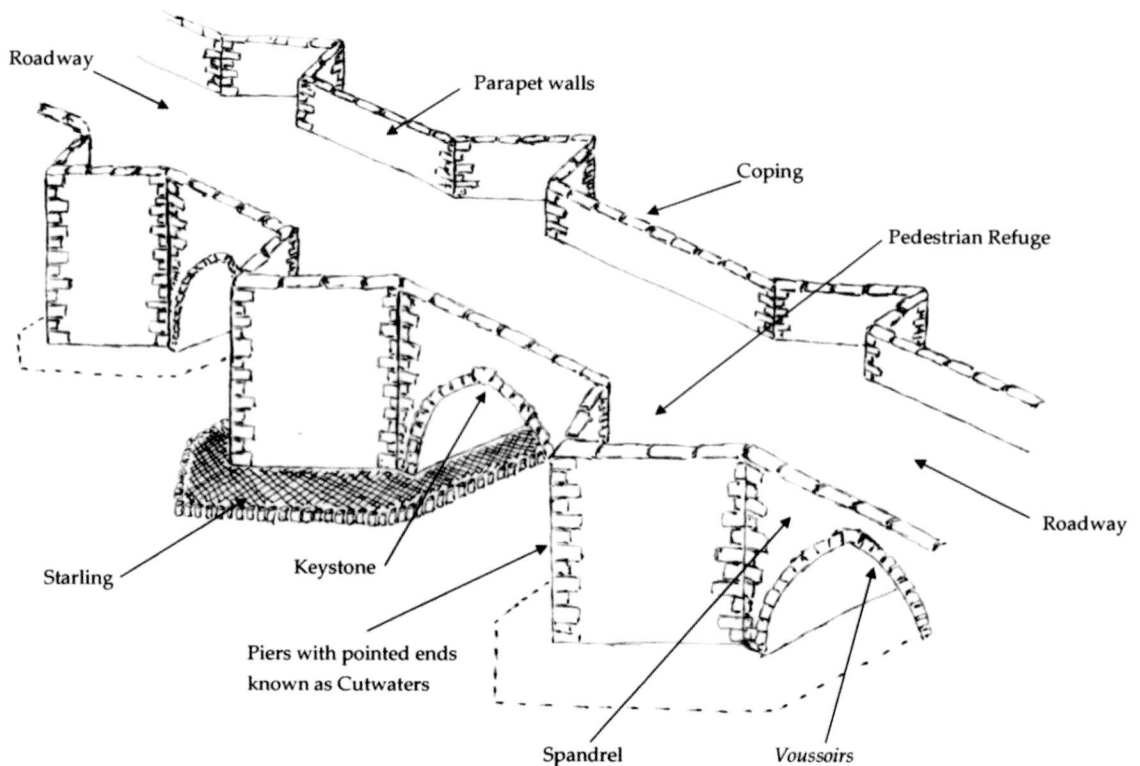

Fig 1 Parts of a Medieval bridge.

Most medieval bridges have piers with cutwaters – which have angular or pointed ends to them, to force the flow of water either side of the piers, thus reducing the pressure of water and damage from scouring. Cutwaters were of particular importance if the river was either tidal or fast flowing. If the bridge had cutwaters, these pointed piers were usually extended upwards to form angular recesses used as pedestrian refuges, as at Wade-Bridge. The majority of medieval bridges in Devon and Cornwall have this feature, which must have been essential when the bridges were so narrow.

The arches of a bridge spring from their stone piers. These arches were sometimes ribbed beneath or vaulted, creating a very strong structure, for example in the Exe Bridge at Exeter and Yeolm Bridge near Launceston. The faces of the arches are usually constructed with dressed blocks known as *voussoirs*. It is not known whether all bridges originally had stone parapets: they may not have been so important during the medieval period when there was no wheeled traffic other than hand-carts.

Foundations

The construction of firm foundations was the most difficult part of building a bridge in the medieval period. Many medieval bridges have quite shallow foundations and relied on substantial piers to spread the weight across the river bed. These piers were normally much wider than the width of the roadways they supported, thereby unintentionally aiding widening projects in the eighteenth and nineteenth centuries.[19] Constructing piers in the river was both a difficult and hazardous job and by the fifteenth century some accounts of bridge building schemes mention the use of primitive coffer dams so that the foundations could be built in the dry.[20] More often, stone transported on barges would be dumped in the river in areas where the piers were required, until the stone was raised above the low water mark and then the piers were raised on these stone platforms. Alternatively long wooden piles might be driven into the river bed, close together then bound and filled with natural materials, before raising stone piers on them. The piers could be protected from erosion by starlings (sterlings), artificial 'boat-shaped' platforms, which were built around them. The construction of starlings was also based on wooden piles driven into the river bed, which were bound or woven together with wattle branches; the platform area was then infilled with rubble, boulders and rab.

The Influence of the Church

Multi-span bridges across estuaries and rivers were normally well documented because of the enormous amount of effort required to build them. Finance had to be obtained and this was usually helped with the grant of an indulgence by a bishop. An indulgence was a pardon, or remission of time in purgatory, given in return for donations and gifts to the Church.[21] According

---

[19] See Warkworth Bridge in plate 5a and 5b.

[20] Harrison, D, 2007. 123 - Mentions that both the building of the bridges at Catterick and Sheffield used some form of coffer dam to hold back the water.

[21] A number of Cornish bridges were built or repaired with funds raised from Indulgences, Charles Henderson mentions several in his work *Old Cornish Bridges and Streams*.

to Duffy,[22] a great number of people left money in their wills, not only for direct relief of the poor, sick or imprisoned but also for many more general and secular works, and: *'the upkeep of roads, causeways and bridges was one of the commonest forms of such secular bequests'*. Henderson stated that *'at the close of the middle ages there was hardly one important bridge in Christendom, which had not been built, or maintained, by means of the indulgence system.'* The majority of pardons or indulgences were only for forty days and were often renewed. Orme indicates that the majority were for churches, chapels and public works, including bridges. He also notes that by far the largest number of references to indulgences for building projects were during the period from 1400 to 1450 - though this may only represent the popularity of indulgences at this time, or their survival rate.[23] During the building of the original Looe Bridge, no less than three indulgences were granted in the years 1411, 1415 and 1418. Further indulgences survive for Cornish bridges at Lostwithiel (1437), Treverbyn (1412) and Horse Bridge (1437). Of course, as many roads and causeways directly linked the parish church with its parishioners, or were used by pilgrims, it was in the churches interest to maintain them.

Fords, bridges and causeways were often associated with chapels. Recorded in the early fifteenth century, Chapel Rock at Marazion is beside the causeway to St Michael's Mount and was the site of a chapel dedicated to the Blessed Virgin Mary.[24] On occasions, chantry chapels were licensed to collect tolls with perhaps a hermit in residence to receive donations towards the repair of the bridge. With the Reformation most chantry and bridge chapels were abandoned. On occasion a cross might be set up instead: at Bideford a Maltese cross with an image of the Virgin Mary and Child carved in relief stood at the centre of the bridge on the south side.[25] Another Devon bridge at Horrabridge still has a cross built into its fabric, just above its central arch.

Pontage and Trusts

Pontage, or the right to collect tolls solely for the maintenance of a bridge, was usually arranged by the charity, or trust, set up to maintain the bridge. Sometimes this was a religious guild, or parish and sometimes a secular body or corporation. The larger multi-span bridges were usually maintained by an established trust, corporation or charity. Bridge Trusts or charities were in turn sometimes responsible to a religious house or civil corporation and therefore accounts were kept of repairs and grants to the bridge. Some bridge trusts were endowed by benefactors with land which was rented or leased out to raise funds for the bridge.

---

[22] Duffy, E, 1992. *Stripping the Altars*, 367.

[23] Orme, N, 1992. 'Indulgences in Medieval Cornwall' *Journal of the Royal Institution of Cornwall*, 154.

[24] Herring, P, 1993. *An Archaeological Evaluation of St Michael's Mount*, 76.

[25] Harrison, B, 2001. *Dartmoor Stone Crosses*, 195 and Whiting, F E, 2006. *The Long bridge of Bideford through the centuries*, 27.

1 *'Menne sum tyme passing over by horse stood often in great jeopardie'*

The Camel, Wade and the growth of the town.

The River

The river Camel rises on Hendraburnick Downs near Davidstow on Bodmin Moor and flows down through Camelford, passing through the parishes of Michaelstow, St Breward, St Tudy, St Mabyn, Helland, Lanivet, St Breock and Egloshayle before flowing under the medieval arches of Wade-Bridge. On its way down from Camelford it acts as a parish boundary in many places. At Tresarrett the river Camel is met by one of its tributaries the De Lank river, while another tributary, the Allen, joins it near Pendavey in Egloshayle. The estuary of the river (the tidal section from Padstow up to Wadebridge) was known as the Hayle (*Heyl*, Cornish for estuary). Up until the eighteenth century, the name Camel was only associated with the upper reaches, near Camelford, while the main length of the river between St Breward and Wadebridge was known as the river Alan. The change in names can be attributed to Ordnance Survey who incorrectly named the rivers on their maps. The river Allen (not to be confused with the stretch of the river Camel that was formerly called the Alan) was formerly known as the river Layne (Laine) and flowed under Laine Bridge (Sladesbridge).[1] The name Camel can be traced back to 1259 when Camelford was granted its charter, and according to Padel, it may combine *camm* 'crooked' with perhaps a river name *el* or *ell*, - simply meaning the 'crooked one'.[2]

The name Wade-Bridge

Until the building of the bridge that united the two parishes, there was only a small settlement or village on the St Breock bank, known as Wade. The name Wade is derived from the Old English *wæd*, 'a ford', and the Old English *brycg*, 'bridge' was only added once the bridge had been constructed: hence Wade-Bridge, or 'the bridge at Wade'. Another village called St Nicholas-at-Wade on the Isle of Thanet in Kent, also takes its name from *wæd*, 'to ford', and the parish church of St Nicholas. The Charter of Endowment of lands for the maintenance of the bridge that was vested in twelve trustees in 1476 calls the bridge *Wada-Bridge*; it was also known as *Wardbridge*, before a standard form of spelling had been adopted. A list of the various spellings of Wadebridge from documentary sources can be found in the appendices.

---

[1] Padel, O J, 1988. *Cornish Place Names*, 176.
[2] Padel, O J, 1988. 63.

Tintagel

River Camel

River Allen
formerly
the Layne

CAMELFORD

Hayle, Padstow
Haven or
Camel Estuary

River De Lank

St Kew

St Tudy

Rock

St Minver

PADSTOW

St Mabyn

Tresarrett

WADEBRIDGE

Sladesbridge

River Camel
formerly the Alan

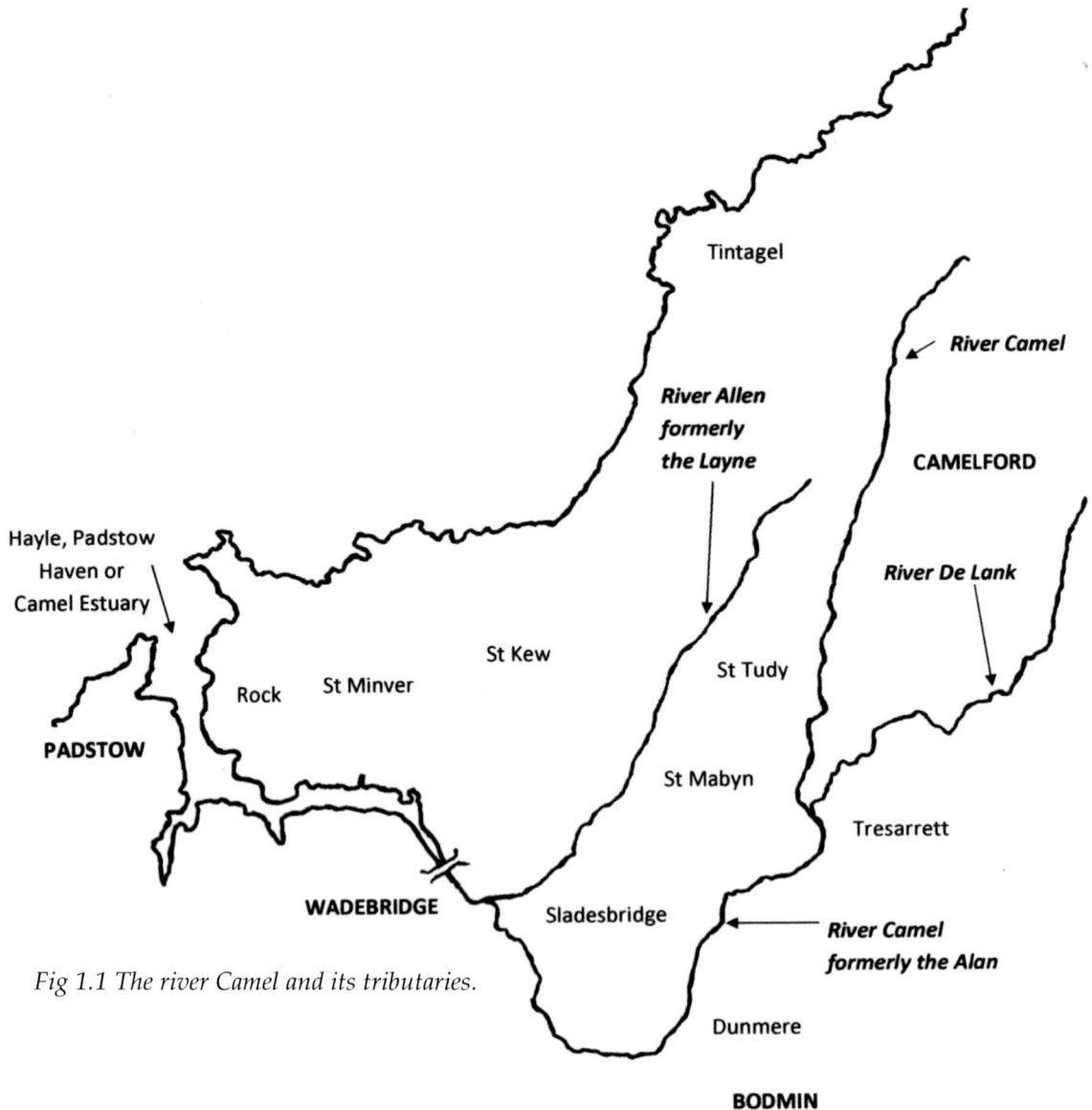

Fig 1.1 The river Camel and its tributaries.

Dunmere

BODMIN

Early references to the village of Wade

In 1312, Edward II granted Walter de Stapledon, Bishop of Exeter, the right to hold a market within the manor of Pawton on a Friday. Two fairs could also be held, one on the festival of St Vitalis the Martyr (28th April) and the other at Michaelmas (29th September).[3] West considered that this market and also the fairs were held in the village of Wade.[4] Clearly a market in a village

[3] Hingston-Randolph, F C, 1901. *The Register of Walter de Stapledon, Bishop of Exeter (AD 1307-1326), 373.*
[4] West, J, 1991. *St Breock and Wadebridge: A Contribution to a History of Parish and Town, 31.*

adjacent to a river would make good sense, as during this period the majority of goods were transported by water. The first reference to the village of Wade by its name was in 1382 during the reign of Richard II, when Bishop Brantyngham of Exeter gave a license to one Sir Thomas Stayndrope, Rector of the parish church of *Poutone* (Pawton) now St Breock, to celebrate the mass at a chapel in Wade.[5] The chapel was situated on the western side of the river. This suggests that even at this early date, before the building of the bridge, the village of Wade was beside an important crossing point, or at least a popular route-way through the northern part of the county. According to Shepherd, the village of Wade was again documented in 1484 when John Carowe was named in a legal action, although by this time the bridge had been constructed.[6]

Wade or Wadebridge during the fifteenth century

At the time that the bridge was built during the 1460s and probably for a few decades after, the village was known as both Wade and Wadebridge. In 1499, the heirs of Richard Criff of Wade are recorded in the manor of Perlees rental as Free tenants and also one John Leche as a Conventionary tenant at *Wadebrigge*, again suggesting that both names for the village were being used.[7] When the bridge was still under construction, a medieval reference in the Bodmin Churchwardens Accounts dated between 1469 and 1472, refers to timber being shipped up to *'Wadebrygge with yn the parish of Egloshayle'*, for building work at St Petroc's Church, while additional references in the same document record, *'cariage for barelles of lyme'* to Pendavey in Egloshayle.[8] Pendavey was held by the Priors of Bodmin and had a quayside for trading. These references would suggest that the bridge was in existence, if not completed, by 1472. It is not known whether there were any lime kilns at Wade or Padstow during the fifteenth century, or if the lime was shipped in from elsewhere. Once at Pendavey the barrels of lime would have been taken overland to Bodmin. In 1501, the accounts for the building of Berry Church at Bodmin record payment to William Cok for bringing a crane from St Issey to Pendavey, probably up the river and under the newly completed bridge, after which it would have been taken overland to Bodmin.[9] This is another indication that the river was in use as a highway and that Wade or Wadebridge, as the village became known once the bridge was built, is likely to have been profiting from this traffic, particularly bringing goods upstream to Egloshayle and beyond.

The dangers crossing the river and the need for a bridge

The river Camel has always been dangerous and even in recent years several people have fallen foul of the river's deceiving currents. An entry in the Egloshayle parish registers states that nine parishioners drowned in January 1617 and were buried in the churchyard the same day, five men

---

[5] Hingeston-Randolph, F C, 1901. *The Register of Thomas de Brantyngham, Bishop of Exeter (AD 1370-1394)*, 485.

[6] Shepherd, P, 1980. *The Historic Towns of Cornwall: An Archaeological Survey*, 61. Shepherd unfortunately does not state where he found this reference.

[7] Fox, H S A, and Padel, O J, 2000. *The Cornish Lands of the Arundells of Lanherne, fourteenth to sixteenth centuries*, 140-41.

[8] Wilkinson, J J, 1874. *Receipts and Expenses in the Building of Bodmin Church AD1469 to 1472*.

[9] Cornwall Record Office, B/Bod/314/1 Payments account, Berry tower, 4th October 1501.

and four women.[10] Presumably they were drowned in the river, although this is not made explicit. Perhaps they were strangers to the area trying to avoid a toll? It seems probable that before the bridge was built, even more people are likely to have lost their lives fording the river.

During the medieval period, the river Camel would have been much wider than it is today. All the area now covered by the Town Quay properties and the Bridge Surgery were part of the river until the early nineteenth century, whilst the north-east side of the Platt would have been marshland and mud banks. Crossing the river at low tide today is not easy as even with less than two feet of water flowing it can be difficult to stand up when wading across. In the winter months or during spring tides, crossing the river would have been impossible, but walking inland several miles to cross in shallower water could be a great inconvenience. For travellers, a bridge would have been a great benefit, saving many hours on a journey by not having to wait for low tide, locate an alternative safe crossing point or queue for a ferry.

Ferries on the Camel

In 1535, Leland noted that prior to the bridge being built there was *'a Fery a 80 yeres syns, and Menne sumtyme passing over by horse stood often in great jeopardie'* (a ferry eighty years since and that sometimes men crossing on horseback stood in great jeopardy).[11] Henderson, in his notes on Cornish ferries, does not mention a ferry at Wade, but does record the Black Tor or Black Rock ferry. The Black Rock ferry belonged to the manor of Penmayne in St Minver parish and linked the village of Rock with Padstow as early as 1337.[12] This was at the estuary of the river Camel and was used for both foot-passengers and horses. In 1808, when the Reverend Richard Warner and a friend crossed the river at Padstow, his friend's horse climbed into a boat and was ferried across the estuary, but Warner's horse refused to go on board. He was persuaded to allow the horse to swim across the estuary: a journey he bitterly repented afterwards, as although the animal survived, it was exhausted and near to death.[13] At Wade, the passage from the Egloshayle bank to St Breock was much narrower than at Padstow and therefore a larger flat-bottomed ferry with a rope to either bank would have been possible. This would have enabled foot-passengers, horses and hand-carts to be transported. One can imagine that on a high tide a frightened animal on the ferry could have caused panic amongst travellers on board. On the western bank at Wade there may have also been some form of pontoon-like walkway across the mud flats to allow travellers to reach the water's edge at low tide. A chapel stood on either bank of the river crossing near the village of Wade enabling prayers to be made for a safe crossing.

---

[10] Cornwall Record Office, P52/1/1 Egloshayle parish registers, deaths 1617, nine people drowned and were buried in Egloshayle churchyard at the same time, they were Robert Mychell, John Garrett Jun., Jane, wife of Air Hawlys, Jane Cowling, wydowe, Jane Braddon, wydowe, Margarett Pears, Richard Gritton, John Lander of Lenkinhorne and Nicholas Frovot. Buried 21st day January 1617, Ralphe Holden, Minister.

[11] John Leland's Itinerary was published in the appendices of Polsue, J, 1872. *A Complete Parochial History of Cornwall* **IV**, 67-92.

[12] Henderson, C., 1963 ed. 'Cornish Ferries' *Essays in Cornish History*, 167.

[13] Warner, Revd. R, 1809. *A Tour through Cornwall in the Autumn of 1808*, 328-9.

The Funnel effect – Trading opportunities

According to West, the town grew up by the river Camel at the highest point where large vessels could reach, but also at almost the lowest point where the river could be forded.

It was quite common in the middle ages for a town to develop on the banks of a river, where a major route-way existed. According to Beresford traders would be attracted to fords, ferry-crossings and bridges, where traffic was funnelled to a narrow point to cross the river.[14] The delaying factor was of great importance to trade: the longer travellers had to wait, prior to crossing the river, the better to persuade them to buy goods. Wading a ford might entail an even longer wait if the river was tidal, or flooded. If a ferry existed, there would still be delays, loading and unloading goods and queuing at busy times. Both ferries and bridges made a charge for crossing, and the collection of tolls or pontage was in itself a delay. It was not only the sale of goods on the river bank that travellers grew to expect, but also the sale of any goods which happened to be transported up or down the river. In addition, the sale of services such as stabling, and lodgings for overnight stops, blacksmiths' shops and farriers to maintain the traffic or shoe a horse, would have all been in great demand. Whether at a ford, ferry crossing or bridge, small communities tended to develop beside river crossings. It is not surprising that the former fair plot and market house at Wadebridge were situated close to both the bridge and the river to catch the passing trade.

Many such towns acquired names pertaining to their location: some like Stratford, Camelford, Chelmsford and Oxford have names which reflect their importance before a bridge was constructed; others like Uxbridge, Cambridge, Trowbridge and Bridgwater are named after the bridge and Wadebridge, of course is named after both ford and bridge. Despite the trading opportunities presented by the funnel effect, the town of Wadebridge progressed very little until the nineteenth century and perhaps was hampered in its development by never gaining formal urban status through the acquisition of a town charter.

Growth of the town

Wadebridge is a modern town compared with most in Cornwall. It has no early Christian origin like its neighbours Padstow and Bodmin, or the borough status boasted by Camelford and St Columb Major, so for these reasons alone, the small village of Wade may have been held back in its development. Padstow with its early monastic site grew mainly due to its maritime trade, while its position at the mouth of the estuary would have given it control of all the trade on the river Camel. Even today it is the Padstow Harbour Commissioners that control the tidal river, while the Lords of the Manor (the Prideaux family) would have formerly controlled the maritime trade. A further reason why Wadebridge may have been slow to develop is that it has always been difficult to navigate the river from Padstow because of the many sand banks that exist, and far easier to dock at Padstow and send the cargo up to Wadebridge on barges.

It is difficult to gauge the size of Wade village prior to the building of the bridge, or of Wadebridge afterwards. Most early travel writers mention the existence of the bridge but few

---

[14] Beresford, M, 1988. *New towns of the Middle Ages*, 115.

comment on the town that grew up beside it.   From the Lay Subsidy Rolls that recorded those eligible to pay tax during the reign of Henry VIII, the parish of St Breock appears quite prosperous compared to the majority of Cornish parishes.   In 1525 there are eighty-five parishioners named as paying tax and in 1543 there were seventy-three men.   However these returns do not stipulate if any of those paying tax lived in Wadebridge itself.   In 1586, Edward Arundell of Lanherne left twenty nobles in his will to the poor of Wadebridge (as well as leaving money towards the maintenance of the bridge) – a fact which suggests a sizeable population.

The growth in maritime trade is indicated by Bartlett who, referring to the Maritime Survey of 1626 in the reign of King Charles I, stated that there were twenty-nine bargemen in the parishes of St Breock and Egloshayle.[15]   King Charles had requested a survey of all the ships in the realm due to the war with France and Spain.   In 1755 while George II was King, the Reverend William Wynne's itinerary recorded seeing clay ovens for sale on the river bank beside the bridge.[16]   He was told that they were made at Bideford, suggesting trade links with other coastal towns in the area.   Wynne also states that there was a 'pretty good Inn' on the side of the river, close to the bridge, probably where the Swan Hotel stands today.   In 1830 the building on this site was known as the Wadebridge Inn and was in the tenancy of John Thomas, by 1847 Thomas had renamed it the Commercial Hotel.[17]

On the St Breock, or western, side of the river much of the early development was on Molesworth Street, Whiterock Hill and West Hill, where a rocky foundation could be found.   Development on the quaysides would have probably consisted of timber built warehouses. According to Gilbert, even as late as the beginning of the nineteenth century there were only fifty houses at Wade with about another fifty on the Egloshayle side of the bridge.[18]   The earliest houses surviving today on the Egloshayle side of the river are at Bridge End and Bradfords Quay Road.   These include the Manor House at Bridge End and Spring Gardens at the junction of Flora Place and Bradfords Quay Road.   Some older properties were casualties of road improvements to the approaches of the bridge including Bridge House (1853) and Riverside House (1954).[19]   On the town side there was formerly St Michael's chapel and by 1838 the Wadebridge Institution was built at the junction of Harbour Road and Molesworth Street and adjacent to the first arch of the bridge.   By the end of the eighteenth century most of the property on either side of Molesworth Street between its junction with the Platt and Whiterock Road had already been built.   The Molesworth Arms Hotel dates from the seventeenth century as do the houses known as the Elms, Mulberry Cottage and Pridham House at the top of the street.[20]   According to James West, the Elms and Pridham House

---

[15] Gray, T,(ed.) 1990. *Early-Stuart Mariners and Shipping: The Maritime Survey of Devon and Cornwall, 1619-35*, 55-6, and Bartlett, J, 1996. *Ships of North Cornwall*.

[16] Wynne, W, 1755. 'A visit to Cornwall in 1755' by William Wynne, edited by Colin Edwards *Journal of the Royal Institution of Cornwall*, 1981, pt.4 **VIII** NS.

[17] *Pigot's Directory of Cornwall* 1830, and *William's Commercial Directory of the Principal Market Towns in Cornwall* 1847.

[18] Gilbert, C S, 1817. *An Historical Survey of the county of Cornwall* **II,** 642.

[19] The Manor House or Mansion House is grade II listed (67868), while Spring Gardens is also Grade II (67842) and Gonvena House is grade II listed (67838).

[20] Reference to Listed Building reports at www.britishlistedbuildings.co.uk.

date from 1580, although he does not provide a reference or evidence for this.[21]   The schedule and parish Tithe map for St Breock published in 1841 shows that almost all the property on Molesworth Street at this time was owned by Sir William Molesworth and leased out to individuals. The Tithe map also shows the start of further development on Whiterock Road, Park Road, Chapel Street and Trevanson Street, but nothing on Eddystone Road which started a few years later (see plate 1).

The development of quays on both sides of the river increased and by 1817, Gilbert recorded that, *'Wadebridge had commodious cellars and timber yards with good anchorage for boats, barges which come up daily from Padstow and supply the inhabitants with goods.'* [22]   Yet in 1801, Britton and Brayley did not see the maritime trade and state that *'Wadebridge is an inconsiderable village, only noted for a stone bridge of seventeen arches'*.[23]   Nevertheless the journal of Thomas Pope Rosevear, a merchant, quarry owner and landowner from Boscastle, suggests that Wadebridge was a thriving place.[24] During 1826 he visited Wadebridge from his home in Boscastle many times, either by gig or horse and much of his business in the town was overseeing shipments of grain like barley and wheat to vessels in the port. He also regularly visited Mr Symons the Attorney, staying overnight at an Inn or with Mr Pollard at Clapper.   Rosevear also records visiting Wadebridge Fair on numerous occasions.   This suggests that even by the 1820s the town was growing due to its trade links.

The area around the Platt, which was always prone to flooding, did not develop fully until the late nineteenth century. The area where the Co-op stands today was formerly the market place and where Boots the chemist is the fair plot or park. The hamlet of Treguddick (the Health centre and Brooklyn House area) was separated from the village of Wade by the Polmorla River, a tributary of the river Camel. The ground level and quay side was over six feet lower than it is today, and if one looks across from Treguddick Bridge to the back of Eyres Garage, one can still see where the former road level was.   Until 1888, many of the buildings on the railway side (east) of the Platt were timber-built workshops. Although a row of cottages did exist between Treguddick Bridge and where the Molesworth Exchange (now known as the Town Hall) was built, they must have often flooded.   Slowly during the twentieth century the ground level was raised and more substantial stone-built properties emerged on the Platt.

Which route to take?
Even after Wade-Bridge was built, travellers continued to use the Black Rock ferry at Rock when travelling down the north coast and today the ferry is still in daily use.   Until the turnpike road was constructed across Bodmin Moor (the modern A30 trunk road), the main route from Exeter avoided the moors, entered the county at Launceston went across Laneast Downs to Hallworthy, St Teath and St Endellion, through St Minver to Rock and crossed the estuary to Padstow. This is made clear from John Ogilby's map of 1675, a strip map that shows travellers were routed to Rock

[21] West, J, 1991. 33.

[22] Gilbert, C S, 1817. *An Historical Survey of he county of Cornwall* **II**. 642.

[23] Britton, J, and Brayley, E W, 1801. *The Beauties of England and Wales*. 520.

[24] Raymond-Barker, J and Clark, C, (ed.) 2006. *The Boscastle Journal by Thomas Pope Rosevear 1825 – 1846*.

to cross the Camel estuary rather than to Wadebridge to use the bridge (see plate 2b).[25] At Long Cross in St Endellion parish there is an eighteenth century direction post, which displays a four-sided granite head and instead of indicating the route to Wadebridge, has Padstow clearly marked on it - pointing the way to Rock and the ferry (see plate 2a).[26] This is a testimony to the fact that the route via Padstow to St Columb was both quicker and cheaper (the ferry toll compared to the bridge toll), or influence was being exacted on travellers – perhaps by Padstow traders, or local landowners with a vested interest. Another reason may have been that the road to Wadebridge was too rough until the turnpike was created through the town in 1760. When the turnpike was completed we see more references to routes across the bridge.

---

[25] The strip maps drawn by cartographers such as Ogilby only showed one route, indicating road junctions to other destinations, but giving the traveller only one way to his or her destination.

[26] The granite direction post, which is 1.8 metres high, records the direction to Padstow, Port Quin, Roscarrock and Port Isaac.

2 'he layed pakkes of wolle for fundation'

The building of the bridge

The building of Wade-Bridge took place at the time of the Wars of the Roses, when the Houses of Lancaster and York were each fighting for the Crown. In 1461, when the work on the bridge is thought to have started, Henry VI had just been deposed and Edward IV had taken the throne of England. He in turn was deposed in 1470 by Henry VI, but returned to the throne again in 1471. Despite this political turmoil, Cornwall appears to have been uninvolved, although after Henry Tudor took the throne in 1485, Cornwall became disaffected when the King imposed heavy taxes and in 1497 the Cornish marched to Blackheath in protest.

Reverend Lovibond – Thomas or John?

Lovibond, a vicar of Egloshayle, has traditionally been given the credit for organising and raising the funds necessary for building the bridge. Yet there has always been some confusion in parochial histories about whether it was a John Lovibond or a Thomas Lovibond who was responsible (see below). It was Sir John Maclean in his *Parochial and Family History of the Deanery of Trigg Minor* who first recorded that John Lovibond was granted a licence in 1468 to draw stone from a quarry at the manor of Penmayne in St Minver parish.[1] The author has been unable to locate the source of Maclean's information, which may be in the Duchy of Cornwall Archives; however an even earlier reference to Lovibond drawing stone has been discovered in a document at the National Archives at Kew, showing that Lovibond was taking stone from a quarry at Penmayne for a number of years.

Licence to draw stone

This reference, found in the Ministers' Accounts for the first and second years of Edward IV's reign, provides a date of 1461-3, some six years earlier than the date given by Maclean.[2] It records that John Lovibond received a licence to draw stone from a quarry on the Duchy manor of Penmayne (see plate 3). The reason the stone was required is not stated, but it seems likely that it was intended for building the bridge, which may have been started as early as 1461. The reference is written in medieval Latin and is abbreviated, but in full the text reads, '*Et de:- iiijd de Johanne Lovibond cleric pro licencia habenda fodendi lapides in quadam quarraria ibidem iuxta Penmayn habenda sibi quamdiu domino Regi placuerit prout patet per rotulum curie anni quarti precedentis*'.

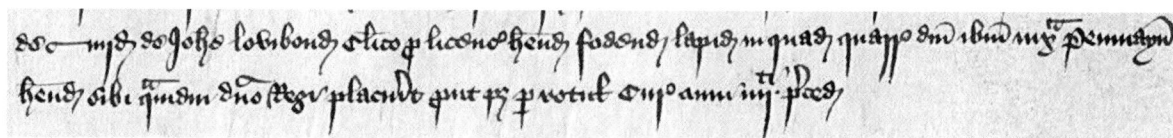

Fig 2.1 - Ministers' Accounts 1st & 2nd Edward IV with John Lovibond reference © National Archives.

---

[1] Maclean, John, 1879. *The Parochial and Family History of the Deanery of Trigg Minor in the County of Cornwall*, **III**, 55.
[2] National Archives, SC6/821/1 (Ministers Accounts 1st & 2nd Edward IV).

Translated, this reads: 'And [he renders account] concerning 4d from John Lovibond, clerk, for having a licence of digging stones in a certain quarry of the lord there by Penmayn, for him to hold as long it shall please the lord king, as is shown by the court roll of the preceding 4th year'. [3]

John not Thomas

It is also a John Lovibond whose name appears on the Charter of Endowment setting up the Wada-Bridge (Wade-Bridge) Trust in 1476. We learn of John Lovibond's death in January 1477-8 in a dispute concerning his estate between his executor John Forde and John Raskarrek (Roscarrock) over land at Lemail in the parish of Egloshayle.[4] There are according to Maclean at least another three further documents that name John Lovibond as vicar of Egloshayle during the 1460s and 1470s when the bridge was being constructed. In 1461-2 and 1475 he is recorded suing individuals in Egloshayle and St Erme parishes, while his name as vicar of Egloshayle occurs in an Inquisition dated 15th January 1461-2.[5]

Inaccuracies in Parochial Histories

Although most nineteenth century parochial histories of Cornwall record Thomas Lovibond as the mastermind behind the project, documentary evidence (shown here) suggests that it was in fact a *John* Lovibond who was involved. According to the list of incumbents on the north wall of the nave at Egloshayle church, John Lovibond became vicar of Egloshayle in 1461 and was succeeded by one Thomas Marshall in 1475. Below Thomas Marshall on the list is Thomas Lovibond, but with no date against his name; this is followed by John Ime in 1476.[6]

Most of the errors appear to stem from the historian William Hals who in 1736 stated that the bridge was built by a Thomas Lovibond and that he was granted an indulgence to raise funds in 1485 to build the seventeen arch bridge. Since then, the majority of

Fig 2.2 - List of Rectors and Vicars of Egloshayle Church.

---

[3] I am indebted to Oliver Padel for transcribing and translating this reference.

[4] National Archives, C1/59/309 (Court of Chancery Edward IV or Richard III) .

[5] Maclean, J, 1879. **III**, 17.

[6] Another list of the Egloshayle incumbents published in Polsue's *Parochial History of Cornwall*, 1867, **I**, 314, does not mention John Lovibond, but records Thomas Lovibond stating that he does not appear in the registers of the diocese.

parochial histories have just reproduced this account, including Lake's Parochial History of Cornwall by Joseph Polsue.[7]

Hals account reads:

> *'Now this licence of all spiritual benedictions, collections, and commutation of penance, throughout the counties of Cornwall and Devon, was there granted by Dr Peter Courtenay, Bishop of Exeter, to Thomas Loveybound, then vicar of Egles-hayle, his chaplain or vicar, in 1485, who raised a considerable sum of money by that means, viz. absolution, as also from charitable and well-disposed Christians. The undertaker, that expert mason John de Harlyn, and the treasurer Loveybound, brought the bridge's building to that perfection as it now stands'* [8]

Sir John Maclean on the other hand questioned whether Thomas Lovibond ever actually existed, for there is no record of either his name, or the Indulgence referred to by Hals, in the Episcopal Registers of the Bishop of Exeter. Existing documentation also disproves the date 1485, for William of Worcester, visiting Cornwall in 1478, noted its existence seven years before the date claimed by Hals. In addition, there are transcripts of the original Charter of Endowment dated 1476 that set up the Bridge Trust and trustees on completion of the bridge.

The author could find no references to a John Thomas or a Thomas John Lovibond in any of the surviving records, which would have perhaps cleared up the discrepancy.[9] According to Gilbert,[10] with the funds and stone left over from building the bridge, Lovibond built the tower at Egloshayle Church. Today, on the north side of the west door to the tower, an escutcheon bearing the arms of Lovibond held by an angel can still be seen. On the shield are three hearts linked by a ribbon and inscribed, *I Loveybound*: the 'I' being an old fashioned 'J', therefore it refers to John Lovibond rather than Thomas.

Fig 2.3 - Lovibond Shield on the west door of Egloshayle Church tower.

---

[7] Polsue, J, 1867. **I**, 128-9.

[8] Hals, W, in Polsue, J, 1867. **I**, 311.

[9] The Lovibond family came from the Salisbury area, in the Charter of Endowment John Lovibond is recorded as being a Canon of the Cathedral Church of Salisbury and even today there are still Lovibonds living in the Salisbury area, including a Lovibond Brewery.

[10] Gilbert, D, 1838. *The Parochial History of Cornwall*, **I**, 373-374.

Hals also appears to be the only historian to name John de Harlyn as the builder of the bridge. Obviously John Lovibond would have needed a master craftsman and architect to design the structure and organise the large work force needed for such a massive project; but there is no record of the actual building of the bridge, or accounts of the labour and materials required, or who paid for it. We only know that the original stone is likely to have been brought from a quarry belonging to the manor of Penmayne. Hals, however, must have learnt this name from somewhere so perhaps he was repeating a local tradition or folk memory. Furthermore, although Hals suggested that Lovibond raised funds by an Indulgence, no record of such a document exists for Wade-Bridge. This is not to say that Lovibond did not raise funds by this means, which was a normal way of raising money for such a project, but no documentary evidence survives to prove it.

Charter of Endowment

In 1476, John Lovibond created a Charter of Endowment, choosing twelve gentlemen from the area as *feoffees* or trustees to the bridge, and giving them responsibility for twenty pounds worth of land, which was donated by John Carminowe of Glynn in Cardinham and Thomas Cayne of Henson in St Minver, to provide an income for the maintenance of the bridge. The trustees included members from many of the most influential Cornish families in the district at the time. During January 1928, a nineteenth century transcript of this document was found by historian Charles Henderson in the attic of the Manor House, the former offices of Symons and Reynolds, Solicitors, at Bridge End, Wadebridge (now Macmillans). Henderson wrote that 'I could not find the original of this charter, though it was apparently in the custody of Mr Symons as Solicitor to the Trust in 1845. I found several certified transcriptions *c*1830'.[11] Today, one copy is housed in the Courtney Library at the Royal Institution of Cornwall and another at the County Record Office.[12] There is now no knowledge of the whereabouts of the original document.

The Transcript found by Henderson is titled 'Grant from John Loveybound of certain messuages in Egloshayle for repairing Wada Bridge, with powers of Attorney to deliver seizin', and reads as follows:

> *'Know yr present and to come that I John Loveybound a Canon of the Cathedral Church of Salisbury and perpetual vicar of the parish church of Egloshayle have given, granted, and by this my present Deed intended, confirmed, to Thomas Arundell Esquire, Edward Courtnay Esquire, John Carmynowe Esquire, John Reskarack Esquire, Michael Pedyt, Richard Bylyon, Thomas Bera, Thomas Lymbery of Padstow, Thomas Bera Junior, Richard Tomeow, Richard Trefry otherwise Tremer, Robert Loveybound and John Forth, all those messuages lands and tenements in Egloshayle with their appurts [appurtenances] which I have of the gifts and grants of John Carmynowe and Thomas Cayne of Henson to me severally made.*

---

[11] RIC.HP14 - Charles Henderson's notes dated 1928 on Wade-Bridge can be found in the Courtney Library at the Royal Institution of Cornwall, they have been written in a small account book, which has Wade Bridge on its spine and General Account 1826 on the front cover.

[12] Cornwall Record Office, DDX.450/181.

To have all the aforesaid messuages lands and tenements with all their appurts [appurtenances] to the aforesaid Thomas Arundell, Edward Courtnay, John Carmynow, John Reskarack, Michael Pedyt, Richard Bylyon, Thomas Bera, Thomas Lymbery, Thomas Bera Junior, Richard Tomeow, Richard Trefry otherwise Tremer, Robert Loveybound and John Forth, their heirs and assigns for the support and repair of a certain bridge called Wada Bridge and if it shall happen that any of the aforesaid Feoffees be impleaded by writ of the Lord the King, and the aforesaid Feoffees so impleaded in such action in the court of the said Lord the King shall acknowledge, render up, or make default, for the tenements aforesaid, or for any parcel thereof, or shall do any other thing by which the same shall be lost in the court aforesaid, from which my will in no wise can be observed, that from thence forth the possession and freehold in them, of the aforesaid messuages lands and tenements, shall totally cease and be annulled.

In witness where of the one part of these Indentures remaining in the possession of the aforesaid Thomas Arundell, Edward Courtnay, John Carmynow, John Reskarack, Michael Pedyt, Richard Bylyen, Thomas Bera, Thomas Lymbery, Thomas Bera Junior, Richard Tomeow, Richard Trefry otherwise Tremer, Robert Loveybound and John Forth. I the aforesaid John Loveybound have put my seal, and to the other part remaining in the possession of me John Loveybound, the aforesaid Thomas Arundell, Edward Courtnay, John Carmynow, John Reskarack, Michael Pedyt, Richard Bylyen, Thomas Bera, Thomas Lymbery, Thomas Bera Junior, Richard Tomeow, Richard Trefry otherwise Tremer, Robert Loveybound and John Forthe have put their seals, these persons being witnesses Nicholas Roche, John Treglyzghy and John Somon.'[13]

One mystery is that although at the bottom of the transcription of the Charter of Endowment it is stated that there were twelve seals affixed, thirteen names appear on it. It is also interesting to note that Henson or Hensons was close to Penmayne and was probably part of the manor during the fifteenth century. [14]

It is assumed from this Charter of Endowment that the bridge was completed, or was nearing completion when it was drawn up. Lovibond may have wished to set up the endowment of land and create the Trust while he was fit and able and, as previously recorded, he died within two years of the Charter being written.

Local Benefactors

Wade-Bridge was not the only bridge to have been built through the inspiration and drive of one man. History has often accredited individual benefactors who were perhaps also concerned to speed their passage through purgatory by good deeds and actions. At Barnstaple, Sir Henry de Tracey was benefactor to the bridge: he, like Lovibond, endowed his bridge with land and

---

[13] John Lovibond notes Robert Lovibond, but does not mention whether he is his son? No further references to Robert Lovibond have been found.
[14] According to Collin Brewer there is a small cottage known as Henson between St Minver and Amble.

property (at West Lyn) to help its future maintenance.[15]   At Bideford, legend suggests that another local clergyman, Sir Richard Gurney, was responsible for the building of their bridge.[16] The Exe bridge was built by Nicholas Gervase and his son Walter, who was mayor of Exeter during the 1230s.[17]   Although it is not known who was responsible for the building of Looe Bridge, it was perhaps a clergyman as a chapel was built over its central arch; in 1436 Sir John Gynys obtained a licence from the bishop to celebrate mass there, he may perhaps have been responsible for building the bridge too.[18]

Master Masons and workforce

When looking at the original medieval bridge at high tide one has to admire the medieval craftsmen who built it. Building such a massive structure on a tidal river must have taken a great deal of organisation and technical expertise. Yet where did the master mason or architect John de Harlyn (if Hals is correct) and Lovibond find their inspiration for such a construction? Wade-Bridge was a late medieval bridge and there were already three long stone bridges existing in Cornwall and Devon when Wade-Bridge was started. These were at Barnstaple, Exeter and Looe, and a wooden bridge at Bideford, across the river Torridge, was being converted into a stone bridge between the years 1459 and 1474, the work starting just before the construction of Wade-Bridge began. It seems likely that John de Harlyn, John Lovibond and other organisers of the Wade-Bridge scheme would have travelled to Bideford, Barnstaple and possibly others such as the Exe Bridge (*c*1196 – *c*1238) and Looe Bridge (*c*1411) to look at these structures and consider the type of problems that they could encounter.

During this period many parish churches throughout Cornwall were also being enlarged or re-built with aisles and towers, and workmen and equipment would have been moving between different building projects. There would therefore have been many skilled masons as well as labourers available and it is probable, although not possible to prove, that some men may have worked on both Bideford Bridge and Wade-Bridge during the 1460s and 1470s.

In the Town Hall in Wadebridge is a mural depicting the building of the bridge. If the stone masons shown there could speak, would we have understood them? A linguistic map of Cornwall at the time of the building of the bridge, shows the eastern half of Cornwall as English speaking, while the western half was still Cornish-speaking. The dividing line was between the river Camel and the river Fowey, suggesting that those building the bridge (who may already have been involved in building bridges elsewhere) might have spoken both English and Cornish. We might expect that the master masons were English-speaking while the labourers, bargemen and the local population communicated in a mixture of Cornish and English.[19]

---

[15] Cruse, J B, 1982. *The Long bridge of Barnstaple*, 6.
[16] Kingsley, C, 1855. *Westward Ho!* 231.
[17] www.exetermemories.co.uk/em/exebridge.phb.
[18] Keast, J, 1987. *A History of East and West Looe*.
[19] Spriggs, M, 2003. 'Where Cornish was spoken and when: A provisional Synthesis', *Cornish Studies* XI, 228-269.

Where was the original stone quarried?

Although no records of the building of the bridge survive, the reference to John Lovibond obtaining a licence to draw stone from a quarry on the Duchy manor of Penmayne, near Rock in St Minver, suggests that the quarry was probably coastal and that the stone was barged up the river to the site of the construction. At this time there would have been few roads in the area, and transporting large amounts of stone over land would have involved mule trains with panniers, as no wagons existed at this time in Cornwall. The obvious choice would have been to use a coastal or riverside quarry to supply the stone, saving on double handling stone from a local inland quarry. Modern maps of the river Camel and its estuary show numerous quarries in St Minver, for example near Cassock Hill, at Rock, Cant, Trevelver, Tregenna and Dinham, and any one of these quarries may have been part of the Manor of Penmayne during the fifteenth century. In a report in the *Cornish Guardian* about the second widening of the bridge, it is suggested that the stone used to build the original bridge came from a quarry behind the Rock Hotel, although no reason was given for this assumption.[20] Where the original stone came from may never be conclusively proved.

The Town Hall Mural

This mural, depicting the building of the bridge forms the backdrop to the stage in the main hall of Wadebridge Town Hall (see plate 4). It was painted in 1962 by Mr Victor M. Harvey of St Mabyn as a feature of the restored Town Hall and was unveiled on the 11th July 1962 by the wife of Mr James Scott-Hopkins the MP for North Cornwall. The scene depicts five of the original seventeen arches in construction. On the far left of the picture in the foreground is a stonemason dressing a piece of stone, while behind him another workman brings a second piece of stone in a wheel barrow. These workmen are being watched by a third man leaning on a staff - perhaps the foreman. To the right and centre of the foreground in a fenced off area of the river bank are sheep grazing, symbolic of the 'bridge on wool' legend. Two arches on the right hand side of the picture have timber scaffold supporting them, while many workmen can be seen above the bridge building the parapet walls and pedestrian refuges. Although this depiction may contain some artistic licence, it is certainly a wonderful impression of the building of the bridge.

Frequency of building

Although it may not be possible to give an exact date for when the bridge was started, or when it was completed, documentary evidence indicates that building could have begun as early as 1461 and was not finally completed until at least 1476: altogether a period of fifteen years. Although this may sound a long time, building projects in medieval Cornwall often took many years, depending on the availability of funding, the weather and the time of the year. According to Joanna Mattingly, the aisles of Cornish churches in poorer areas could sometimes take more than ten years to complete, with long gaps during building.[21]

---

[20] Cornish Guardian, July 12th 1962, 'Major Operation in Progress at Wadebridge'.
[21] Mattingly, J, 2005. *Looking at Cornish Churches*, 27.

Similarly, the building of Wade-Bridge would have been seasonal with building work suspended during the winter months, unless the weather was exceptionally mild or dry. Work would also have to be halted at times when the river was in full flood or during spring tides, particularly during the early stages of creating the foundations and building the piers. The most important factor in preventing delay was funding. It is unlikely that Lovibond had all the necessary funds to complete the project in 1461 and it is much more probable that finance had to be raised from time to time to allow the building to continue. When work was suspended, builders may have obtained employment on church projects, or if the delays were long, they may have worked on the building of Bideford Bridge.

According to Smyth, *'medieval bridges were built one arch at a time. This meant that at each pier, during construction, the arch which had just had its centring (or support) removed exerted a horizontal force which was not yet balanced by an opposing thrust from the next span. To cope with this force the piers had to be very wide, and - where it crossed a river – they considerably obstructed the flow'*.[22] If this is the case it would suggest that the bridge would have been built from the Egloshayle bank, westwards towards the village of Wade, as firm rocky foundations that would have formed a rigid construction for the first arch could be secured at the Egloshayle end. This is the reasoning behind numbering the arches on plans of the bridge from the Egloshayle end towards the town end. Warkworth medieval bridge in Northumberland clearly shows the width of the piers in relation to the narrowness of the roadway, it also shows how large the pedestrian refuges would have been at Wade-Bridge before it was widened (see plate 5a and 5b).

Early reports of the bridge

The first visitor to Cornwall to mention the bridge was the English Chronicler, William of Worcester, who travelled to Cornwall in 1478, only two years after the Charter of Endowment. He made only a brief reference to it, calling it *Wade-brygge,* being situated upon and by the town of Wade (*quod pons Wade-brygge scrita super et prope villam Wade*). His entry is vague and in one place he talks of the bridge being of stone construction and having twelve arches (*Wade-brygge qui continent 12 archuatas de lapidibus constructas*), in another as having eighteen arches (*continent 18 arches; et longitude pontis est north and south*) and in a third entry as having sixteen piers, i.e. seventeen arches, which is in fact the correct figure (*Wade-brygge de XVI peres*). William of Worcester did not visit the north side of the county, and did not personally see the bridge which explains why his reports are conflicting: it was all hearsay as he travelled the county. However the fact that he mentions the bridge three times in his *Itinerarium*, would seem to indicate that the bridge was already well known and the talk of the county.[23]

It was John Leland, King Henry VIII's Royal Antiquary who in 1538 gave the first accurate account of the bridge. Leland had been commissioned by the King to travel the kingdom in search of England's antiquities.[24] He wrote:

---

[22] Smyth, B, 1998. 'Changing materials, changing bridges' *British Archaeology*, November no. 39, 6.
[23] William of Worcester's Itinerary, in Polsue, J, 1872. *Complete Parochial History of the County of Cornwall*, **IV**, 93-112.
[24] Polsue, J, 1872. **IV**, 67.

'Thens 3 miles by good corne grounde, but no wood, to Wadebridge. Wher as now Wadebridge is, ther was a fery a 80 yeres syns, and menne sumtyme, passing over by horse, stoode often in great jeopardie. Then one Lovebone, vicar of Wadebridge, movid with pitie, began the bridge, and, with great paine and studie, good people putting ther help therto, finishid it with xvij fair and great uniforme arches of stone. One told me that the fundation of certein of the arches was firt sette on so quick sandy ground, that Lovebone almost despairid to performe the bridg, ontyl such tyme as he layed pakkes of wolle for fundation.'

Leland was the first person to record the legend of the wool packs and the first to describe the bridge correctly as having seventeen uniform arches.

The Wade-Bridge legend

During the nineteenth century, the legend was repeated and further embellished by popular folklorists Robert Hunt[25] and Beatrix Cresswell.[26] They both record that Lovibond had difficulty building firm foundations for the bridge and that pier after pier was built and then lost in the sands. They suggest that masons built piers during the day, but that there would be no trace of them next morning. So hard was the task that Lovibond was about to abandon it when one night he had a dream that an angel with a flock of sheep came to the river, sheared the sheep, let the wool drop into the water, and as the wool sank the angel raised a bridge upon it. On waking, Lovibond followed his dream and gathered packs of wool from local farmers, which he placed thickly upon the sand, then raised the piers above. This account of the legend is also recorded by Cornish author Joseph Hocking in his novel *Roger Trewinion*.[27]

Wool Legends nationally

Leland was the first to record the legend of the 'bridge on wool' and today it is still very much alive, despite examinations of the bridge foundations in 1956, 1962 and 1975 which found no real evidence to support Leland's claim. Is the legend that Wade-Bridge was built on a foundation of wool packs just a myth, or is there any tangible or documentary evidence to support such a claim? Wade-Bridge is one of a number of bridges associated with this legend and many have been elaborated on and perpetuated by Victorian folklorists and guide book writers. The following bridges boast the same legend: Old London Bridge,[28] St Ives Bridge in Cambridgeshire, formerly Huntingdonshire,[29] and Munhin Bridge in Ireland.[30]

---

[25] Hunt, R, 1903. *Popular Romances of the West of England*, **II**, 445.

[26] Cresswell, B F, 1915. *The Homeland Handbooks, Tintagel, Boscastle and the North Coast of Cornwall*, 14.

[27] Hocking, J, 1905. *Roger Trewinion*.

[28] Fearnside, W G, and Harrel, T, 1838. *London Bridge*, 64.

[29] Iago, W, *Notes & Queries* , **X** , 299 quoting Burn-Murdoch, B, 1988, 9.

[30] *Western People* Newspaper, 2002. at www.westernpeople.ie/news/story.asp?j=11025.

Further claims to the legend

Closer to home, in north Devon, Whiting claims that Bideford Bridge also has a legend about being built on wool. [31] Kingsley in his novel *Westward Ho!* goes on to say that because Bideford Bridge is built on wool, it shakes at the slightest step of a horse. Both Whiting and Kingsley embellish the Bideford story by describing a dream similar to that of Lovibond. At Bideford the parson or vicar was Sir Richard Gurney and it is said that the bridge was originally intended to be built half a mile further upstream from the present site. However as the construction progressed the stones were removed downstream by an invisible hand. Sir Richard, 'on going to bed one night in some perplexity and fear of an evil spirit who seemed so busy in his sheep-fold, beheld a vision of an angel, who bade him build the bridge where he himself had so kindly transported the materials; for there alone was sure foundation amid the broad sheet of shifting sand'. [32] Yet according to Whiting, Bideford Bridge is built on a ridge of rock some eleven feet below the surface of the sand.

At St Ives in Cambridgeshire, Burn-Murdoch states that the bridge is built on oak piles, although he also records that there is a legend to the effect that its foundations were formed of woolpacks. In more recent times, the construction of foundations for Munhin Bridge, County Mayo in Ireland, involved the use of bales of wool to restrict the flow of underground water and assist ground support. [33] In their *History of London*, Fearnside and Harrel record that Peter, the minister of St Mary Cole Church, who was the architect of London Bridge also built his bridge on packs of wool.

This type of legend is also popular across the country, in connection with the building of churches and chapels. For example, the massive tower of the parish church of St Botolph in Boston, Lincolnshire that is 272 ft (83m) high and popularly known as the 'Boston Stump' is traditionally said to have been built on wool packs, as is the church of Our Lady at Salisbury. [34]

Symbolic of the Wool trade

Fearnside and Harrel have suggested that the 'Bridge on Wool' was a play on words, implying a tax was imposed on the wool trade towards the cost of building London Bridge. Similarly it has also been suggested that the legends for Wade-Bridge and Bideford Bridge relate to this fact: that they were funded from the sale of wool. The wool trade was clearly an important industry in England during the fifteenth century, and was responsible for a great deal of wealth; however it was not necessarily the most important industry in Cornwall at the time of the building of Wade-Bridge. The medieval tin industry in Cornwall was more profitable than the wool industry and Smedley notes that Cornish wool during this period was of poor quality, being very coarse in texture. [35]

---

[31] Whiting, F E, 2006. *The Long Bridge of Bideford: through the centuries*, 21.

[32] Kingsley, C, 1855. *Westward Ho!* 231.

[33] *Western People* Newspaper, 2002 (Dec 24th) 'Work on new Munhin Bridge in Erris nears completion'.

[34] Westwood, J, 1992. *Albion: A Guide to Legendary Britain*, 216-217.

[35] Smedley, J, 1994. 'A History of the Cornish Wool Industry and its people', *Journal of the Royal Institution of Cornwall* ,**II**, 86.

Despite this, the wool trade did expand in Cornwall in this period, with hand carding of wool being gradually replaced by mechanised Tuckingmills or Fulling mills. Henderson has recorded documentary evidence of fifty-eight Tuckingmills, Cornish name *Melyn Drucky* or *Velyn druckya*. The nearest to Wade-Bridge was at Hingham in Egloshayle parish, first recorded in 1420.[36] But without any records surviving of the sponsors of this vast project, it is difficult to state with any certainty that the wool trade helped finance the building of Wade-Bridge. The original trustees of Wade-Bridge came from some of the most powerful families in the county at that time: the Arundells, Courtnays, Carminows and Roscarracks. These were all large landowners who would have certainly kept sheep and been involved in the wool industry, but were just as likely to have also been involved in the tin industry.

In support of Wool being used in foundations

In talking of Bideford Bridge, Whiting admits that he hesitates to refute this wool legend, as it is possible that wool was used around the starlings to collect and bind the sand against the scouring river. Natural materials were used far more often than they are today and as late as the 1920s at Wadebridge faggots of furze (gorse) were staked out in the river with stone as training walls to divert the water flow.[37] At Bideford the rubble stone forming the starlings was held together in windlasses (baskets) made by plaiting together branches of holly and hazel. Alluvial clays were also used to waterproof medieval coffer dams and in the foundations of a bridge may have been used with a mixture of natural materials to secure a foundation. At Wade-Bridge there is no evidence that starlings were originally built to protect the piers, even though concrete starlings were constructed around them in 1975-76. Nevertheless wooden piles (possibly iron tipped) would have been driven into the river bed and bound together in some way to create the original foundations. These would have been in-filled with rubble stone and the piers would have then been raised on them. It is not impossible that wool along with other natural materials could have been used in small quantities to bind everything together.

Investigations into Wade-Bridge foundations

It is quite probable that Lovibond had difficulty in finding firm foundations for the bridge, particularly on the western side. In 1956, when consideration was given to widening the bridge for a second time, test drillings revealed that the bedrock in the river varied from between 20ft (6.1m) and 60ft (18.2m) below alluvial sands, silts and clays.[38] There were also problems in finding firm footings for the new bypass bridge in 1993, where drilling found rock on the western side of the river at 100ft (30m) depth.[39] The foundations of the original bridge would not have gone down to a depth of 60ft (18.2m); probably no more than 8ft (2.4m) to 10ft (3.05m) into the river bed. Harrison states that 'during the Middle Ages piers were laid on rock when it was convenient, sometimes on piles, but shallow foundations continued to be employed, even for

[36] Henderson, C, 1963. 'Cornish Tucking Mills and Windmills' *Essays in Cornish History*, 207.

[37] Luke, F, 2006. *Reminiscence of Wadebridge and the River Camel* (ed. Eric Tatlow), 25-6, see also fig 9.8.

[38] Stephens, R L C, and Carlyon, J L, 1994. 'The history, repair and upkeep of a highway structure Scheduled as an Ancient Monument' *Proceedings of the Civil Engineers Municipal Engineer*, **103**, 158.

[39] Hoyle, R, 1993. 'Crossing the Camel' *North Cornwall Advertiser*, 10.

major bridges'.[40] In March 1955, the *Western Morning News* wrote a short report on a proposed examination of the bridge foundations, with a headline, '*Was it built on rock or on wool?*' but no results of the examination were ever published. Again in 1962 the foundations of the old bridge were examined and core samples taken, yet there is no report about the findings. It should have been possible for some organic material to have been preserved in the alluvial clays, yet nothing is reported. According to West, when the bridge was widened in 1963 a piece of wool was brought up with one of the cores from the bed of the river - a practical joke by a local man![41]

Since the 1950s, a public house on the Platt at Wadebridge, formerly known as the 'Cornish Arms', has been renamed the 'Bridge on Wool', in honour of the town's legend. The modern pub sign depicting the legend shows a bishop with a crozier (rather than a priest) in the foreground, holding a lamb in his hand on one side of the river, while opposite him on the other bank is a shepherd shearing a sheep, with the wool flowing down the river towards the bridge in the background. The modern Cornish name *Pons war Gwlan*, for 'Bridge on Wool' is also displayed.

In all probability we will never be able to prove conclusively whether the building of Wade-Bridge involved the use of wool in its foundations. The suggestion that wool mixed with clay was in some way used to bind together some of the wooden piles used in the foundations may have some credence, but it seems no evidence has ever come to light.   However, the more I write about the bridge, the more I come to realize that it does not matter whether the legend is true or false: what matters is that the people of Wadebridge hold on to these stories as they are very much part of the town's identity today.

Fig 2.4 - The Bridge on Wool Public House.

---

[40] Harrison, D, 2007. *The Bridges of Medieval England*, 146.
[41] West, J, 1991. *St Breock and Wadebridge: A Contribution to a History of Parish and Town*, 55.

Who paid for the building of the bridge?

The building of Wade-Bridge was one of the biggest building projects undertaken in Cornwall during the fifteenth century. The resources needed to build it would have been substantial, including quarrymen, stonemasons, labourers, bargemen and thousands of tons of stone. This ambitious project would have been far beyond the income of the two rural parishes of St Breock and Egloshayle and would have needed the financial support of wealthy and powerful patrons. This suggests that the reason for building the bridge was much more than to simply link two parishes; it must rather have been to facilitate communications and trade along a much longer distance route through North Cornwall and Devon. It was surely someone's vision for a medieval 'Atlantic Highway', and with the bridges of Bideford and Barnstaple already in existence, Wade-Bridge was the missing link.

Looking at the names of the first trustees to the Wada-Bridge Trust it immediately becomes clear that although Lovibond may have been credited with masterminding the building of the bridge, with perhaps John de Harlyn as his architect and master-mason, it was some of these trustees who had the wealth, power, influence and desire for such a project. Of the original twelve trustees, the Arundells, Courtnays, Carminows and Roscarracks were some of the biggest landowners in the county at the time and it is not surprising to find Sir Thomas Arundell at the top of the list. During the second half of the fifteenth century, the Arundell family were the largest landowners in Cornwall. The Arundells lived at Lanherne in the parish of St Mawgan in Pydar and, according to Fox and Padel, by c1400 held the Cornish manors of Treloy, Trembleath (including lands in St Minver parish), Mitchell, Lanherne which also included St Columb Major, and many more manors in the west of the county.[42] They also held land to the east of the river Camel. It is recorded on the 15th May 1343, that the Arundells held the following tenements in the parishes of St Minver and St Kew, Trevanger, Blakes Keiro, Keiro Veor, Gunvenna, Trelawder, Tredrizzick and Treweens, all part of the manor of Trembleath. By 1459 the tenements also included Carlumb, Middle Amble, St Minver, Lemail in Egloshayle and Trethawek.

Thus it is clear that the Arundell family would have had a vested interest in helping provide a bridge to link their lands on either side of the river. It would have enabled their stewards to reach distant parcels of land without waiting for low tide or a ferry. Fox and Padel record that by 1478-79, one Thomas Lymbery was the steward of all the Arundell lands in Cornwall and may already have been acting for the family in 1465, or even in 1459. It is therefore not surprising to find that the original trustees of Wade-Bridge also included Thomas Lymbery. A further trustee of Wade-Bridge, Richard Tomeow (Tomyow) is recorded as a free tenant of the Arundell Estate at St Columb Major between 1451-1464, creating another link with the Arundells.

---

[42] Fox, H S A, and Padel, O J, 2000. *The Cornish Lands of the Arundells of Lanherne, fourteenth to sixteenth centuries*, 24.

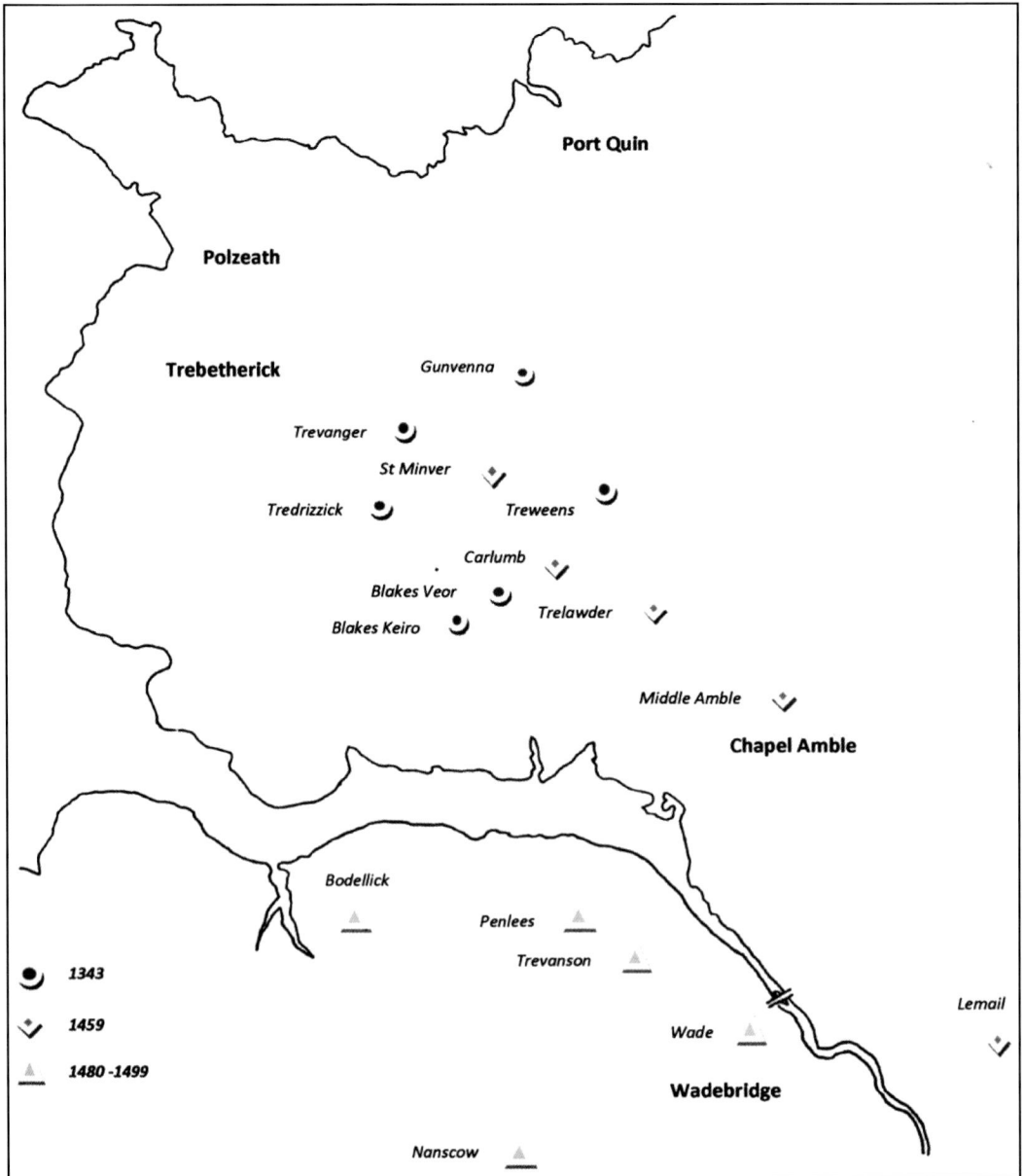

Fig 2.5 - Map showing lands owned by the Arundells on the north and south sides of the river Camel.

Furthermore, the manor of Perlees (St Breock) and Trevisker (Padstow), which included land in St Breock parish at Bodellick, Nanscow, Trevanson and Wade was formed by the Arundells between 1480 and 1499.[43] Perlees was formerly part of the great manor of Pawton and although it did not

---

[43] Fox, H S A, and Padel, O J, 2000. 140.

become a separate manor until near the end of the fifteenth century, it is quite possible that Perlees (including Wade) was owned by the Arundells at the time the bridge was built.

Although the author has found no further records to indicate that members of the Arundell family continued as trustees after Thomas Arundell (Charter of Endowment 1476), additional records suggest that the family remained interested in the bridge. Later in 1586, Edward Arundell left money in his will for the maintenance of the bridge, while at Trevelver in St Minver parish - formerly an Arundell holding - one of the earliest depictions of the bridge survives (see chapter 3). All this indicates that the Arundell family may have played a major role in influencing the building of Wade-Bridge.

The Duchy of Cornwall owned the manor of Penmayne and was therefore responsible for giving Lovibond a licence to draw stone from a quarry on its estate for several years. The Duchy would also have benefited greatly from the bridge since it held manors on both sides of the river, at Talskiddy near St Columb Major and Tywarnhaile near St Agnes, as well as at Penmayne in St Minver and Helstone in Lanteglos by Camelford.

It is very likely that several of the other trustees may also have benefited through the building of the bridge. Edward Courtenay owned Boconnoc Estate, John Carminow owned Glynn in Cardinham, while John Roscarrock was the owner of Croan and Lemail in Egloshayle. The remainder of the trustees either lived one side of the river Camel or the other, Richard Billing at Trevorder in Egloshayle, John Forth was a husbandman of Egloshayle and another executor to John Lovibond, while Robert Lovibond was possibly a son of John Lovibond. Richard Treffry lived at Tremere in St Tudy, while Thomas Bere lived at Pengelly in St Breock.

3 'the longest, strongest and fayrest that the shire could muster'

The original bridge, descriptions and donations

It is difficult to be sure what the original bridge looked like, as no visual records, like plans, illustrations or paintings survive from the fifteenth or sixteenth centuries. One tends to accept that the bridge looked similar to the images surviving from the eighteenth and nineteenth centuries, but we cannot be sure of this, or even if the bridge was completely finished by the time the Wade-Bridge Trust was founded in 1476. In this chapter we look at various sources of evidence and the fact that Wade-Bridge was once the noblest bridge in Cornwall, its extreme length accentuated by its narrow roadway and lengthy causeway at the western end.

Further accounts of the bridge

Topographer John Norden noted the bridge in *c*1600 as being, '*the fayreste stone bridge in all Cornwall, leading over Padstowe creeke near Breage*' [Breock]. '*It took its name of a foorde adjoining, which affoordeth a way, not so safe as compendious, when the tyde is out*'.[1] The first Cornishman to record the bridge was Richard Carew of Antony in his *Survey of Cornwall* published in 1602 (which incorporated Norden's maps). It is Carew who wrote the most famous description of the bridge. He said it was '*the longest, strongest and fayrest that the shire could muster*', also that, '*the salt water leaving Padstowe, floweth up into the country, that it may embrace the river Camel, and having performed this naturall courtesie, ebbeth away again to yield him freer passage, by which means they both undergo Wade bridge*'.[2] Nearly a hundred years later in 1698, Celia Fiennes, a pioneering female traveller visited Cornwall, riding side saddle, but she only briefly mentions Wade-Bridge in her travels from St Columb Major to Camelford, when she writes, '*from St Columbe I went to Way bridge 6 long miles, There was a river wch was flowed up by ye tyde a Great way up into the Land, it Came from ye north sea, it was broad, ye bridge had 17 arches. thence to Comblefford, over steep hills 9 miles more*'.[3]

Illustrations and paintings of the original bridge

The earliest visual representation of the bridge from the late seventeenth century, is at Trevelver Farm in St Minver parish. But in using this and other surviving illustrations and paintings from the eighteenth and nineteenth centuries to construct a picture of the original bridge, it must be understood that some of these images may have employed a certain amount of artistic licence. Documentary evidence in the form of plans and sketches drawn before the first widening may provide a more accurate basis for reconstruction. Both can be supplemented by the accounts of travellers described in chapter 10.

---

[1] Norden, J, 1966. *A Topographical and Historical Description of Cornwall in 1584.*

[2] Carew, R, 1602. *Survey of Cornwall* edited and re-published in 1953 by F E Halliday. 219.

[3] Fiennes, C, 1698. *Through England on a Side Saddle: in the time of William and Mary, Tour: Lands End to Winchester.*

The Trevelver picture is a very small painted line drawing of seventeenth century date created as a frieze around the cornice of a panelled parlour-room at Trevelver Farm in St Minver parish, overlooking the north side of the river Camel. A further two paintings depicting the bridge hang in Pencarrow House. In one it is the main subject, while the other shows a distant view. An illustration of the bridge was made by William Borlase in 1759 and another by Cyrus Redding in 1842. A further two illustrations of Wadebridge that feature the bridge were published by William Knapp in 1853, one taken from the north and another from the south.

Trevelver - (plate 6a) The area of frieze containing the painting of the bridge only measures 3ins (0.08m) in height by 18ins (0.46m) long. It shows a view of the bridge looking upstream with the houses at Bridge End (Egloshayle side of the river) on the left hand side of the view. Of these houses, one appears to be Bridge House (the property formerly built up against the upstream parapet of the bridge) with the Riverside House depicted below it. The right hand side of the picture is more difficult to make out, as there is a joint in the wooden cornice, but it may depict the former St Michael's chapel on the town or western side of the bridge. All that can clearly be seen is a cross, although its position in relation to the overall picture would suggest it is intended to be a gable cross on a building. A brigantine is shown in front of the last two arches and is possibly intended to be a vessel moored up at Bradford's Quay. One person on horseback can be discerned riding from Egloshayle towards the town, while a small rowing boat with two people aboard can be seen in front of the first arches. This frieze, with an additional painting of the farm house and surrounding estate positioned above the fireplace were both restored by conservators in 1997, with the aid of a grant from English Heritage. Today the house remains a private farm house, and there is no public access.[4] It is interesting to note that Trevelver was purchased by a branch of the Arundell family during the late seventeenth century, while Maclean records that the family were in St Minver parish from 1613 onwards. Was the painting of the bridge at Trevelver commissioned by the Arundell family?

Pencarrow - These two landscapes are painted in oils and although neither painting is signed, they have been attributed to the school of Francis Towne, a landscape artist of the eighteenth century.[5] They are situated on the back stairs of Pencarrow, with the painting of the old bridge hanging above the first flight of stairs and the second hung on the first floor landing. Both present much informative detail.

The Molesworth Family of Pencarrow have been very much involved with the town of Wadebridge as landlords, trustees to the bridge and also as patrons to Egloshayle Church, therefore it is not surprising that the family commissioned these two paintings.

---

[4] Tuthill, P, 1997. Trevelver Farm, open day 3rd August 1997, *North Cornwall Advertiser*, July 1997, 37, also *Cornish Guardian*, 31st July 1997.

[5] Francis Towne (1739 or 1740 – 1816) was an English watercolour landscape painter. According to one source he was born at Isleworth in Middlesex in 1740, while another records that he was born in Exeter in 1739. He is known to have taken commissions from Devon families including Sir Thomas Acland of Killerton, but it is not known if he ever painted in Cornwall. Both paintings measure 6ft 1in (1.85m) wide by 3ft 3 ½ins (1m) high (inside frame measurements).

The first painting (plates 6b, 7a and 7b) shows Wade-Bridge from upstream with its seventeen medieval pointed arches spanning the river Camel. It shows a large building on the town or western approach and several large properties on the eastern or Egloshayle side (Bridge End).

In the foreground can be seen the river, with the arches reflected in the water. On the left hand side of the river small cottages can be discerned nestled beside woodlands; some of the cottages appear to be thatched. The foreground also shows a large area of marsh and mud banks. On the right hand side of the painting a small rowing boat can be seen tied up at a quayside. High quay walls are shown below a group of large houses at the beginning of Egloshayle Road where today Bridgend Garage stands; all are three storey properties.

Close to the bridge, a person stands on the river bank in front of arch 1, while the heads of several people can be seen walking or riding across the bridge. Behind arches 5 and 6 can be seen two tall ships' masts and above arch 3 Riverside House is visible. Bridge House, which was built against the upstream Egloshayle side of the bridge, is not shown, probably because the artist wanted to show all the arches. To the left of centre on the hillside can just be made out the old windmill at Trevelver, a prominent landscape feature that can still be seen from the bridge. The back drop to the painting shows wooded hills, but no sign of Gonvena House which was built in c1790.

On the western side of the bridge the ramped and walled causeway is shorter as in the illustration by Borlase described below. At the end of the causeway, a building with tall chimneys appears to be on the site of the present Swan Hotel, which was formerly the Wadebridge Inn and later the Commercial Hotel. Stables can be seen to the rear of the Inn and some post and rail fencing to a small enclosure or paddock. In front of the stables, there is a man on horseback, with another man standing holding a horse, which is being attended by a farrier or blacksmith.

The artist shows the bridge to be made of stone blocks rather than local stone, highlighting the artistic licence used in producing this painting.

The second painting (plate 8) shows a view of Egloshayle Church and the river with the old bridge in the distance. The artist has viewed the church from fields above Treraven Farm and today it is difficult to imagine capturing such a view, as trees and modern developments ruin the view.

In the foreground is the river Camel, with a reflection of the church tower in the water. To the right are two horned bullocks grazing by the riverside, while there is also a man in a small boat. Central in the painting is a barge in full sail, with two men, one on each side with an oar. The bridge showing sixteen of its seventeen arches can be seen in the distance. Egloshayle Church is shown with mud flats or salt marsh between it and the river bank. To the left the old vicarage can be seen (this was demolished and replaced by the present building on this site).[6] The roofs of cottages can be seen between the trees stretching up Tower Hill and around the Churchtown. The large building depicted behind the aisle of the church is Court Place.

---

[6] Maclean, Sir J, 1873. *The Parochial and Family History of the Deanery of Trigg Minor*, **I**, 419, plate XV. Maclean illustrated the old vicarage at Egloshayle prior to its demolition. It was replaced by the present Victorian building.

Borlase – (plate 9) It was Sir John Molesworth who sponsored the illustration of Wade-Bridge which appeared in William Borlase's 1758 book, *The Natural History of Cornwall*. This illustration shows a view of the bridge from downstream which has more of a maritime flavour with several vessels in the foreground. On the left can be seen several large properties at Bridge End on the Egloshayle side of the river Camel. The large house shown against the parapet wall on the upstream Egloshayle side of the bridge could be Bridge House whilst another house partially blocked by the mast of one of the ships could be Riverside House. The right hand side of the picture shows a short ramped causeway and part of a large property, possibly the Market House or the Wadebridge Inn. In the foreground, one barge is shown in sail and a second upstream of the bridge. On the left of the foreground are another two sail boats and a rowing boat, with people shown in each. A few people are also depicted on the bridge, one on horseback near the town side (above arch 17), another above arch 7, with rolling hills in the background. The illustration was published as a plate and dedicated : *To John Molesworth Esq. this North View of Wadebridge in Cornwall, engrav'd at his expence is most gratefully inscrib'd by Wm. Borlase.*[7]

Redding - (fig 3.1) This illustration published in Redding's '*An illustrated itinerary of the county of Cornwall*' in 1842 depicts the bridge from upstream. On the left it shows the bell turret of the Wadebridge Institution, built in 1838, while the built up area on the right of the picture is Bridge End, and above is Gonvena House shown in silhouette. This view shows the bridge with only 15 pointed arches, as arches 1 and 17 had been blocked by this time. In the foreground women can be seen drying washing on the river bank, while three men in a boat appear to be fishing on the river. Another small boat can be seen in the distance near the Egloshayle bank. The tall masts of several ships downstream at the quay sides can be seen over the top of the bridge parapets.[8] The artist has rather exaggerated the pointed arches of the medieval bridge.

Fig 3.1 - Redding's illustration depicting the pointed arches of Wade-Bridge.

Knapp's Lithographs – (fig 3.2) This artist has viewed the scene from the fields where Bridge View Estate now stands, looking down on the town and bridge. The picture is inscribed 'Wadebridge, from Trenant' and dated 1853 (at the time these fields were part of Trenant Farm). A coach drawn by four horses is seen crossing from Egloshayle. The long causeway is also shown

---

[7] Borlase, W, 1758. *The Natural History of Cornwall*, 46, plate III.
[8] Redding, C, 1842. *An Illustrated Itinerary of the County of Cornwall*. 42.

stretching from the last arch to near the former site of the railway level crossing.[9] By this time the bottom of Molesworth Street is far more developed, while many more properties can also be seen to the left of the picture. High above on the opposite hillside can be seen Chapel Terrace and Whiterock Terrace on Whiterock Road and what appears to be the original chapel. Tall masted ships can be seen moored on the downstream quays on either side of the river, while some railway trucks can just be discerned to the right of the Wadebridge Institute.

The second illustration (fig 3.3) is from Dunveth and looks down on the roofs of property in the town and across to Bradfords Quay Road and Egloshayle Road. The bridge is shown with thirteen visible arches. To the left of the illustration the Manor House can be identified along with additional buildings at Bridge End, and to the right the Methodist Chapel (known as Forty Windows).

Fig 3.2 - Knapp's Lithograph of Wadebridge from Trenant 1853.

Length of the Bridge

A plan still hangs in the Town Hall at Wadebridge which accurately assesses the original length of the bridge (see plate 10).[10] It was commissioned in April 1852, before the first widening of the bridge took place. This is of fundamental importance as it is the earliest accurate plan of the structure that is known, although by this time, two arches, one at each end of the bridge, had already been blocked up, reducing its length to 15 arches. The plan was intended not only to

[9] Knapp's lithographs were produced by Rook & Co. London and published by William M. Knapp, Bookseller, at Wadebridge in October 1853.

[10] This plan of Wade-Bridge was hanging in the Council chamber in the Town Hall, however in recent years it has been locked away. In November 2010 it was re-framed and now hangs on a wall at the top of the main stairs.

show the extent of the bridge prior to widening, but to ascertain the ownership of all the property on or adjacent to it.

At this time the total length of the bridge, including the blocked up arches, was 503ft (153.3m) from western abutment to the eastern abutment. However if the additional walled causeway at the western end was included and the road junction at the Bridge End on the eastern side, then the total distance was 680ft (207.3m). This is far more than the 320ft (97.5m) reproduced by most parochial histories. In c1736 William Hals recorded that the bridge was only 320ft (97.5m) long and almost every parochial history and guide book since, has reproduced this figure without checking.[11] On a dark, wet, winter night it must have seemed a long way across the bridge as there was no lighting provided until 1854, and records suggest there were trees at both ends of the bridge, shading its approaches. The decking or road surface of the bridge was made up of pitched stone (stone set on edge) and may have also had river gravel on the surface. There was certainly no tar macadam until the early twentieth century.

Fig 3.3 - Knapp's Lithograph of Wadebridge from Dunveth 1853.

The length of the seventeen arch Wade-Bridge is comparable with Barnstaple's bridge of sixteen arches which was 520ft (158.5m) and originally also had long causeways on either side of the bridge. An unusual feature of the original Barnstaple Bridge was that it was not built in a straight line, but curved slightly, the central arches being set slightly upstream from the ends of the bridge. The twenty-four arch Bideford Bridge and the Exe Bridge of eighteen arches were

---

[11] A number of parochial histories of Cornwall and guide books featuring Wadebridge have copied Hals' statement that the bridge is only 320ft long including Lyson (1814), Gilbert, C S, (1817), Hitchins (1824), Stockdale (1824), Penaluna (1848) and Polsue (1867).

700ft (213m) and 750ft (229m) long respectively, while Looe had the shortest bridge at only 384ft (117m) consisting of fifteen arches.

With the exception of the original Looe Bridge with fifteen arches, no other Cornish bridge came close to the length of Wade-Bridge. After these, the closest were New Bridge and Horse Bridge on the Tamar both with seven arches, Greystone Bridge (Tamar) six arches and Lostwithiel and Respryn on the Fowey with five arches each.

Arches

Wade-Bridge is the only bridge out of the five long medieval bridges of Cornwall and Devon to have arches of a uniform width. The arches are all 18ft 6ins (5.64m) wide and were raised 9ft (2.74m) above the spring tides. The original pointed gothic arches of Wade-Bridge still survive today, sandwiched between nineteenth and twentieth century masonry. We know that the bridge originally had large cutwaters that protruded out each side of each pier, and that they formed pedestrian refuges above, where people could stand to avoid traffic.

As previously mentioned, Bideford Bridge was converted from an earlier timber bridge and the width of the original arches was determined by the length of the timbers available. When it was re-built in stone the same positions for the piers were used and the arches of the bridge therefore vary in width considerably. According to early illustrations of the Looe Bridge the arches were also of different widths, while measurements of the eight surviving medieval arches of the Exe Bridge vary between 15ft (4.57m) and 18ft 2in (5.55m).[12] Cruse states that the width of Barnstaple's arches ranged from 18ft 4ins (5.6m) to 22ft 6ins (6.86m). It is therefore surprising that the builders of Wade-Bridge managed to construct arches of a uniform width, considering that it was so difficult to find a firm foundation for each pier. This suggests that the technical skills involved in building a bridge across a tidal river were advancing by the 1460s and that the builders overcame problems with the foundations.

Width of the roadway

Prior to being widened in 1852-53, the width of the Wade-Bridge roadway on the 1852 plan, was 10ft (3.04m) from parapet to parapet. Previous to this the width had been recorded as 9ft 8ins (2.95m). During the mid nineteenth century, curbs or buffer stones were set against the parapet walls, presumably at either end of the bridge, to restricted the width of vehicles entering on to the bridge, so that their wheels would not scrape against the parapets. In 1845 the width was limited to only 8ft 10ins (2.69m) between the curbs.[13] Though apparently very narrow, the width of Wade-Bridge was greater than Looe whose original bridge varied in width from between 10ft 3ins (3.1m) to just 6ft 8ins (2m), with scarcely two arches the same size.[14]

---

[12] The width of the arches of the old Exe Bridge at Exeter were measured on 27th February 2011.
[13] *West Briton and Cornwall Advertiser,* 17/10/1845 - The width of the roadway was measured by Magistrates from the Cornwall County Sessions on the 19th August 1845.
[14] Bond, T, 1823, *East and West Looe,* 8.

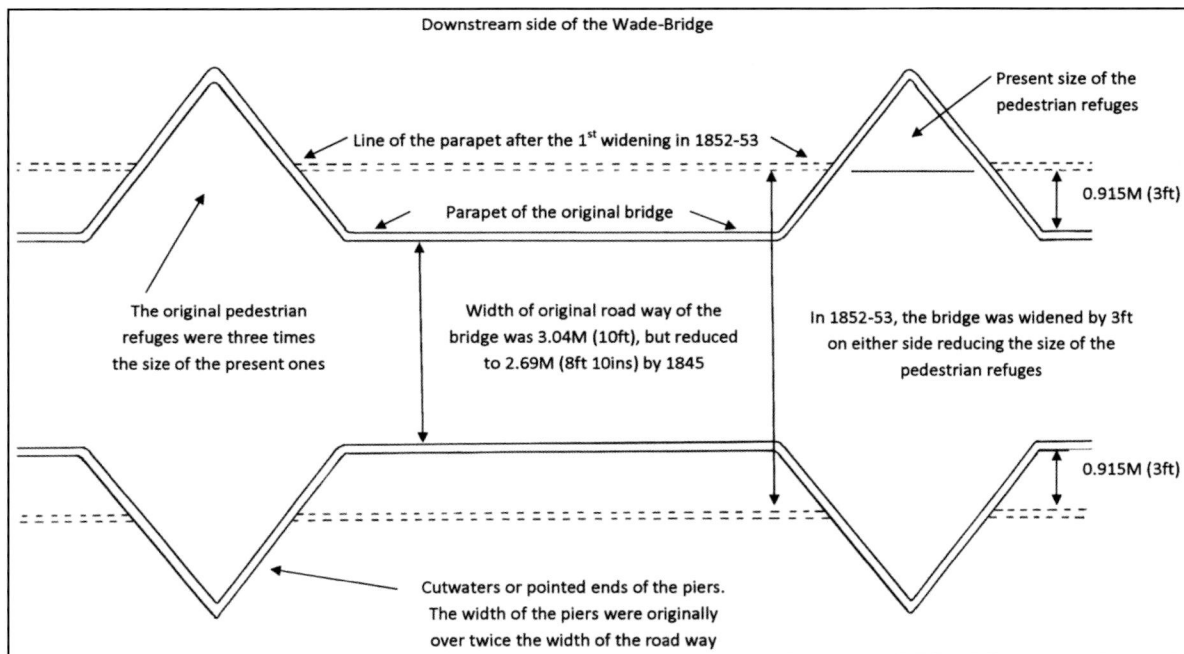

Downstream side of the Wade-Bridge

Line of the parapet after the 1st widening in 1852-53

Present size of the pedestrian refuges

Parapet of the original bridge

0.915M (3ft)

The original pedestrian refuges were three times the size of the present ones

Width of original road way of the bridge was 3.04M (10ft), but reduced to 2.69M (8ft 10ins) by 1845

In 1852-53, the bridge was widened by 3ft on either side reducing the size of the pedestrian refuges

0.915M (3ft)

Cutwaters or pointed ends of the piers. The width of the piers were originally over twice the width of the road way

Fig 3.4 - The original size of the cutwaters and pedestrian refuges prior to the first widening.

The narrowness of Wade-Bridge in proportion to its length, linked with its walled causeway, made Wade-Bridge a very impressive structure across the river Camel. At the time of building, it was wide enough to meet the needs of all the local traffic, and long enough to stretch over the whole river, with its highest spring tide. The original character of the bridge no longer survives, but prior to its first widening, the width of the piers with their cutwaters was far in excess of the width of the roadway above. Each pier was 23ft 5ins (7.14m) in width, and of a solid construction, each arch measuring 12ft 1in (3.7m) with each cutwater protruding another 5ft 8ins (1.72m) out from the roadway. During the fifteenth century the only traffic to pass over the bridge would have been horses, pack-animals, pedestrians and hand-carts. In Cornwall, there were few wagons, and no coaches or carriages during this period; this was due to the poor state of the roads in the county.[15] Almost all goods would have been carried by horses, mules or donkeys, either across their backs or in panniers on each side of the animal. The original width of the bridge was sufficient to allow two laden pack animals to pass at the large pedestrian refuge points. There were very few horse drawn carriages and coaches in Cornwall until the late eighteenth century, and therefore for the first three hundred years the bridge's roadway was quite adequate for the traffic of the day.

---

[15] Although it is believed that there was very little wheeled transport in medieval Cornwall, there is a thirteenth century reference in the Cartulary of Launceston Priory to 'the great way of waggons' in St Breward parish in Hull, P L, 1987. *The Cartulary of Launceston Priory*, Devon & Cornwall Record Society, NS **30**, 39.

Donations to the bridge

Before the Reformation, it was quite common for people to leave money in their wills for churches and chapels, to provide lights on altars, and for secular works such as the maintenance of bridges, causeways and roads. Although such bequests to religious foundations ceased after the Reformation, the documentary evidence suggests that people still continued to support the maintenance and upkeep of the bridge.

In the will of Christopher Tredeneck (Tredinick) of St Breock,[16] dated April 1531, three shillings and four pence was left to the store of Wade-Bridge, as well as various sums of money to the Friaries of Bodmin and Truro and chapels of St Lawrence and St George at Bodmin and to St Antony. The 'store' would have been a fund for the maintenance of Wade-Bridge. During Henry VIII's reign, Christopher Tredeneck was High Sheriff of Cornwall on more than one occasion and also a county magistrate. The site of his family home is now part of the Royal Cornwall Agricultural showground.

In July 1586, during the reign of Elizabeth I and a year before Mary Stuart was executed, Edward Arundell of Lanherne in St Mawgan in Pydar left twenty shillings a year towards the maintenance of Wade-Bridge for as many years as he should live.[17] At this time Edward held several manors including the manor of Penlease (Perlees) in St Breock which included Wadebridge. He died in the same year that he made his will (1586) at the age of 47 years and therefore payments of twenty shillings continued until 1633.

According to North, his will read:

> 'to the maintenance of Wade bridge, 20s yearly to be paid to the feoffees and guardians of the bridge out of the rents and profits of Treveliew lands, for so many yeres as I shall accomplishe in age at the daye of my deathe, being now in this present yere of our Lord God fortie and seaven yeres olde at St Margarets daye last past, payable at Treveliew each year on his birthday, subject to 'sufficient acquitance' being first made.

In an undated memorandum from the seventeenth century found in the Bridge Wardens' accounts for Wade-Bridge, the terms of Edward Arundell's bequest were repeated by the trustees of Wade-Bridge, signed by trustees William Prideaux, Thomas Castell and Christopher Collyer vicar of Egloshayle (1614-1633) and witnessed by William Kestell and R. Randell. A note in another hand states that this bequest had been paid to the year 1632 with one year to go, suggesting that the memorandum is dated 1632.[18]

---

[16] Dunkin, E H W, 1882. *Monumental Brasses in Cornwall*, 94.

[17] North, C, 2001. 'The Will and Inventory of Edward Arundell of Treveliew and Lanherne, 1539-1586', *Journal of the Royal Institution of Cornwall*, 38-63. Treveliewe is now known as Trebelzue and is in St Columb Minor and close to the western end of RAF St Mawgan, also Dunkin, E H W, 1882. *Monumental Brasses in Cornwall*, 48-51.

[18] Cornwall Record Office. DDX 450/167.

Also during Queen Elizabeth's reign, the Blanchminster Charity Accounts show that, one James Cater in 1577 received a collection of two shillings and six pence from the parishioners of Stratton towards Wade-Bridge.[19] The Blanchminster accounts further record that donations were often made towards the maintenance of bridges in north and east Cornwall. In 1693, one pound, seven shillings and seven and a half pence was given towards the repair of six un-named bridges, while donations are also recorded for Dunmere Bridge near Bodmin, Yeolm Bridge near Launceston and Notter Bridge near Liskeard.

According to Lorigan, in 1611 during the reign of James I, one George Juell of St Teath a 'helier' (a slate worker) left five shillings in his will towards the *mayntenance of the Wad brige*. George Juell may have owned his own small slate quarry at Newhall in the parish.[20]

Although only a few references of donations to the maintenance of Wade-Bridge survive, it is possible that many such donations were made to the store of Wade-Bridge, particularly before the Reformation which have simply not survived. The surviving references suggest that people throughout north Cornwall benefited from the building of Wade-Bridge. The fuller records for Barnstaple, show that funds for their bridge were collected from many parishes. In 1458 to 59, a typical list of donations at Barnstaple recorded small amounts from thirty-nine villages and parishes.[21]

---

[19] Goulding, R W, 1898. *Records of the Charity known as Blanchminster's Charity.*

[20] Lorigan, C, 2009. *Connections: Aspects of the History of North Cornwall*, 8, also Cornwall Record Office, Probate Record AP/J/154/ 1-4.

[21] Cruse, J B, 1982. *The Long Bridge of Barnstaple & Bridge Trust*, 7.

4 'St Mychall chapel and the Kynges chapel, lying on the west and east side of Wade bryge'

The causeway, bridge approaches and medieval chapels

The Causeway

The area of Wadebridge known as the Platt, where the Town Hall, Bridge on Wool and the Swan public houses are situated, is much lower than the height of the present roadway on the bridge. The river side or northern side of the Platt is all reclaimed ground which was formerly salt marsh and mud flats at the time the bridge was constructed. Both the Town Hall and the existing Treguddick Bridge (over the Polmorla River) were not built until 1888. Before this period the ground would have regularly flooded, and has continued to flood periodically until the 1990s when the river banks were raised as part of a flood alleviation scheme. The Platt has flooded many times within living memory, with perhaps the worst occasion in 1965.[1]

When the bridge was constructed during the fifteenth century this low-lying flood-prone ground was crossed by a raised or ramped causeway built from roughly where the old railway crossing was once sited (the site of the old Market House), 152ft (46.33m) to the abutment of the bridge, where the junction of Harbour Road is now. Today, the road rises 6ft 4½ins (1.94m) from a position at the junction of Eddystone Road with Molesworth Street to the western abutment of the existing bridge.[2] It is now impossible to tell how much the levels have changed since the bridge was built; although there was always a significant difference in height.

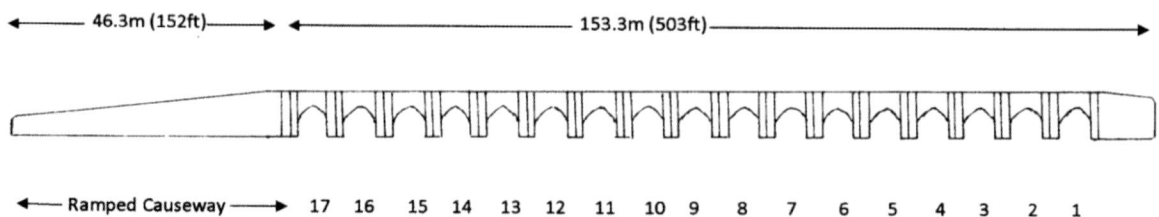

Fig 4.1 - Shows the full extent of the original bridge and its ramped causeway.

A causeway or 'causy' is not a term that is used much today, although causeways still do exist with perhaps the most well known being those linking the islands of St Michael's Mount and Holy Island, Lindsfarne to the mainland. They were a common structure across marshy ground in the past and many modern roads crossing broad valley bottoms, marshes or boggy moorland started out as medieval causeways.

---

[1] The last major flood in Wadebridge was on the 14th July 1965.
[2] The levels of the road between the junction of Eddystone Road and Molesworth Street and the western abutment of the bridge were taken by my brother Martin Langdon on the 31st January 2010.

The best unspoilt example of a causeway in Cornwall that still survives is at Horse Bridge near Callington on the river Tamar. This causeway stretches two hundred feet (61m) in length across low lying fields before reaching the six-arched bridge. At Tregony, although the medieval bridge has been superseded, the road leading up to it from the northern side is built on a causeway across the marsh. The eighteenth century bridge at Trewornan across the Amble River has a causeway running from the bridge and aligned with the driveway to Trewornan House.

The ramped causeway that stretched from where the old railway line crossed Molesworth Street, up to the bridge abutment, was formerly walled on either side and can clearly be seen extending towards the town in William Knapp's early lithograph of the bridge, printed in 1853 (fig 4.2). This depicted the bridge before it was widened and shows sand quays in the area now known as the Platt, as well as a number of houses further inland. An illustration by William Iago of Bodmin (c1860) featured in Maclean's *Deanery of Trigg Minor* also shows the wall of the causeway extending westward towards the town (fig 4.3), while the wall can also be identified on the Ordnance Survey map of 1880 (fig 4.4).

Fig 4.2 - William Knapp's Lithograph showing the causeway running beyond the arches.

What made the original bridge appear much longer particularly in some of the earlier paintings and illustrations of the eighteenth century is the ramped western approach to the bridge. The wide flat valley bottoms needed some form of causeway to raise the approach roads above the flood plain and connect with the bridge. At Barnstaple on the town side, there was a causeway of 300ft (91.5m) and on the Tawstock side of 1500ft (457m). There is no record of any causeway at Bideford, perhaps because the original long bridge spanned the whole width of the valley. The river valley at Looe was much narrower and therefore a causeway was not required, however at Exeter with its very wide valley bottom the approaches must have originally been linked by causeways.

Fig 4.3 - William Iago's illustration showing the causeway wall running west beyond the last arch.

The Causeway Wall

In the well known and much published Victorian photograph taken from the bridge during the 1860s, a view looking west towards Molesworth Street is seen (fig 4.6). The end of the bridge and causeway wall can be clearly seen on the left or upstream side of the bridge, continuing to the old Market House, which fronted the railway crossing. On the right-hand or downstream side can be seen the Wadebridge Institute with part of its arched doorway and bell turret showing. To the west of the Institute and adjoining can be seen Mallet's Ironmongers (now a sports shop). Two pedestrian refuges can be identified on the upstream side of the bridge casting shadows across the road and between these refuges is the last arch of the bridge, which aligns with the junction of Harbour Road. It is only the causeway wall which extends to the old Market House near the railway crossing. Many people have misinterpreted this photograph, mainly due to the angle it was taken from, and have suggested that the arches of the bridge extended to the old Market House. This is definitely incorrect as the medieval arches are uniform in both height and width and it is therefore quite easy to identify where the buried arches are by simple measurement.[3]

One of the first publications to include this photograph was *Old Wadebridge* by Ronnie Hoyle in 1983, and it was Mr Hoyle who suggested that the arches of the old bridge could be seen from in the cellars of some of the shops and that the bridge itself extended to near the old level crossing. Both these statements are incorrect; the cellars of the shops do not extend out into the road as far as the line of the old bridge. In 1999, the author gained permission from the owner of no 3 Molesworth Street, formerly Chapman Jewellers, to examine the cellar and check these claims.[4] It

[3] On 14th November 1999, the author measured the decking of the bridge and its arches to ascertain where the first arch of the bridge would have been.

[4] The author gained permission from Mrs Thelma Riddle to examine the cellar of no 3 Molesworth Street, the former premises of Chapman Jewellers, on Saturday 4th December 1999.

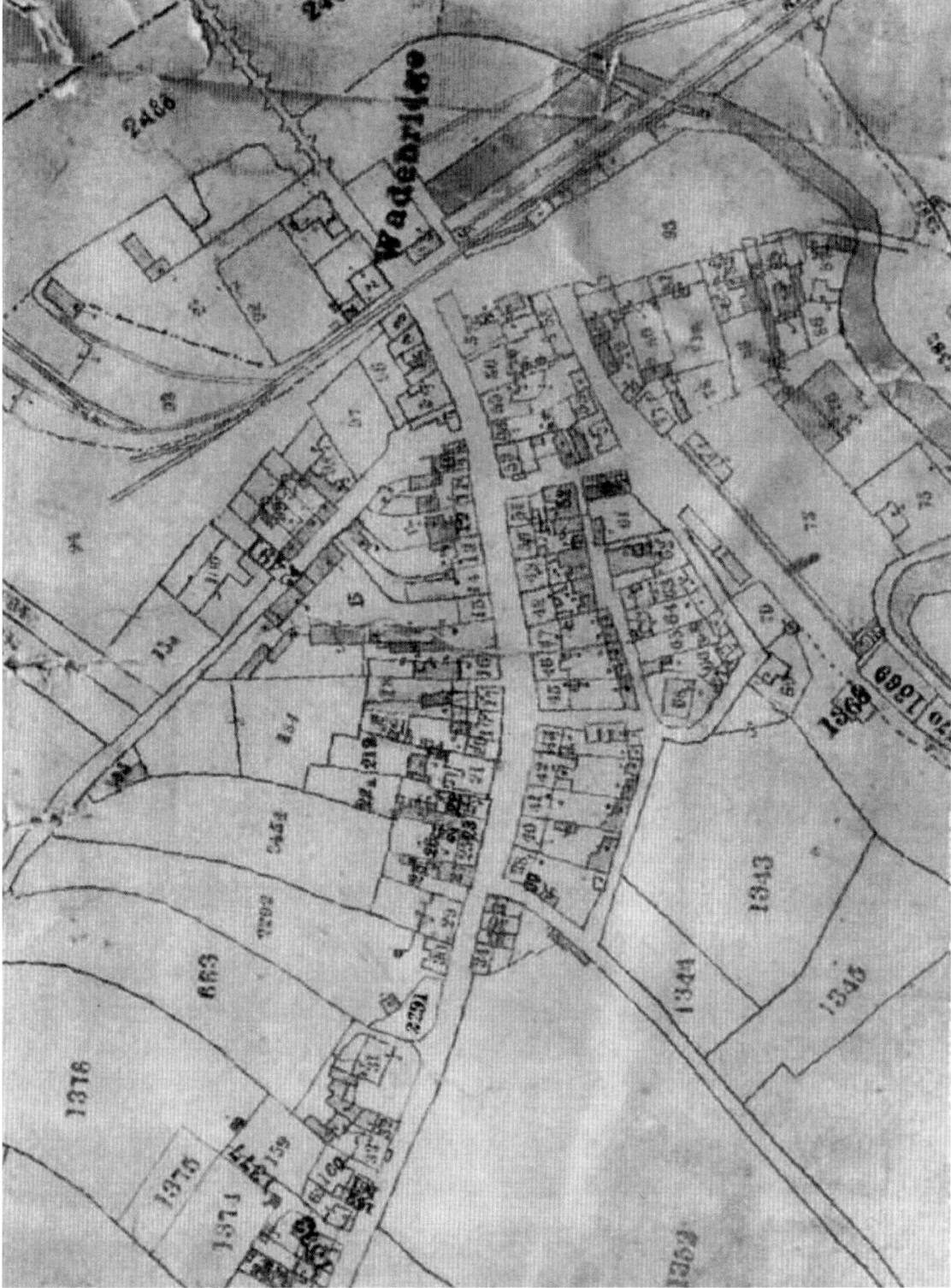

Plate 1 – *St Breock Tithe Map 1841, showing the development of Wadebridge, Courtesy Cornwall Record Office.*

Plate 2a – Eighteenth century direction post at Longcross, pointing the way to Padstow rather than to Wadebridge.

Plate 2b - John Ogilby's 1675 map showing the passage across the Camel estuary from Rock to Padstow, Courtesy Andrew Eddy.

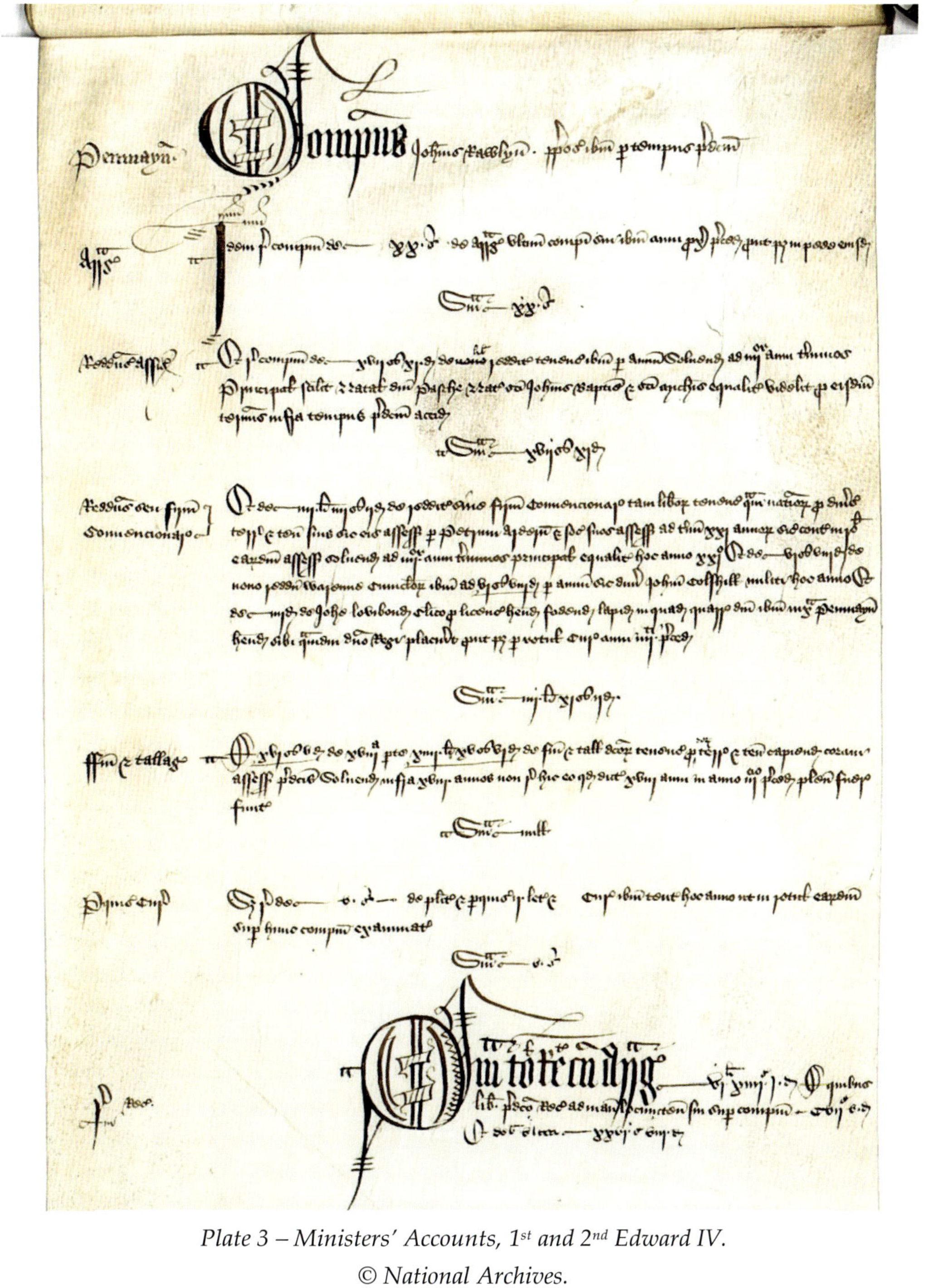

Plate 3 – Ministers' Accounts, 1st and 2nd Edward IV.
© *National Archives.*

Plate 5a – Warkworth medieval bridge in Northumberland, which clearly shows the width of the piers in relation to the narrowness of the bridge.

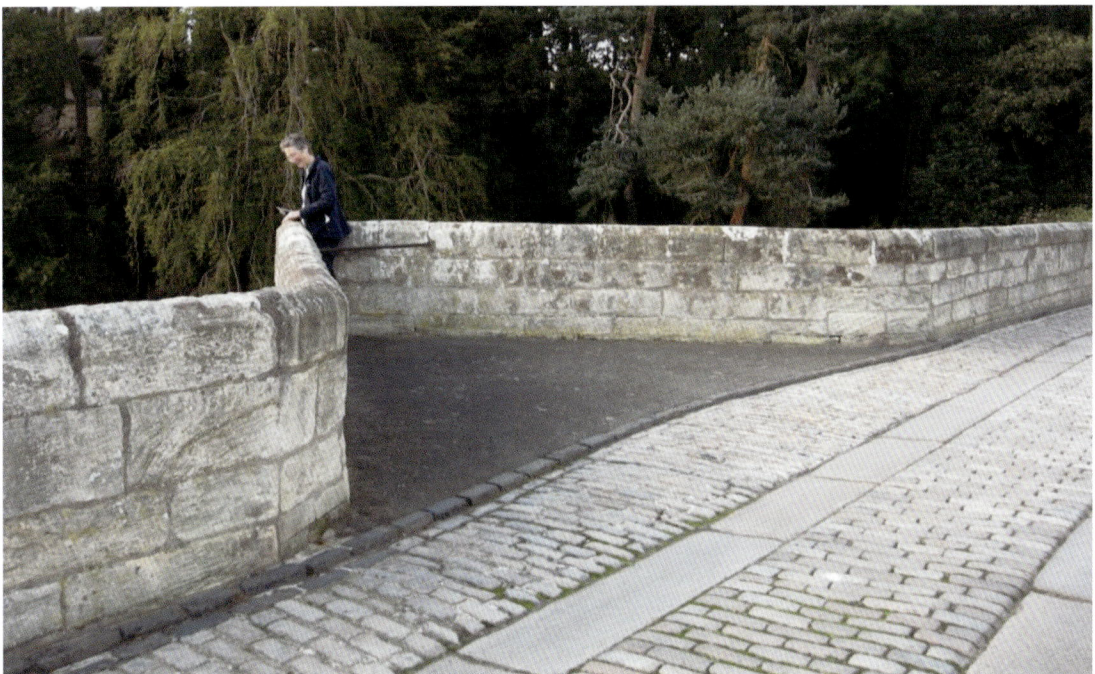

Plate 5b – Warkworth medieval bridge showing the massive pedestrian refuges similar in size to those at Wade-Bridge prior to the first widening scheme.

Plate 6a – The painted seventeenth century image of Wade-Bridge at Trevelver Farm, St Minver, Courtesy Mr & Mrs Anthony Wills.

Plate 6b – The eighteenth century landscape oil painting of Wade-Bridge at Pencarrow House, Egloshayle, Courtesy Lady Molesworth St Aubyn.

Plate 7a - The Wadebridge Inn at the western approach to Wade-Bridge, depicted in the Pencarrow painting, Courtesy Lady Molesworth St Aubyn.

Plate 7b – Bridge End at the eastern approach to Wade-Bridge, depicted in the Pencarrow painting, Courtesy Lady Molesworth St Aubyn.

Plate 8 – The second painting at Pencarrow depicting Wade-Bridge, this time in the distance with Egloshayle Church in the foreground,
Courtesy Lady Molesworth St Aubyn.

was discovered that the cellar did not extend any further than the front of the shop, whereas the alignment of the original bridge and its walled causeway were several feet further into the road.

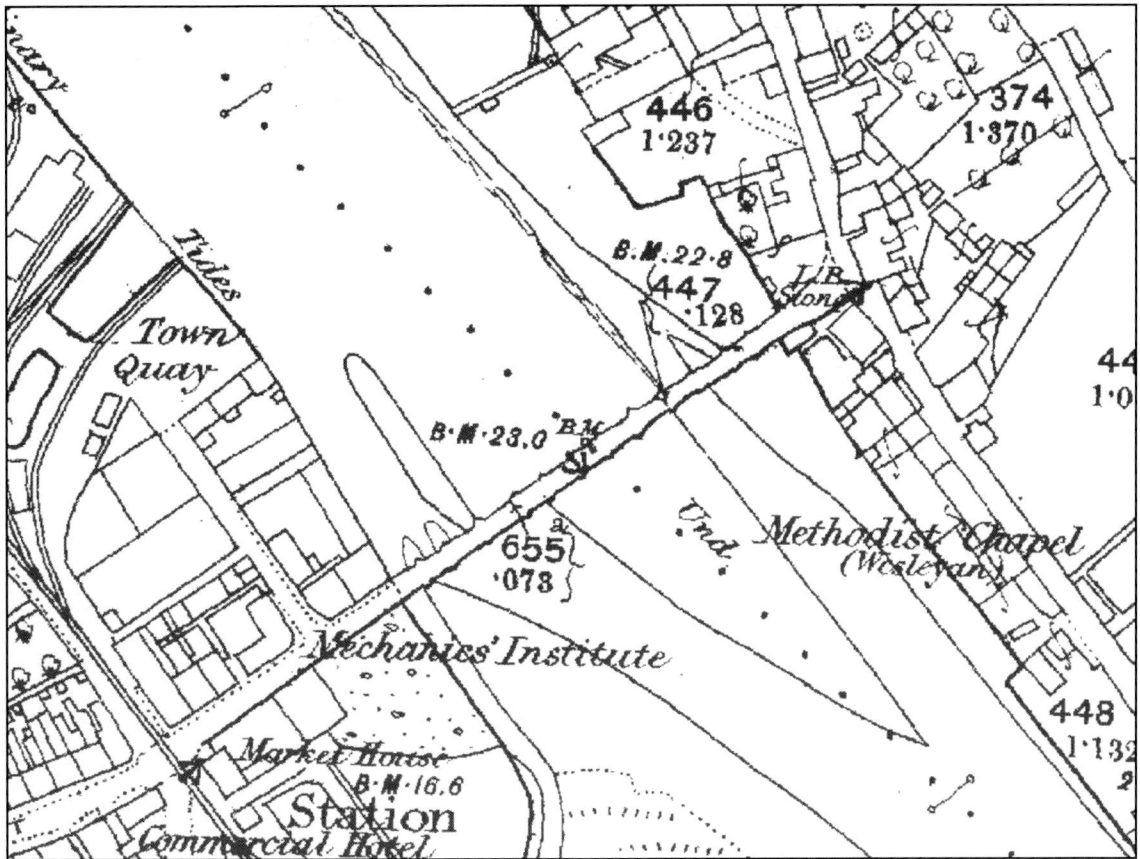

Fig 4.4 - Ordnance Survey Map 1880, showing the causeway wall upstream extending west to the site of the Market House, © Crown Copyright.

Several of the early illustrations and at least one painting show the bridge in a picturesque setting with rolling hills in the background, ships and smaller vessels in the foreground and buildings at either end of the bridge. Some of the artists may have used artistic licence to enhance the scene, masking reality, so it is often only the ramped causeway depicted on the western end of the bridge that indicates whether the artist illustrated the bridge from downstream or upstream. As the causeway was ramped to raise the road level to connect with the bridge, a wall had to be built on either side to protect the traffic of the day from falling off the edge of the causeway into the mud and marsh below. Pedestrians, cattle and sheep being driven to and fro to the market, pack-horse trains, travellers on horseback and handcarts all needed to be safe. It was only when properties started to be built up against the causeway that the walls were no longer needed. This is why in fig 4.5, the causeway wall is seen on one side only. The Wadebridge Institute building had already been built in 1838, the cellar rooms of which are at the former mud-flat level, with the windows and front entrance at the same level as the causeway. The author gained permission in 1990 to examine the cellars under the Wadebridge Institute when Malletts Ironmongers closed, but no sign of any arches or the causeway wall was found, reinforcing the view that the last arch is under the junction of Harbour Road.[5]

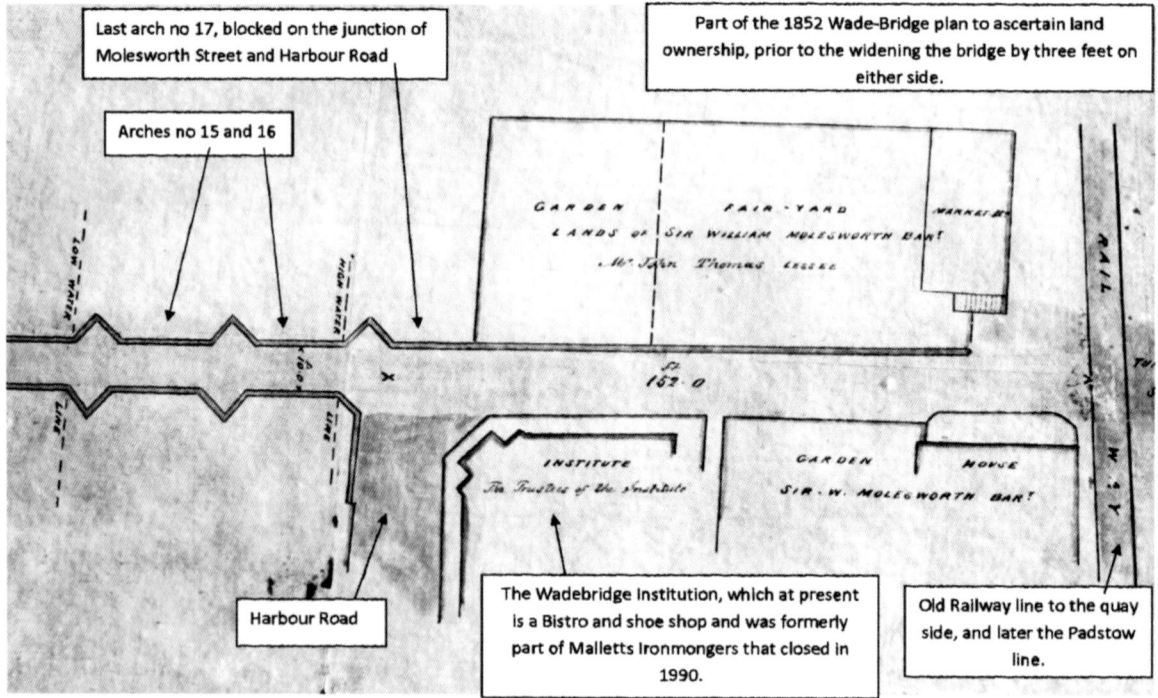

Last arch no 17, blocked on the junction of Molesworth Street and Harbour Road

Arches no 15 and 16

Part of the 1852 Wade-Bridge plan to ascertain land ownership, prior to the widening the bridge by three feet on either side.

Harbour Road

The Wadebridge Institution, which at present is a Bistro and shoe shop and was formerly part of Malletts Ironmongers that closed in 1990.

Old Railway line to the quay side, and later the Padstow line.

Fig 4.5 - Part of the 1852 plan to ascertain land ownership prior to the first widening of the bridge. This shows the causeway wall extending to the Market House. Courtesy Wadebridge Town Council.

Kink in the alignment of the bridge and causeway

The properties on the upstream side of the causeway were not built until 1873, and those nearest the bridge also have cellars. These properties, known as nos. 1, 3, and 5 Molesworth Street, were built on the land of the old fair plot and gardens owned by Sir William Molesworth. When built in 1873 they were roughly in line with the upstream parapets of the bridge after its first widening in 1852-53. However since the upstream widening of the bridge in 1962-63, they have formed a restriction or kink in the roadway leading west from the bridge, over the old causeway (now the beginning of Molesworth Street).[6]

---

[5] The author gained permission from Mr Philip Mutton who purchased Mallett's shop (the old Wadebridge Institute) to view the building and cellar rooms prior to re-development on 9th December 1990.

[6] When the bridge was widened for the second time in 1962-63, one local person suggested that the houses at the beginning of Molesworth Street that were built in 1873 should be demolished to remove any restriction to traffic. Clearly this did not go ahead.

Fig 4.6 - A view looking towards Molesworth Street from the bridge, showing the Wadebridge Institute and Malletts Ironmongers on the right and the causeway wall on the left.

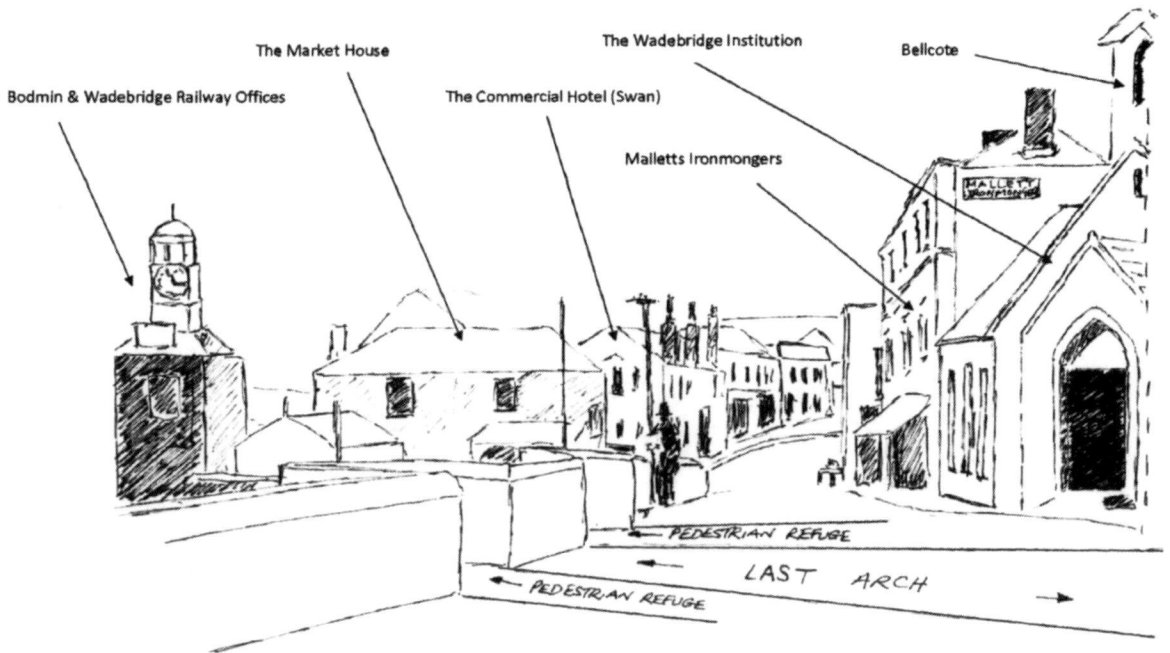

Fig 4.7 – A sketch identifying some of the buildings seen in fig 4.7 (above) and indicates where the last arch of the bridge is situated.

It has been recorded by Maclean that the first and last arches of the bridge were formerly used as cellars. Today, the last arch is beneath the road junction between Harbour Road and Molesworth Street, while the first arch over at Bridge End is still a cellar - although unused and locked. The plan of the bridge drawn in 1852 prior to the first widening, supports this view, and shows the causeway wall only on the upstream side. No records survive to indicate when the western wall of the causeway was removed. Nor is there any evidence to suggest that there were ever any small flood arches within the ramped causeway.

The pre-Reformation chapels.

The sites of the two ancient chapels which stood on either bank of the river, before the bridge was built, are not precisely known, although according to Henderson the bridge was built from chapel to chapel.[7] There are several documentary references to St Michael's chapel which stood on the town, or western bank, but little is known about the King's chapel on the eastern, or Egloshayle, bank. There are no early illustrations or maps of the bridge that identify either of the two chapels, with the possible exception of the Trevelver painting.

All five of the medieval long bridges in Cornwall and Devon had pre-Reformation chapels associated with them. At Barnstaple there was a chantry chapel dedicated to St Thomas on the town side of the bridge, while at Exeter another chapel of St Thomas stood at the western end of Exe Bridge and a chapel dedicated to St Edmund on the opposite, city end. Today, alongside the eight ruined and dry arches, can be seen the Victorian tower of the medieval chapel of St Edmund. Similarly, Bideford had a chapel situated at either end of its bridge: All Hallows or All Saints chapel at the west or town side of the bridge, and St Anne's at the east end. Perhaps the most interesting chapel, also dedicated to St Anne, the mother of the Virgin Mary, stood over the centre arch of the original Looe Bridge. Although no other chapels in Cornwall and Devon are recorded in the middle of a bridge, a few do still survive in other parts of England.[8] At St Ives in Cambridgeshire a chapel still stands on a central pier of the bridge, while a more elaborate chapel rebuilt in the eighteenth century stands on the bridge at Wakefield in West Yorkshire.[9] Further bridge chapels stood on Rochester Bridge and the Elvet Bridge at Durham.[10]

---

[7] Henderson, C G, and Coates, H, 1972. *Old Cornish Bridges and Streams*, 2nd ed. 116.
[8] Harrison, D, 2004. *The Bridges of Medieval England*, 199.
[9] Cook, M, 1998. *Medieval Bridges*, 40.
[10] Harrison, D, 2004. 200, Robins, F W, 1947, *The Story of the Bridge*, 145, 148, and De Mare', E, 1975, *Bridges of Britain*, 121.

St Michael's Chapel

As noted in chapter 1, St Michael's chapel was first licensed on the 6th September 1382, during the reign of Richard II, by Bishop Brantyngham of Exeter, to Thomas Stayndrope, rector of the parish church of Poutone (Pawton) now St Breock. The licence granted Stayndrope or his chaplain the right to hold a mass in the 'Capella de Wade' (the Chapel at Wade). In 1385, William Piers, rector of Poutone, had a licence to celebrate the mass in the sacred chapels of St Michael (at Wade) and at St Bruerdus at Burlawn. At the Reformation, both St Michael's chapel and the King's chapel were abandoned along with thousands of others across the country. After the Reformation, St Michael's chapel was never claimed by the Crown, but continued to be managed by the St Breock churchwardens who rented the building out for secular purposes.[11] In 1556, *St Mychall Chapell* was rented to M. Vyell for three years at a cost of twelve shillings and in 1565 to William Well for a term of seven years. According to the Churchwardens' Accounts, M. Vyell also rented the chapel in 1568 and again in 1571 for a further two years. In 1569, five hundred helying stones (roofing stones or slates) were paid for by St Breock churchwardens along with a helyer (slater or roofer) to re-roof the chapel. In 1575 the chapel is referred to as, *'the store howse at the bryge'*, suggesting that the chapel may have been close-by. In 1576, a John Martyn rented the chapel for a term of seven years paying eighteen shillings per annum, and he is referred to as renting the property again in the Churchwardens' Accounts for 1578.

Messrs. Tipper and Dawe

In 1591, St Michael's chapel was finally relinquished by St Breock churchwardens to William Tipper and Robert Dawe, gentlemen of London, who also seized the King's chapel on the Egloshayle bank. It is on this deed of sale that the chapels are described as being 'on the east and west ends of Wade-Bridge'. This appears to be the only direct reference to the sites of the chapels in relation to the bridge. These acquisitions by Tipper and Dawe are fully reported in the Calendar of Patent Rolls during the thirty-fourth year of Queen Elizabeth's reign (1591-92). The document states that both chapels were, for good service of Edward Dyer, granted *inter alia* to William Tipper and Robert Dawe, gentlemen of London. These gentlemen were speculators who went in search of pre-Reformation chapels and other redundant ecclesiastical property, concealed lands and tenements that had not been declared to, or forfeited to the King at the time of their dissolution. Tipper and Dawe were granted a licence by Queen Elizabeth I to search out these buildings, and then claimed them under the licence and sold them on. Records surviving in the Patent Rolls indicate that these gentlemen acquired hundreds of old pre-Reformation chapels and small parcels of land throughout the whole country.[12] As well as purchasing St Michael's chapel and the King's chapel either side of Wade-Bridge they purchased a chapel at Dunmeer that was formerly owned by the Prior of Bodmin, a chapel at Burlorne Eglos in St Breock parish, plus land in St Kew and Padstow.

---

[11] Cornwall Record Office, DDP19/5/1.
[12] National Archives, C66/1384 m24 - Calendar of Patent Rolls 34th Eliz. Part 4, m.24.

The reference in the Calendar of Patent Rolls in 1591, reads, '*recently in the tenancy of John Martyn or his assigns and others adjacent to their chapel called St Michael's chapel lying and existing above the west side of Wadbridge in the parish of Sainte Breke in the county of Cornwall with all lands, tenements and hereditaments belonging to the same chapel*'.

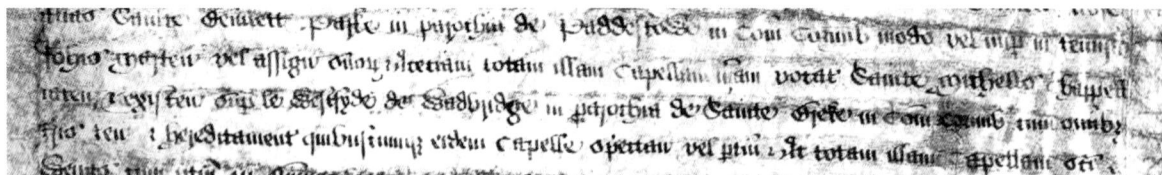

Fig – 4.8 Extract from the calendar of Patent Rolls showing the reference to St Michael's Chapel on the west side of Wade-Bridge, © National Archives.

The Chappell

Forty-two years later in a schedule of leases for the manor of Pawton dated 1633, Sir A Gorges granted the right to hold a fair in Wadebridge to John Tredenick for 30 shillings along with the lease of the '*Wadebridge Chappell*' for 12 shillings.[13] One assumes this to be the redundant St Michael's chapel although this cannot be substantiated. In 1650, the manor of Pawton, Trevose and Ide was sold to merchants Nich Opy of Plymouth and Richard Lobb of Milar (Mylor) for £7000; it included the '*Wadebridge Chappell*'.

A hundred years later, on the 2nd August 1758, the manor of Pawton is recorded leasing a property known as '*The Chapple situated and lying near Wade-Bridge*'.[14] The property consisted of a '*dwelling house, together with curtilage, back, side and herb garden, together with commons there unto for pasturing Pigs, Geese and Ducks.*' Is this the same St Michael's chapel? The lease refers to the property being near to Wade-Bridge, although in this case it is difficult to tell if they are referring to the town or the bridge. It is also difficult to identify where there would be room for a herb garden and commons, although the latter could just mean a common right to allow pigs, geese and ducks to graze on the marshes. The freehold of this property was owned by John Molesworth, son of Sir John Molesworth of Pencarrow, and it was leased to John and William Collins. Further leases of the Chapple to John and William Collins dated 29th September 1762 and 28th October 1784 also survive.[15] This could suggest that once St Michael's chapel was abandoned for religious devotion and its later use as a store, it may eventually have been converted into the dwelling house known as the Chapple. Another possibility is that this dwelling house was built on the former site of the chapel and thereafter adopted the name Chapple due to its location. In 1790 a rental for the manor of Pawton includes Wadebridge, Fair Park, the Old Chapple and the

---

[13] Henderson Calendars 18, 85 (Molesworth Records) in the Courtney Library, Royal Institution of Cornwall.
[14] Cornwall Record Office, DDCF 904.
[15] Cornwall Record Office, DDCF 905-906.

Market House.[16] The last reference we have to the Chapple is in a lease dated December 1826, when Mr Thomas Werry leased the property for £23.[17]

The Wadebridge Institute

Could the Wadebridge Institute building, which stands on the downstream western approach to the bridge, be on the site of the chapel?   In 1838, the Wadebridge Institution was formed and the new Institute building erected close to the last arch of the bridge. Again, the freehold was owned by the Molesworth family, a fact which may suggest that the Institute was built on the site of the former chapel - though the Molesworths owned much of the property in the town during this period.   The site was leased to the trustees of the Institute and funds to build the Institute building were raised by public subscription, selling shares at £2 10s each - with originally forty-six shareholders.[18]   This Institute – alternatively known as the Literary Institute, Wadebridge Public Institution and later the Mechanics Institute, held its first lecture in January 1839.

Fig 4.9 - Wadebridge Institution Building, today used as a shoe shop and bistro.

The building contained a meeting room, a reading room with included the town's first public subscription library and a gentlemen's smoking room. In 1881, a report describing the Institute was published in a North Cornwall guide; it reads:

> *'We should not be doing justice to the intelligence and public spirit of Wadebridge did we not mention its Literary Institution and Reading Room, a very important and substantial*

---

[16] Henderson Calendars 18, 95.

[17] Cornwall Record Office, DDCF 909.

[18] The original share certificates and account books were until recently in the possession of Wadebridge Old Cornwall Society, but in 2000 were deposited in the Cornwall Record Office for safe keeping. Ref. CRO/5798.

building of comparatively modern erection and triangular shape, occupying the corner of streets facing the ancient bridge and leading to the wharves. The reading room is large, handsome, and well-ventilated; two-thirds of the walls are occupied by an excellent library of ancient and modern literature and the remainder is filled with large maps, the latest addition being the new map of Africa. The table is strewed with the leading daily and weekly newspapers, and the presence of such monthlies as 'The Nineteenth Century' 'Blackwood's' and other magazines testifies to the mental calibre of the 70 or 80 members whose names hang suspended near the portrait in oils of a truly old-English-looking, beneficent gentleman, who, we suppose, was the founder or patron of the institution'. Was this gentleman Sir William Molesworth?[19]

Closure of the Institute

The Institute closed in 1912 and the trustees leased the building to Malletts who already occupied premises adjoining its western side.[20] Later in 1938 when the lease ran out, the Molesworth family relinquished their claim to the freehold, allowing the trustees finally to sell all the shares and wind up the Institution. Malletts then purchased the freehold for £380 allowing them to extend their premises.[21] Today, this building still survives and is occupied by a shoe shop and a Bistro. A large metal ceiling rose vent in the ceiling of the shoe shop (now above a modern false ceiling) indicates that this was the former smoking room. The building is L-shaped in plan and has rooms below the level of the present road. The original entrance was through an arched doorway that still exists and above this was a bell turret, removed during the 1980s. Malletts continued to trade until 1990, when the shop finally closed, and at this time the author was given access to examine the rooms below the shops. Among the items left in Malletts shop were a number of plaster heads, some face-less, which must have been connected to the building's former use as an Institute; speculations about their meaning or purpose include death masks, or some scientific or medical study.

The King's Chapel

The only named reference to the King's chapel standing at the eastern end of the bridge is in the deed of sale in the Calendar of Patent Rolls to William Tipper and Robert Dawe, Gent. of London who acquired both the King's chapel and St Michael's chapel in 1591-92.[22] This reads: *'recently the chapel with pertinences called the kynges chapel above the east part of Wadebridge in the parish of Sainte Egglishayle in the aforesaid county of Cornwall and also one part of our Lords garden adjacent'*. The reference to *Sainte Egglishayle*, suggests that the recorder at the time did not understand the meaning of the name Egloshayle (church by the estuary or river). Maclean in his *Deanery of Trigg*

---

[19] Anon, 1881. *A Picturesque guide to North Cornwall*, Cater, Launceston.
[20] *Cornish Guardian*, 5th April 1912, 'Wadebridge and its Institute: The Closing Scene'.
[21] Records held by Wadebridge Old Cornwall Society.
[22] National Archives, C/66/1384 m24.

Minor suggests that the King's chapel may be the chapel that Lysons records as St Wence in Egloshayle parish, however its site was not known.[23]

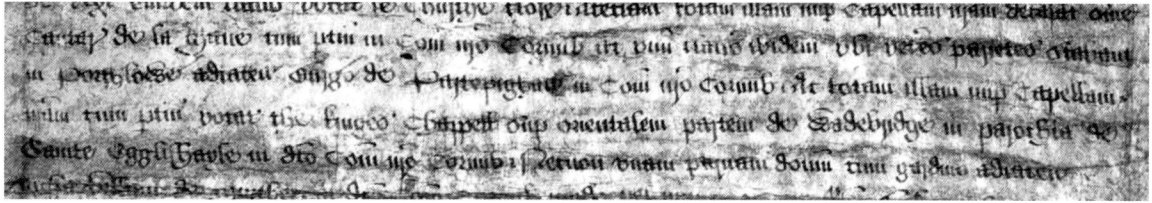

Fig 4.10 - Extract from the Calendar of Patent Rolls showing the reference to the King's Chapel on the east side of Wade-Bridge, © National Archives.

No records survive to indicate when the chapel was first licensed, who it was dedicated to, or which King is referred to. This is not the only reference to a King's chapel in the county. At the King Harry Passage near Trelissick there was once a chapel dedicated to Our Lady and King Henry (Harry); the King in this instance was King Henry VI.[24] There are also references to a King's chapel at Maidenhead in Kent, which formerly stood close to the medieval bridge in the main street; this was dedicated to King Edward I.[25]

The eastern end of the bridge is founded on rock, unlike the western or town side. This is why the Bridge End area at Egloshayle is always depicted with many more substantial buildings on early prints. The exact site of the King's chapel is not known and it could have been on either the up or downstream side of the bridge, on the site of any of the buildings on the north side of the bridge approaches. It is doubtful whether the chapel site will ever be confirmed conclusively; however the possibility that it was below Riverside House appears on present evidence, to be the best suggestion.

Riverside House

If we examine part of the 1852 plan of the Egloshayle end of the bridge, we can see that on the downstream side of the bridge, there was a slipway nearest to the bridge owned by Padstow Harbour Commissioners, with Riverside House to the west of this. By tradition, this has always been regarded as the site of the King's chapel, or that the chapel was incorporated into the fabric of the house as a basement or cellar to the property.

According to Mrs Sedding who lived here in the early twentieth century the property was owned in 1769 by the Fox family, who built Gonvena House during this period.[26] The 1852 plan of the

[23] Lysons, D & S, 1813. *Magna Britannia* , **III**, 83.

[24] Henderson, C, and Coates, H, 1972. 90.

[25] Walker, J W, 1931. *A History of Maidenhead,* 2nd. Ed. 22.

[26] Sedding, E, (Mrs) *c*1909. *The Riverside House: A Tale of Wadebridge*, 3. - According to Mrs Sedding, in 1769, one John Fox enlarged Riverside House and scratched the names of some of the Fox family of that time, with the date 1769, on a pane of glass in the drawing room.

bridge shows that Riverside House and the Manor House on the opposite side of the road were both owned by Richard Symons the solicitor to the Wade-Bridge Trust at the time.

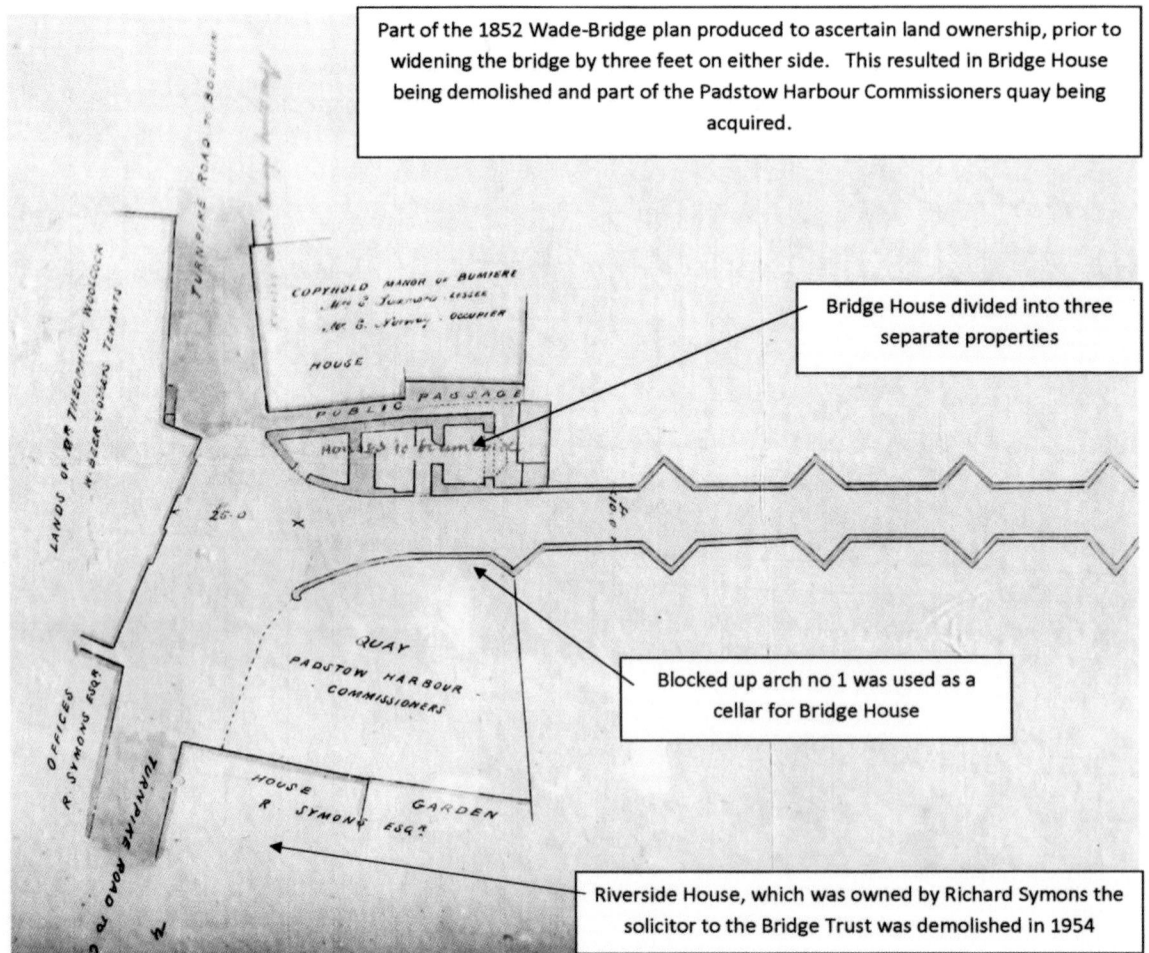

Part of the 1852 Wade-Bridge plan produced to ascertain land ownership, prior to widening the bridge by three feet on either side. This resulted in Bridge House being demolished and part of the Padstow Harbour Commissioners quay being acquired.

Bridge House divided into three separate properties

Blocked up arch no 1 was used as a cellar for Bridge House

Riverside House, which was owned by Richard Symons the solicitor to the Bridge Trust was demolished in 1954

Fig 4.11 - Part of the 1852 plan of the bridge, which shows the sites of both Riverside House and Bridge House, Courtesy Wadebridge Town Council.

By 1909, Riverside House or a part of it was the home of the architect Edmund H Sedding, author of *Norman Architecture in Cornwall*. By the twentieth century and up until its sad demise in 1954 (see below), it was the home and surgery of the town's General Practitioners, Dr J B O Richards and later Dr A Wilson-Gunn, as well as being the Central Hospital Supplies Service sub depot during the second World War.

Fig 4.12 - Riverside House situated on the east side of Wade-Bridge, demolished in 1954, Courtesy Collin Brewer.

A Tale of Wadebridge

While the Seddings were resident, Mrs Sedding wrote a romantic short story entitled *The Riverside House - a tale of Wadebridge*. This fictional story tells of Cuthbert Mayne the young Catholic priest, administering the Mass in secret in a basement chapel below Riverside House and his love for a girl called Anna Trehaine who lived there.[27] Some of the footnotes Mrs Sedding adds to the book give a good insight into what the old house was like, although her reference to Cuthbert Mayne being executed on the bridge is fiction rather than fact.[28]

The house had a room in the centre of the hall that was considered to have been the chapel. It was enclosed by a high railing, while at each end of the passage were doors with heavy bolts, fastening on the inside. Mrs Sedding records a holy water stoup in the house, although she does not describe it. The kitchen had an old hatch door leading direct onto the road, while the two rooms above, that belonged to the oldest part of the house, contained several windows with old 'green bottle' glass. There were supposed to be forty cupboards in the house, some of which had already been sealed up by 1909, however large cupboards in the bedrooms had their fastening on

[27] Sedding, E, c1909.
[28] Sedding, E, c1909. 32.

53

the inside and were large enough to hold several men. Mrs Sedding also describes a stone cellar or dungeon with a door, in the centre of which was a square opening, iron barred. It had a stone bench at one end and a small window looking out towards the river, which was also barred. There was also talk of a room being blocked up and a secret staircase leading down to the cellars. Large wooden double doors with massive bolts led out onto the marshy ground between the house and the bridge (the slipway).

Fig 4.13 - Another view of Riverside House showing the eastern end of the downstream parapet, Courtesy Collin Brewer.

Demolition of Riverside House

When Riverside House was demolished in 1954 to make way for the widening of the eastern approach to the bridge, an archaeological 'watching brief' was undertaken by Miss Dorothy Dudley. On examination of the cellars during the demolition, she found that at the core of the foundations was a small rectangular building, 40ft (12.2m) long and 20ft (6.09m) wide, with its long sides running parallel with the river. The building had been erected on a platform cut out of the slaty rock of the river bank, while the northern and eastern walls of the building were formed by rock cut sides. The western and southern walls were approximately two feet thick and carried an external string course about 4ft (1.22m) high above the ground level. The slate-built walls were consistently well executed in dry walling. [29]

---

[29] Dudley, D, 1954. 'The demolition of Riverside House, Wadebridge' *Devon and Cornwall Notes and Queries* **XXVI**, and Cornwall Record Office DDX364/20.

Miss Dudley went on to report that a strange feature for a cellar was a small erection built into the sides of a rock-cut alcove 10ft (3.05m) long by 7ft (2.1m) wide at the south end of the east wall. Again this was well built in smaller slabs of slate than elsewhere in the cellars. Two doorways were on the west wall, another in the south wall and each was 7ft (2.1m) high and 4ft (1.22m) wide, while a deeply splayed window or possibly two were set in the western wall.

Miss Dudley concluded that such features as the deeply splayed window and the string course on the west and south walls were not what one would expect in a cellar. She considered these walls to have been the external part of a much earlier building, possibly of an ecclesiastical nature, although the doors and windows were all flat topped not arched, perhaps indicating secular building rather than a chapel. On the other hand it was suggested by Miss Dudley that this part may in fact have been the crypt of a building above this level. Perhaps it was a lodging place for the use of pilgrims and travellers who had to await time and tide here before they could continue on their journey.

Today, all evidence of Riverside House is gone and part of the site is now beneath the roadway, while the remainder acts as a small public garden with seats, from which one can admire the bridge. Further archaeological work in the area might yet confirm the original site of the King's chapel. Another contender for the former site of the King's chapel is Bridge House, which was situated on the upstream side of the bridge at Egloshayle end, although this was demolished in 1853 when the bridge was first widened and the second widening on the upstream side would have erased all archaeological evidence of it.

Bridge End

The community of houses and businesses on the Egloshayle, or eastern approach to the bridge is known as Bridge End. By the 1930s this area had a butcher, wine & spirit merchant, hairdresser, garage with petrol pumps, boot repairer, grocer, builders merchant and fishmonger.

On 3rd November 1993, while gas pipes were renewed at Bridge End, two small stone built arches were discovered, buried beneath the surface of the road, at right angles to, and slightly above the level of the bridge. These were sadly reburied on the same day they were discovered, and little photographic evidence was obtained. The arches appear to have been culverts, perhaps used to drain water from the fields above, where the Bridge View estate stands today.

5 'where after he shall be dead and quartered, a quarter to be set on a poale at Wade bridge'

Historical accounts

If the old bridge could speak, it would tell us so much about those who passed over it; and events on or near it, but today all we have are a few incomplete historical documents that give clues, or perhaps a brief reference to some colourful events that the bridge has witnessed. These snippets of information give only the bare bones of an occasion or happening and historians are left to add the flesh, make a story and place things in their historical context. Here are examples of a few of the more exciting incidents in the life of Wade-Bridge.

Armed assault on Wade-Bridge

One series of documents which survives at the National Archives at Kew, albeit not a complete record, reports an affray, armed assault or attack that took place on Wade-Bridge on the 18th June 1542, the 34th year in the reign of Henry VIII. This attack eventually found its way to the Court of Star Chamber in Westminster Hall, London.[1] Henderson is the first historian to make a reference to this event, which involved John Tredenek (Tredinick), the local squire of St Breock, and George Wolcoke (Woolcock), a constable of the parish.[2]

This was the year when Henry VIII executed his fifth wife Catherine Howard, marrying Catherine Parr the following year. In 1543, England was again at war with France, while three years earlier the Cornish monasteries of Launceston, Bodmin and St Germans had been dissolved.[3]

The clash of arms appears to have been premeditated; for we hear from witnesses at the court case that John Tredenek came across the bridge with five servants or retainers, who were all on horseback with full apparel. In other words they were fully armed with swords and bucklers, bows and arrows and also daggers. George Wolcoke, Thomas Wolcoke and Martyn Hyden (Hayden) blocked Tredenek's passage, verbally insulting and taunting him, while further men who had lain in wait ambushed them. Wolcoke's men also had a number of weapons including an eight foot staff, short swords and bucklers, daggers and a halberd. Was Tredenek pre-warned to come prepared for trouble? Had they been lured to the bridge to be attacked? Or were they simply passing over the bridge? The witness depositions suggest that they may have had a dispute earlier in the same day, so perhaps this was unfinished business? Even though there were no fatalities, Tredenek decided to take the matter to court.

---

[1] Six documents survive at the National Archives at Kew, not all of them complete or readable, however enough can be transcribed to give an insight into the event. Documents REQ 3/20, STAC 2/18/3, STAC 2/18/5, STAC 2/18/22, STAC 2/18/255 and STAC 2/31/11.

[2] Henderson, C G, and Coates, H, 1972 Ed. *Old Cornish Bridges and Streams*, 118. The names of these individuals are spelt in several different ways in these documents: Tredeneck, Tredenek, Wulcoke, Wolcok, Wolcoke, but all refer to Tredinick and Woolcock.

[3] Orme, N, 2010. *A History of the County of Cornwall II : Religious History to 1560*, 98.

Although the disagreement was primarily between John Tredenek and George Wolcoke, each had a group of servants, retainers and family members with them; however it is interesting that not all family members were on the same side in this dispute. Tredenek had five men with him, Petroc Parnall, John Wolcoke (the brother of George), William Joell, Thomas Tredenek (another relative) and Edward Hydon. George Wolcoke's men included another relative, Thomas Wolcoke and his stepson Martyn Hydon (possibly a relative of Edward who was fighting on the other side). A further three men lay in wait including a Henry Bromston, Thomas Capell and John Pakett.[4] Another nine men are named as witnesses to the affray suggesting that in total there must have been at least twenty-one people on the bridge at this time.

The Tredenek family held a mansion at Tredinick, half a mile to the north-west of St Breock churchtown. Today the site is part of the Royal Cornwall Agricultural Showground. According to Polsue writing in the late nineteenth century, the house boasted the largest windows of its kind in the kingdom; it has long been destroyed and the farmhouse which was later built on its site has also been demolished, so that today only a few cut stones survive, built into the present Boscawen House which now occupies the site on the showground.[5] At the time the Tredeneks also held the neighbouring farms of Trelill and Dunveth. George Wolcoke was a yeoman farmer and gentleman landowner and holding the office of parish constable must have also been influential in the parish. According to the Lay Subsidy Roll of 1543, both Tredenek and Wolcoke were taxed at the same amount, indicating that they were both large landowners in the parish.[6] It is not recorded where in St Breock or Wadebridge Wolcoke and his family lived.

Tredenek decided to petition the court about the affray and the preliminary hearings were held at Lostwithiel, probably at the old Duchy Palace. The court listed a number of questions they wished to establish answers to, which included the following:

1   Whether George Wolcoke was a constable of the parish of St Breock?

2   Whether George Wolcoke as a constable of the said hundred obeyed and kept the king's peace according to his oath?

3   What words were said by George and Thomas Wolcoke and Martyn his son to John Tredenek and why?

4   Who struck the first stroke or blow, George Wolcoke, John Tredenek or other persons?

5   Whether George Wolcoke had in his hand an eight foot staff, or a sword?

6   Whether Thomas Wolcoke did strike John Tredenek and if so with what weapons?

7   Whether George Wolcoke did fall at distance with Edward and whether he was likely to be in danger of death?

---

[4] Some of the names of the servants and witnesses to this assault are difficult to read on the original documents.

[5] Polsue, J, 1867. *Parochial history of Cornwall*, I, 130.

[6] Stoate, T L, 1985. *Cornwall Subsidies in the Reign of Henry VIII 1524 and 1543 and the benevolence of 1545*, 85. John Tredeneck and George Wolcoke were taxed as landowners in St Breock parish, while John Wolcoke and Michael Wolcoke were taxed for the goods they held.

On the 28th May 1543, a hearing was held at Lostwithiel, where witnesses provided sworn depositions to representatives of the King's Council who included Humfry Arundell,[7] William Carnsnyowe (Carminow),[8] William Bere and Nicholas Glyne. Ten witnesses were examined and interrogated of whom at least one, Edward Hyden (Hayden),[9] was involved in the affray; however it is difficult to tell whether the others named were involved or were simply bystanders. Depositions were provided by Henry Trefrye, Gentleman, Michell (Michael) Wolcoke, William Watts aged 30 years, John Wacome, John Hore and Edward Hyden aged 58, all supporting Tredenek, while Edward Clyker Gentleman aged 40 years, Henry Hocker aged 40 years, Richard Polstag aged 38 years and John Wayte aged 50 years upheld Wolcoke's position.[10]

Henry Trefrye stated that he could not tell who started the affray between John Tredenek and George Wolcoke, although be claimed that he saw George Wolcoke with a staff of five feet in length. He also saw George deliver a blow to Edward Hyden and that they both fell at a distance. Michell Wolcoke who was George's brother testified against him and claimed that on Christmas Day in the 33rd year of the reign of Henry VIII (1541), George had drawn a dagger against another of his brothers, John, and assaulted him and that John was in despair of his life. This reference may have been added to suggest George Wolcoke was an aggressive man who would even turn on members of his own family.

Both Michell Wolcoke and William Watts stated that George was a constable of the *pryshe of seyne Breoke* (parish of St Breock) and that he had not always kept the King's peace according to his oath. They stated that George told John Tredenek to take a weapon as he was going to fight him and that Tredenek took his servant's sword and buckler (shield). Both Edward Clyker and Henry Hocker stated that after Wolcoke had taunted Tredenek, Tredenek set an arrow in his bow and aimed it at Wolcoke and that it was then that Wolcoke challenged him to take a weapon and fight.

Nevertheless, as one would expect, each witness gave a slightly different account of the event so that, for example, George Wolcoke's staff is recorded as five feet, six feet and eight feet long. What is clear is that there was a clash with swords and that there were a few strikes between them. William Watts claimed that Thomas Wolcoke struck Tredenek with his sword; however their depositions state that no one was hurt.

The depositions of Edward Clyker and Richard Polstag read as follows:

> **Edward Clyker** *Gentilman of the age of xl yeres or there aboute sowrn and examyned uppon a booke by his outh sayth that he was present at Wade brygge when the ffraye was betwene George Wulcok and John Tredeneck and herd the said George Wulcok call aft the said John Tredenek saying Tredenek here is he that thou callest knave and churse to daye and thou wylt*

---

[7] Two Humphry Arundells are recorded in the Lay Subsidy Roll for 1543, one at Withiel and another at Helland; both were substantial landowners.

[8] One William Carnsuyow is recorded as a landowner in St Kew parish during 1543.

[9] One Edward Hydon is recorded in the Lay Subsidy Roll for 1543 under Egloshayle parish.

[10] All the deponents' ages quoted were estimates, for example William Watts is recorded as '30 years or there abouts', also all the other ages noted were also recorded as 'there abouts'. Not all the deponents have ages recorded in the document.

evy thyng with hym here I am there uppon the said John Tredenek came bake aynst hyme with a bowe bente and an arrow yn hyme and then the said George said lene the bowe yf thou wilt fyght and then he putt his bowe frome hyme and toke his servants sword and buckler and soe they drewe to geders a halfe a dosyn strypes but hoe gave the fyrst stripe he knoweth nott. Also he sayth that he herd the one calle the oder knave and churell and sayth that as he herd saye Fyr Mathewe Polden priste should have a chylde by a woman of the parish of seynt Breoke and sayth that the said John Tredene doth vexe and trobyll the said George Wulcok for malice as he surposith and for noe cause els and more this deponent cannot saye.

Richard Polstag *of th age xxxviij yeres sowrn and examyned uppon a booke by his outh saith that he was uppon Wade brygge when John Tredenek and George Wulcoke dyd mete and saith George Wulcoke did saye to the said John Tredenek thes words here comyth the same man that thou dydest calle knave and chorell to daye and the said John Tredenek ys more that is true and with that he sett an arrowe in his bowe and then the said George sayd here be nor kyttys nor crowes but if than be a man take a wepon and make a knave of me or els I wyll make one of thou and there was nor iij strypes betwene them but there was not hurte don betwene them. And saith that he herd the saith John call to the saith George gorbelly and knave and saith that in his consyens that Fyr Mathy Polden begate a woman with chylde within the said friary and more the deponent cannot saye.*

From these depositions one learns perhaps the true reason for the clash of arms. Both witnesses allege that one Friar Mathew Polden, a priest, had fathered the child of a woman in the parish of St Breock and that this woman was in some way connected to John Tredenek, either a servant or perhaps even a mistress. Is it possible that Friar Polden found a home in St Breock parish after the friary at Bodmin closed in September 1538 and then embarked on a more worldly life which involved an affair which offended Tredenek. Clearly Polstag and Clyker's statements indicate that Tredenek and Wolcoke had both previously met earlier in the day. Wolcoke's taunts about Polden's conduct included calling Tredenek a *'knave'* and a *'churell'*, both derogatory and disparaging terms to call the Lord of the Manor. By the same token, Tredenek had also called Wolcoke a *'knave'* and a *'gorbelly'*. According to the Oxford English Dictionary, a knave could be described as an unprincipled man, given to dishonourable and deceitful practises, a base and crafty rogue; while churl means an ill-bred person, a peasant or of low status. A gorbelly means someone with a protruding belly or fat stomach.

Court of Star Chamber
In Tudor England there were no courts dealing with violent crimes except for the King's Court at Westminster Hall. It was known as the Court of Star Chamber because its ceiling was painted with stars. In November 1543, George Wolcoke, Thomas Wolcoke, Martyn Hyden and others

were subpoenaed to appear in person before his Majesty King Henry VIII in the Star Chamber at Westminster, to answer to his Majesty and his Council for their actions.[11]

The journey from Wadebridge to London would have been long and hazardous as there were no stage coaches in those days and the roads, particularly in Cornwall and Devon, were nothing more than dirt tracks. There were only two ways to travel to London from Cornwall, either by sea or on horseback. If the weather was fine and with a good horse a traveller could travel thirty miles in a day during the summer and twenty in the winter, however the court case at Westminster was in November and a journey in poor weather could take much longer. The journey could therefore have taken them at least ten or twelve days each way at a leisurely pace.[12] It would seem unlikely that all the witnesses were called to Westminster, as their sworn statements were taken down at Lostwithiel. The documents suggest there was more than one hearing at Westminster although the one we have record of was dated 28th November 1543.[13]

Although witnesses stated that there was some contact between swords, and that Thomas Wolcoke struck John Tredenek with his sword, there were no reports of anyone being seriously injured and the damage appears to have been more to do with their pride. The reference to George Wolcoke and Edward Hayden falling at a great distance and in danger of death may indicate that they fell off the bridge down into the river. During this period, Wade-Bridge was long and narrow with its eastern or Egloshayle approach wooded. According to the court report the attack took place at the Egloshayle or eastern end of the bridge: did Wolcoke's men lie in wait under one of the dry arches of the bridge or in amongst the trees on the wooded approach?

The outcome of the court case is unknown and it is disappointing to find that the most important document, the judgement appears to be missing. Some of the documents are incomplete, while others are damaged or too dark and faded to read, but enough has been transcribed to give the gist of the story. What is certain is that both men appear to have survived the King's judgement. The two feuding families had further disputes which ended up at the Court of Star Chamber. Plaintiff George Wolcoke took Henry Tredeneck, Joan his wife and others to court on an allegation that they forcibly entered a property at St Breock,[14] while William Tredeneck took

---

[11] National Archives, STAC. 2/18/3.

[12] Jenkins, A K H, 1983 Ed. *Cornwall and its People*, 135-37 and 144-46. Jenkins gives some idea of how long it would take to travel from Cornwall to London during the middle ages. He suggests that if you were well equipped and riding for your life in the King's service, one could reach London in 6 or 7 days. In 1342, a messenger with letters for the Receiver left Restormal Castle for London, making the return journey in 12 days. However it is not known whether he changed his horse enroute. Jenkins also notes that in 1605 pack horses with bullion would take 10 days to reach Truro from London and the post still took 8 days from London to Penzance in 1663. Mortimer, I, 2009. *The Time Traveller's Guide to Medieval England* suggests that a single traveller alone could ride 30 miles a day in the summer and 20 miles a day during the winter months.

[13] Regnal Year: Henry VIII is ascended to the throne on 22 April and therefore the regnal year goes from April 22nd to April 21st each year, and the 34th year of Henry VIII was between 22nd April 1542 and 21st April 1543. Henderson in *Old Cornish Bridges* quoted 1543, but the affray must have taken place in June 1542 according to the regnal year.

[14] National Archives, STAC 3/1/109.

George Wolcoke and others to court regarding the seizure of sheep in Padstow and St Issey and no doubt there were other incidents for which records have not survived.[15]

Cuthbert Mayne

At the beginning of December 1577, a quarter of Cuthbert Mayne's body and possibly also his head were set up on a pike or pole on the bridge as a warning to those who continued to follow the Catholic faith. This was perhaps the most gruesome episode in the history of our bridge. It is the only recorded occasion that an event like this happened at Wade-Bridge; though it is possible that there were other times when bodies were displayed on the bridge as an example.[16]

Most punishment during this period was performed in public at the market square, and the bodies of the convicted were often set up on a gibbet as a warning to others on the main thoroughfares of the day, either beside roads, bridges or at the entrances to towns and cities. Presumably a proclamation would have accompanied the piking of the body, with word then spreading by word of mouth amongst local people. The practise of displaying the heads of traitors, thieves and those who offended the authorities on London Bridge started in 1305 with the head of Scottish patriot William Wallace and continued for nearly four hundred years.

Fig 5.1 - Cuthbert Mayne by Daniel Fournier,
© National Portrait Gallery.

At the Southwark end of Old London Bridge, the entrance to the City of London, the heads of traitors were continually on display above the drawbridge gateway. According to Pierce, visitors recorded seeing as many as thirty-four heads at one time and the city even employed a Keeper of Heads who disposed of the old and decaying heads in the river as fresh examples arrived for display. [17] The stench of rotting bodies on Old London Bridge is well recorded.

---

[15]National Archives, STAC 3/4/33.

[16] Daniel Fournier spelt Cuthbert Mayne as 'Cutbert Mayn' and gave the date of his execution as 1579, although the correct date was 1577. Fournier (*c1710 - c1766*) drew this likeness over 170 years after Mayne's death, perhaps this is why Mayne appears much older than his 33 years!

[17] Pierce, P, 2001. *Old London Bridge.* As well as William Wallace, the heads and quarters of people from all parts of society were displayed on London Bridge as well as many prominent people such as Simon of Sudbury, the Archbishop of Canterbury, Wat Tyler and Jack Cade, Kentish rebels, those who opposed Henry VIII, including Sir Thomas More and Thomas Cromwell and later the conspirators in the Gunpowder Plot.

When crossing the narrow bridge, people would have been unable to escape the smell of Cuthbert Mayne's rotting body. As the corpse decayed it would have attracted dogs, seagulls, flies and vermin. Without living through this period of history, it is difficult to know how gruesome the people of Wadebridge would have found this. It is quite likely that they would have seen the executed bodies of criminals from time to time on public display at Bodmin, or hanging on a gibbet elsewhere. Nonetheless, it must have been a potent reminder of the fate awaiting adherents to the Catholic faith in this newly protestant country.

Catholicism in Elizabethan England

Following the Reformation, Henry VIII became the head of the English Church and was succeeded by his son Edward VI, but on the death of Edward VI in 1553 there was a brief and bloody return to Catholicism under Mary I. Mary's reign only lasted five years and with the accession of Elizabeth I in 1558 there was a return to the Anglican Church. For the first ten years of her reign Elizabeth tried to accommodate English Catholics so long as they remained loyal to her and turned a blind eye to the many secret services held in private homes so long as they attended church when required to. Elizabeth followed this policy of religious tolerance until political and religious threats from Europe forced her to become less considerate.

In 1566, Pius V became the new Pope, but as God's representative on Earth for all Catholics, he was far more aggressive than the previous incumbents and his dislike of Queen Elizabeth caused him to issue *Regnans in Excelsis*, a Papal Bull, on the 28th February 1570, excommunicating her and absolving all her subjects from allegiance to her and her laws. It charged Elizabeth with being a heretic, of not being the legitimate Monarch in the eyes of Catholics and stated that those who supported her would also be excommunicated. This was the time of the counter Reformation, and plots against Elizabeth, with the aim of placing Catholic Mary Queen of Scots on the throne of England. Invasion by Spain was a real threat.

In 1568, Elizabeth put Mary Queen of Scots into protective custody where she remained until her execution in 1587. Meanwhile Elizabeth's reaction to the Papal Bull was to persecute Catholics by fining them for non-attendance at church, seizing their assets and estates if they were caught celebrating the mass, imprisoning or executing them. The Government issued a statute making it high treason to publish or act upon the Papal Bull and to be caught with such hallowed tokens as the *Agnus Dei* incurred penalties of *premunure* (loss of lands, goods and liberty for life). The Papal Bull forced many to choose between loyalty to the Queen and State or to the Pope and the Catholic Church. According to Rowse, priests like Cuthbert Mayne who died as traitors to the State were seen as martyrs by Catholics.[18]

---

[18] Rowse, A L, 1941. *Tudor Cornwall*, 342.

Early Life of Cuthbert Mayne

Cuthbert Mayne was born in 1544 at Yorkston near Barnstaple, Devon, he received Anglican orders and became Chaplain of St John's College Oxford in 1573.   Later having made the acquaintance of Catholics like Edmund Campion, he converted to Catholicism. In 1573, Mayne was forced to flee abroad and studied at the English College at Douai in Flanders (now northern France), where he was ordained as a priest in 1575.[19] The seminary at Douai was founded in 1559 by Cardinal William Allen and was the main centre for English Catholics escaping religious persecution. Here hundreds of Catholic priests were trained and then returned to England where they took up clandestine duties administering the mass to English men who refused to give up their Catholic faith.

On returning from Douai at Easter 1576, Cuthbert Mayne took up residence at Golden Manor, the home of Francis Tregian in the parish of Probus. Though employed as steward, he secretly administered the Mass to the Tregian family and frequently visited other manors around the county with his employer. Mayne also performed the Mass at Lanherne in St Mawgan in Pydar, the home of the Arundells, relatives by marriage to the Tregians. Tregian was not discreet about his support for Catholicism or Mayne's presence, and when the authorities decided to clamp down on those who refused to attend church, Golden was one of the first places to be visited.

Mayne's arrest and execution

In June 1577, a party of over one hundred men led by Sir Richard Grenville and ten Justices of the Peace, raided Golden Manor, arresting Mayne and removing him to Launceston Castle, together with evidence of his religious beliefs and proof of his illegal services.[20] Mayne was to spend three months in a dungeon at the castle until the Michaelmas Assizes where he was tried before Sir Roger Manwood and Sir John Jeffreys. Mayne was to be made an example of; he refused to denounce his religious views and was later given the death sentence. His examination the day before his execution was signed by many leading gentry, including William Mohun, John Carminowe, Francis Godophin, Sir John Jeffreys, Richard Edgcumbe, Thomas Chyverton, Richard Trevanion, John Bevill and others.[21] He was indicted with bringing to England a printed copy of the Papal Bull and of publishing this document at Golden Manor. That at Launceston he had defended the claim that the Pope was head of the Church. That he had brought an *Agnus Dei* that was blessed by the Pope and had given it to Francis Tregian and that he had administered the Mass according to the Popish rite at Golden.

His sentence was recorded as follows:

> *'and the place of his execution to be at Lanson uppon a Markett daye, where after he shall be dead and quartered, his hed to be sett uppon a poale, and placed in some emynent place within the saide towne of Lanson, and his IIII quarters to be likewise sett upon IIII poales, and placed*

---

[19] *Douai, Douay* or *Doway* is in the Nord department of northern France and the college site still exists as part of a University.
[20] Rowse, A L, 1941. 347.
[21] National Archives, Domestic State Papers, Elizabeth I, SP12/118 F.105 No. 46, 1577, Gale document no. MC4304187867.

the one at Bodmyn, the second at Tregony, the third at Barnstaple; and the fourth at Wadebridge'.

On St Andrew's day (30th November) 1577, he was dragged through the streets of Launceston on a hurdle, before being hung, drawn and quartered in the market place. After execution, his head was to be set up on the castle gate, while his quarters were to be dispatched as stated in his sentence to Bodmin, the county town, Barnstaple, near where he was born, Tregony, close to Tregian's home and Wade-Bridge, then on one of the most commonly travelled routes in the county. At Barnstaple and Tregony his quarters were probably placed on their respective bridges in a similar fashion to Wade-Bridge, so that all who crossed the river would see the gruesome spectacle, as a reminder to forget the old faith and adhere to the Church of England. Whelan has described the quarters of Mayne's body as *'The grim milestones of the road to Rome'*.[22]

It is a matter of conjecture as to whether the quarters of Mayne's body and his head were distributed according to the letter of the sentence, and leading authorities on the lives of the English Martyrs give conflicting accounts.

Bishop Richard Challoner stated that, *'his quarters were disposed of, one at Bodmin, one to Tregony, one to Barnstaple, and the fourth to remain at Launceston Castle: his head was set upon a pole at Wadebridge, a noted highway'*.[23] Cardinal William Allen gives a different account of the dispatch of the quarters of Mayne's body, *'After he was quartered, one quarter was sent to S. Probus (Tregony) where he was taken, an other to Wade-brig, the third to Bastabile in Devonsheir where he was borne, the fourth and his head remaine in Lanstone where he was executed'*.[24] Allen does not mention that a quarter was sent to Bodmin the county town. Martyrologist Reginald Bede Camm recorded that, *'when the quarters of the holy martyr were distributed, his head was stuck on a pole at Wadebridge'*.[25]

None of these three accounts agrees with the original sentence. So we are entitled to speculate that on Wade-Bridge were impaled both one quarter of Mayne's body and perhaps later his head, as the reconstruction (plate 12) suggests.

Relic of Cuthbert Mayne

Today, part of Cuthbert Mayne's skull is still preserved at St Joseph and St Anne chapel and convent at Lanherne, St Mawgan and until recent years was annually processed around Launceston. This event, was locally known as 'Catholic Sunday', and always took place in June, with a Mass held on the Castle Green. There is some confusion as to how the head or skull was rescued: Challoner records that the martyr's head was set upon a pole at Wade-Bridge and subsequently liberated by an Arundell of Lanherne, but in seeming contradiction also notes that the original terms of the sentence were carried out. Is it possible that having been first set up in Launceston the head was later removed and set upon Wade-Bridge?

---

[22] Whelan, H, 1984. *Snow on the hedges: a life of Cuthbert Mayne.*
[23] Challoner, R, 1803. *Memoirs of Missionary Priests and other Catholics of both sexes.*
[24] Allen, W, 1582. *A Briefe Historie of the Glorious Martyrdom of Twelve Reverend Priests: Father Edmund Campion and his Companions.*
[25] Bede Camm, R, 1914. *Lives of the English Martyrs.*

Whatever the truth, the upper part of Mayne's skull eventually came into the possession of the Rawe's of Trevithick in St Columb Major parish who later gave it to the Carmelite Nuns at Lanherne in 1807. A further portion of the skull was removed by the Weston family to Sutton Place in Guildford, the Westons being cousins of the Rawe's and both descendants of the Arundell family. This portion of skull has since been donated to the local Catholic Church in Guildford.

Cuthbert Mayne was the first seminary priest to be martyred for his faith during the reign of Elizabeth I; but he was not the last, a further one hundred and eighty seven Catholics were executed. Although the majority being priests, some school teachers, scholars, gentleman and even a gentlewoman were put to death. In 1588 alone, thirty-two priests were executed, while throughout Elizabeth's reign hundreds more lost either their estates or liberty. In 1886, Cuthbert Mayne was beatified by Pope Leo XIII and canonized by Pope Paul VI on the 25th October 1970.[26]

Returning to the bridge: a hole in the granite coping and the remains of an iron spike, both in the down-stream parapet of the bridge are alleged to be connected with the fixing of part of Mayne's body. This is supposition, as the parapet walls of the bridge have been re-built several times over the centuries and the granite copings may also have been replaced.

For example, in 1828 a contract was drafted to have the parapet walls pulled down and replaced by new ones with stone from Dunveth Quarry and also to have the moorstone coping replaced; it is not known whether this work was actually carried out. The hole in the coping (fig 5.3) does not appear deep enough to support the weight of a long pike or pole, let alone a quarter of a body, as the hole is only a few inches deep, and the iron spike is more likely to have been used to fix a permanent feature such as a lamp (fig 5.4). But though supposition, the survival of this tradition indicates how deeply ingrained the story remains in the fabric of local life, even after Mayne's body had rotted away or been taken for relics. Superstitions are likely to have attached to the place, particularly amongst those with Catholic sympathies.

Fig 5.2 - The Relic of Cuthbert Mayne.
© John Neale, Launceston.

---

[26] Today the Catholic Church at Launceston is dedicated to St Cuthbert Mayne, it was opened on the 30th November (St Andrew's day) 1911, 334 years after Mayne's martyrdom. The Church was designed by architect Arthur G. Langdon, whose brother was Canon Charles B. Langdon the founder of the Church at Kensey Villa, St Stephen's Hill, Launceston.

Fig 5.3 - Hole in the granite coping, downstream parapet.

Fig 5.4- Iron pin in the granite coping, downstream parapet.

The Civil War and Wade-Bridge

During the Civil War (1642-1646), both Royalists and Parliamentarians saw the advantage in capturing and controlling the bridges. At this turbulent time, the control of the bridges in Cornwall gave control of the county. The landscape of seventeenth century Cornwall was different from today, and particularly difficult for the movement of thousands of troops by either foot or horse. There were no tarmacadam roads and travel during the winter months would have been slow and often treacherous. Rivers were navigable much further inland, and wide marshy valley bottoms would have caused an army great difficulty. Bridges as key crossing places were focal points in the road network.

Throughout the war, both factions placed guards on bridges and skirmishes often took place at river crossings. As far as we know, the area around Wadebridge did not see any major battles, although Wade-Bridge would have been an important bridge to secure to allow troops free passage through north Cornwall. Although the only mention of Wade-Bridge in connection with the Civil War is in its dying days, it must have been guarded at many times of unrest.

The War in the west

By 1645-6, the Parliamentarians with Cromwell's New Model Army were pushing the Royalists further west, with the last major engagement at Great Torrington. Here the Royalists under the command of Lord Hopton were encamped using the parish church to hold their prisoners and barrels of gunpowder. On the 16th February, the Parliamentary troops led by Sir Thomas Fairfax arrived in heavy rain and a full scale fight broke out when Cromwell with his dragoons tested the Royalist defences. A stray spark ignited the gunpowder blowing up the church and killing all the prisoners inside. Hopton with three thousand horse slowly retreated westwards, with Fairfax in pursuit. By 25th February the Roundheads had reached Launceston and by 2nd March they entered Bodmin, which Hopton's army had only left the night before. Although Hopton's army was in disarray, he stayed loyal to the Crown and would not surrender.

On the 8th March 1645-6, Fairfax sent Cromwell to secure 'Ward Bridge' (Wade-Bridge). He took with him a force consisting of one thousand horse and five hundred dragoons, to prevent the Royalists under Lord Hopton from breaking through and escaping to the east (plate 13). [27] He met no resistance at Wade-Bridge which was fortunate for the bridge and for the people of the town. The troops may well have gathered on the fields above the bridge (now Bridge View Estate), where they would have had a good view of the bridge and its approach from the west. Fairfax also placed guards beyond Lostwithiel to prevent any Royalist's horse attempting to break away, as the Parliamentarians had done in 1644. [28]

It was reported in the *Moderate Intelligencer* (1645): *'upon the Lieut. Gen. coming in the enemies 600 retreated to their Body, and so together to Ware-Bridge: The Lieut Generall with the Horse quartered the first at night within a mile of them, in the morning he commanded a party to that Bridge, to gain it, which*

---

[27] *The Western Informer*, 7th March 1645-6, in the King's pamphlets, British Library, 102, a. 69
[28] Coates, M, 1963. *Cornwall in the Great Civil War and Interregnum*, 205.

was done with that resolution, that the enemy retreated, not firing a pistol, what will feare do taken down? The whole Army with the Generall having the night quartered in a field, advanced from Blisland to Bodman, which they quitted the day before, 500 of their Foot quitted Lestithel, whither the Generall sent three Regiments of their Foot, three quarters with him at Bodman, two to Ware-Bridge, our Horse on the east of the River.'[29]

Another contemporary report dated *Munday* March 2nd 1645 stated that: *'Lieut. Gen.Cromwell lay all night about S. Tudde (St Tudy) with 1000 horse and 400 dragoones in case the enemy should attempt to break Eastward and made good Wardbridge over which they were to passé: They quitted Bodman March 1 at ten at night; the Lord Hopton himself brought up the reare; most of their foot were Welshmen (not above 400 in all) were drunke, it being Taffies day (St David's Day)'.*[30]

In this report, it reinforces the importance of Cornwall's bridges in times of war, *'Thus wee keepe Strong Guards at Listithiel, Ward-Bridge, and the Fords upon both Rivers'.*

There is some confusion about the exact number of troops that Lieutenant General Cromwell brought to Wade-Bridge, different contemporary reports stated slightly different numbers and their reports would have depended upon correspondents estimating the number of troops and reporting back to intelligence agents.[31]

In 1645-6, Wade-Bridge was still a bridge in the countryside with a very small community living alongside the river and on the western hillside. The arrival of an army of perhaps fifteen hundred men, including a thousand on horseback would have been seen as an impressive but frightening sight. Landowners would have dreaded an army passing over their land or camping on it. All the troops and their horses would need feeding, blacksmiths to attend to their horses, whilst trees would have been cut down to use as fuel for cooking and for warmth. Luckily for Wadebridge, records suggest that the army's stay was short. Having met with no resistance, the greater part of the troops may have continued west to be present in Tresillian a few days later when the Royalists surrendered.

Shortly after, another bridge was to witness to an historical event. On the 10th March 1645-6, Fairfax based at Tregony with his Roundheads offered Hopton who with the Royalist Army was in Truro, conditions for surrender which were agreed at a conference held at Tresillian Bridge. The Treaty for a complete surrender was signed two days later in Truro.

---

[29] *Moderate Intelligencer* (1645) London, England, March 5th 1646, British Library, Gale Document Z2001391349.

[30] *Perfect Diurnall of some Passages of Parliament*, British Library, Gale Document Z2000099815.
When one researches the Civil War in Cornwall, one can become confused over the dates of some events. The final push westwards through Cornwall during the first three months of 1646, is often recorded as 1645. The contemporary documents are all dated 1645, however this is due to the two different calendars that were in use at this time. In England the Julian calendar was still in use and used March 25th (Lady's Day) as the first day of the year, whereas the new style Gregorian calendar (rest of Europe) chose January 1st as the beginning of the year. Therefore events that were recorded in those first three months are sometimes given both year dates ie. 1645-6.

[31] *Kingdomes Weekly Intelligencer*, March 2nd 1646 records, 'one thousand horse and foure hundred dragoons'.

Cornish bridges and the Civil War

Two other important bridges in Cornwall were those at Lostwithiel and Respryn, due to their proximity to important houses such as Menabilly, Boconnoc and Lanhydrock which all featured prominently in the Civil War. Respryn Bridge was guarded by the Royalists at the outbreak of the Civil War, and when Essex came down to Lostwithiel in July 1644, he put an outpost at Respryn. Essex with his Parliamentary Army took Lostwithiel, leaving some of this army garrisoned at Restormal Castle and on Beacon Hill. The Royalists took the bridge again on 11th August, giving King Charles access from Boconnoc to Sir Richard Grenville who was in Bodmin.[32] Later, the joint forces of King Charles and Prince Maurice seized Lostwithiel, forcing Essex's cavalry to steal away across the bridge at night due to an inadequate sentry.[33]

During the Civil War, Launceston was frequently besieged and captured and Polson Bridge along with other Tamar bridges was constantly guarded, especially when Prince Charles held Court in the town during 1645. Earlier in July 1644, Essex with his Roundheads was alleged to have pulled down two of the Tamar bridges after forcing Sir Richard Grenville and the Royalists back over the border into Cornwall, one of which may have been at Polson. New Bridge was defended by Sir Richard Grenville against Lord Essex on 20th July 1644.

Damage to bridges during the Civil War

In Devon, Barnstaple's bridge did not fare so well. The town's leading families supported Parliament and this led the Royalists to capture Barnstaple in September 1643. In June 1644 the town was taken back by Parliamentarians and re-captured again the following year by Sir Allen Aspley and the Royalists who according to Oliver destroyed *'an arch or two'*, so that he could control entry into the town from the bridge.[34] By removing a couple of arches and installing a wooden drawbridge access could easily be controlled. A similar project took place in late 1645 when sections of the stone bridges at St Ives, Huntingdon and St Neots were removed by Parliamentary troops and replaced with drawbridges.[35] At Wallingford the bridge over the Thames had four arches destroyed and replaced with a drawbridge.[36]

If any resistance had been received by Cromwell at Wade-Bridge, it is likely that the bridge would have also had a couple of arches destroyed and quickly replaced with a timber drawbridge, fortunately this never happened.

---

[32] Henderson, C G, and Coates, H, 1972 ed. 77.
[33] Boger, Revd. Canon E, 1887. 'Lostwithiel Bridge and its Memories', *Western Antiquary* **VI**, pt XII, 281-287.
[34] Oliver, B W, 1946. 'The Long Bridge of Barnstaple pt.1' *Reports and Transactions of the Devonshire Association*, p.178.
[35] Burn-Murdoch, R, 2001. *St Ives Bridge and Chapel*, 19.
[36] Robins, F W, 1947. *The Story of the Bridge*, 153.

6 'their heirs and assigns for the support and repair of a certain bridge called Wada Bridge'

The Wade-Bridge Trust, pontage and tolls

John Lovibond set up the Wade-Bridge Trust, dated 1476, its Charter of Endowment named twelve trustees and endowed an area of land for raising funds to maintain the fabric of the bridge (see chapter 2). The Trust was known as the Wada-Bridge Trust, Wada-Bridge Charity or Lovibond Charity, and functioned from its inception in 1476 until it was wound up in 1853 at the time of the first widening, when ongoing maintenance was taken over by the county. Over the centuries the numbers of trustees occasionally dwindled to as few as four, these being the rector of St Breock, the vicar of Egloshayle, and the Lords of the Manor in each parish, normally a Molesworth from Pencarrow and a Prideaux from Prideaux Place, Padstow (representing St Breock).

Although we have no records of the actual building of the bridge, or the exact source of the original stone, accounts had to be kept once the Wade-Bridge Trust was set up and many documents have survived today, preserved in both the Cornwall Record Office and the Courtney Library at the Royal Institution of Cornwall in Truro. The majority of the surviving Trust documents date from the seventeenth and eighteenth centuries and consist of a wide range of papers. Some are mere scraps of paper containing hand written receipts for payment, while others are more detailed accounts of rentals and leases, naming lessees, those up-to-date with payments and those in arrears. The documents include the Bridge Wardens' Accounts of the reparation of the bridge, detailing their expenditure, leases of named Trust properties and references to the Trust's audit or count days at the local inn where the wardens came to account for the year's work.

When the Bridge Trust was set up, twenty pounds worth of land and property in Egloshayle church-town was donated by John Carmynowe of Glynn in Cardinham and Thomas Cayne of Henson in St Minver and vested in the Trust (see chapter 2). According to Gilbert, there were also lands in the parish of St Breock given by the Prior of Bodmin and other well-respected benefactors to the Trust.[1] The Trust also acquired at least one property in the parish of Padstow. This land and property, was leased out to provide an income for the maintenance of the bridge, while other sources of income would have included donations and occasionally pontage. The joint income was used to pay a Bridge Warden or Wardens to oversee the day to day upkeep of the structure. It was the Wardens who organised the local labour when needed and arranged to draw stone from local quarries. They were in turn responsible to the trustees, who would arrange any contracts for major work such as re-paving, replacing the parapets etc.

---

[1] Gilbert, D, 1838. *The Parochial History of Cornwall*, **I**, 373.

Bridge Trusts

Like Wade-Bridge, both Bideford and Barnstaple bridges had Bridge Trusts to administer the day to day maintenance of the bridge, collection of tolls etc., while the bridges at Looe and Exeter were controlled by Corporations, but with similar aims and rules. All employed Bridge Wardens and provided annual accounts relating to the repair and maintenance of their bridges. The Bridge Trusts of Bideford, Barnstaple and Exeter all had an offical seal of office, and documents survive at both Bideford and Barnstaple complete with seals. At Exeter the original bronze seal survives at the city's Royal Albert Memorial Museum: it is inscribed *S'PONTIS EXE CIVTATIS EXONIE*, 'the seal of Exe Bridge in the city of Exeter', and shows an image of three arches of the Exe Bridge with three buildings above, the central one with two crosses on its roof possibly representing St Edmunds chapel.[2] Similarly, the bronze seal at Barnstaple still survives and shows six arches with a chapel at one end and a large cross at the other. The Bideford seal shows four arches of the bridge with a cross displaying the Virgin Mary and Child above the bridge and a chapel at either end. All these seals emphasize the importance and the relationship between the chapels and the bridge. It is not known whether the trustees at Wade-Bridge had their own seal, but as no seals are affixed to surviving Wade-Bridge documents it seems unlikely.

Egloshayle Lands and Property

The majority of the land held by the Wade-Bridge Trust in Egloshayle parish was at Above Town and in the Greenhill area of the church-town. The tithe map shows that by 1840, this included at least fifteen cottages. The Trust also leased out gardens, orchards, a field known as Long Meadow, and another called Green Hill Meadow; which also included a small quarry, all in the same area of the village, fig 6.1 shows an extract from the tithe map that mentions some of this.[3] Another important property owned and leased out by the Trust was Bridge House.

Cross Park

Part of a tenement in Egloshayle owned by the Trust, called Cross Park, features in a number of surviving seventeenth century leases. It is described as a close and also included Green Hill Park and Rogerland as well as two orchards or gardens and all common of pasture and wastrel.[4]

In *c*1667 the property was leased on a ninety-nine year term to Edward Hawke in an agreement signed by Nicholas Courtney and William Mathew, trustees for Wade-Bridge. Hawke in turn assigned the property to John Mills gentleman of Tregorden in Egloshayle. On the 4th November 1678, the lease of a dwelling house and garden where John Hearle was living at Cross Park was

---

[2] At present (2012), the Exeter Bridge Wardens' seal is on display at the Royal Albert Memorial Museum, Exeter.

[3] The site of Rogerland, alias Radge land is now Marshall Avenue, Green Hill meadow is now cut through by the Egloshayle bypass. Long Meadow still survives directly north of Elm Cottage at Above Town, while the properties known as Orpine Cottage, Bellevue, Chyvean, Pink Cottage and Rose Cottage are all on land that was owned by the Bridge Trust. The Trust also owned land where Molesworth Row stands and also land on West Park Road at Green Gables and the Farthings.

[4] Cornwall Record Office, DDX450/174 –179.

surrendered by John Mills in an agreement signed by John Tregagle Esq. and William Mathew, clerk, a trustee and the vicar of Egloshayle.

In the following year on the 3th November 1679 a house and garden, part of the same tenement was surrendered by Joan Harris, spinster, the ninety-nine year lease was on the life of herself and her two sisters Mary and Elizabeth. Jas. Rawlinge a carpenter from Egloshayle surrendered his lease on the 6th November 1682, the contract being signed by Sir John Molesworth and Jas. Kestell of Kestell Esq. trustees. Jas. Rawling appears again in a lease dated 21st September 1721, when he, or perhaps his son (considering the date), signed a ninety-nine year lease on Cross Park, Green Hill Park and Rogerland. This time the lease is signed by trustees, Sir John Molesworth, of Pencarrow, Carolus Pole, clerk, Edward Hoblyn of Croan and John Hathaway, vicar of Egloshayle.

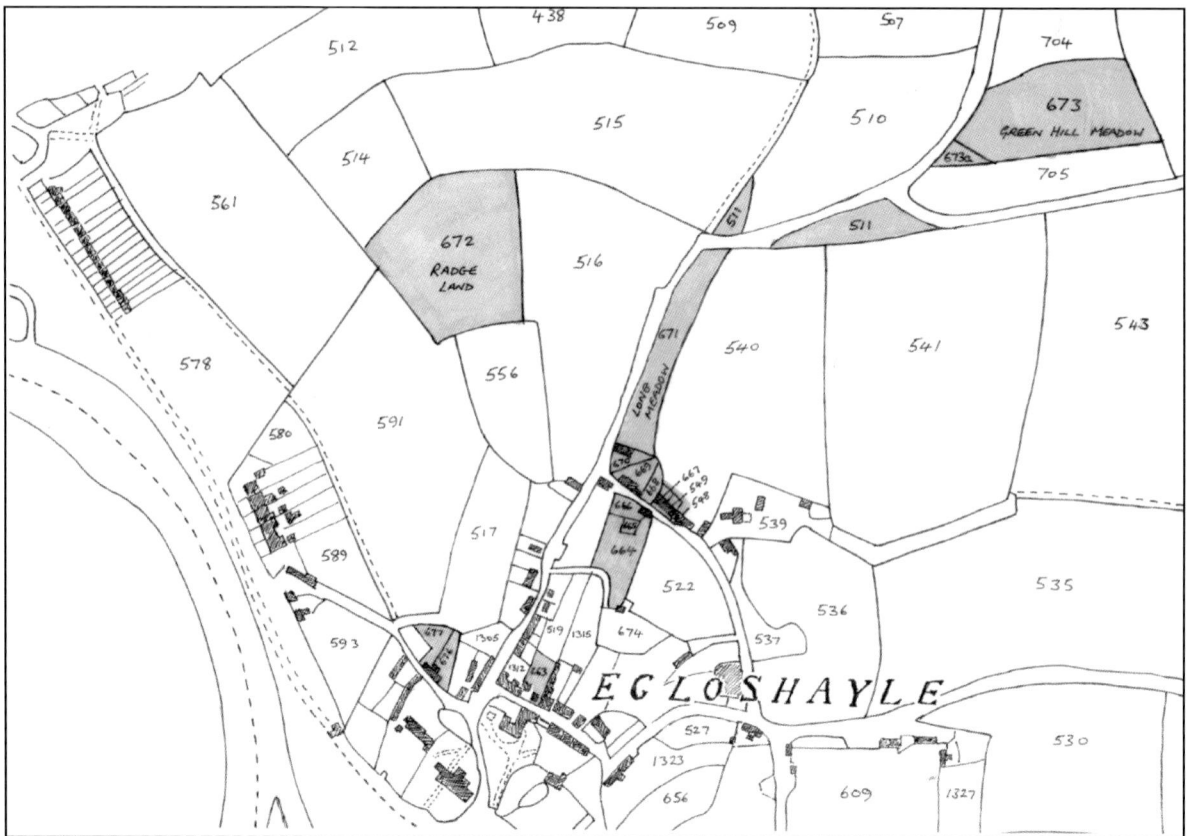

Fig 6.1 - A copy of an extract from the Egloshayle parish tithe map showing Egloshayle Churchtown and the land and property owned by the Wade-Bridge Trust.

A further ninety-nine year lease dated 6th November 1683, was made between the trustees and a Thomas Reede, a husbandman from Egloshayle, who signed the lease on the lives of himself, his wife Mary and son William for part of an orchard assigned to him by John Mills, where he was to build himself a house. It is also recorded that John Mills reserved the right to repair the adjacent houses.

In the late eighteenth century rentals for the Egloshayle lands, some local family names appear that are still associated with the parish. In 1791 Conventionary tenants included John Burt, William Ching, William Hender, John Goodfellow, Thomas Kestle and Thomas Reynolds, and Rack tenants Richard Waram, William Brabin and John Hicks.[5]

By 1840, Cross Park at Bove Town (Above Town) is recorded as being owned by the Bishop of Exeter and leased to William Pollard of Court Place, while Rogerland (recorded on the tithe map as Radge Land), Long Meadow and Green Hill Meadow were still under the ownership of the Trustees of Wade-Bridge and leased to Richard Fradd.

During the late eighteenth and early nineteenth centuries one George Borlase acted as an agent to the *feoffees* (trustees) of the bridge and conducted many of the surveys or auctions for the lease of the Wade-Bridge Tolls. On 29th November 1793, Borlase also arranged the auction of the lease on a property of the late William Chiry deceased. There were eleven bidders; the bidding started at twenty-one pounds and was won by Richard Lean for forty-five pounds.   The bidders included William Prout, Mr Borlase, John Boust?, John Benett, John Pollard, John Colern, Thomas Kestle, Richard Fradd, John Goodfellow, and Mr Andrew. These were already tenants or lease holders of the Trust's property in Egloshayle. The successful bidder had to secure the lease by paying ten guineas immediately on signing, and pay six shillings and eight pence per year rent and thirteen shillings and four pence on the death of each life.

Bridge House

This must not be confused with another property called Bridge House on the 1880 Ordnance Survey map, which stands opposite the eastern approach to the bridge at Bridge End. The Bridge House referred to here was a property or properties built against the bridge on the upstream, Egloshayle side and it is referred to several times in the accounts of the Bridge Wardens.

In the Bridge Wardens' Accounts of 1698 is the first reference to Bridge House. It reads: '*Ye Bridge House built and erected on Wade-Bridge in Egloshayle for the use of the said bridge towards its repair £5 yearly*'. Borlase illustrated the bridge in 1758 (fig 6.2) and shows several buildings on the Egloshayle end of the bridge. He depicts a two-storey building against the upstream side of the bridge, with a chimney at each end of the pitched roof, complete with two dormer windows. Whether this is an accurate drawing and interpretation of the scene is a matter of speculation, but in 1852, an accurate plan of the bridge was produced prior to the first widening of the bridge, which clearly shows a building against the first arch on the upstream, Egloshayle side of the bridge (fig 6.3).   Examination of the plan suggests that this property is different from that illustrated by Borlase, as the plan shows a much narrower, but longer house, divided into three single-room properties. From the plan it is not possible to ascertain whether this building is single storey or higher.

---

[5] Cornwall Record Office, DDX450/108.

Fig 6.2 - Bridge House shown in the centre of Borlase's 1758 illustration of Wade-Bridge.

In 1786, Sir William Molesworth of Pencarrow, James Cory, clerk, the rector of St Breock, Henry Peers, clerk, the vicar of Egloshayle as Trustees of Wade-Bridge, granted to one Thomas Reynolds, a watchmaker from Egloshayle, the lease of a dwelling house built by Humphry Sink deceased, on the east side of Wade-Bridge; it was forty-seven feet long and fourteen feet wide, being part of the lands of the said bridge. From the measurements this appears to be the same as the house shown on the plan of 1852. It is difficult to tell if Reynolds was leasing the whole property or one part of the building. The lease was drawn up after the deaths of Elizabeth Reynolds, mother of Thomas, Osbertus Hamley of the city of London, a watch finisher and his son John Hamley, late of St Mabyn. The ninety-nine year lease set the payment of rent of one shilling and six pence to be paid in equal amounts, 'at the most usual days and times of payment for rent in the year', that is Christmas, Lady Day, Midsummer and Michaelmas. A further clause in the lease stated that as well as maintaining the property, Thomas Reynolds, his executors, administrations or assigns shall and will do 'suit of service' unto all and every Bridge meeting that shall be held on account of the said bridge. It therefore appears that living in the Bridge House obliged Reynolds to attend all the meetings about the bridge and perhaps carry out some duties. Clearly it may have been in

Reynold's own interest to attend, as living on the bridge, decisions made about the structure were likely to affect him.

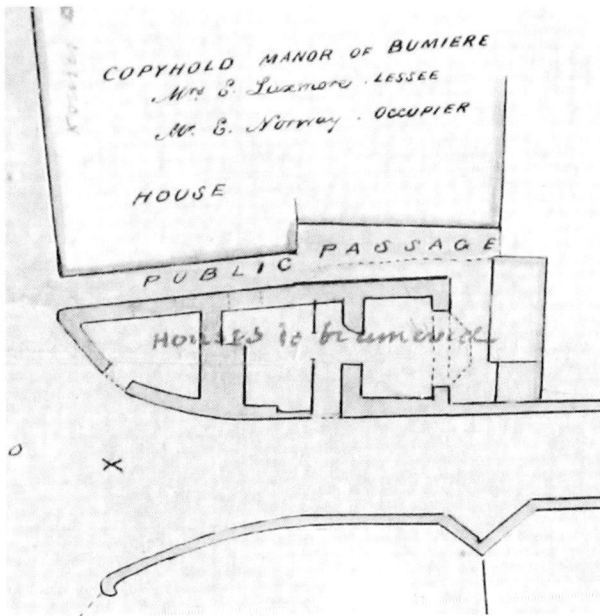

Fig 6.3 - *A plan view of Bridge House at the eastern upstream side of Wade-Bridge on the 1852 plan.*

Another plan of Bridge House was attached to a contract to re-build the parapet walls in April 1818 (fig 6.4).[6] At this time, one part of the property was occupied by the Reynolds family, while another was the home of the Ivey family. An elevation was also sketched above the plan, suggesting that the property was a two storey dwelling.

From some of the leases, it is clear that part of the Bridge House was held as an office for the Wade-Bridge Trust as payments were due to be made there four times a year according to some leases. It also appears that whoever won the lease to collect the tolls would have lived in the house, so that he was available at all times to collect the money from the passing traffic. Furthermore, the 1840 Tithe Apportionment schedule for Egloshayle records that the first Post Office in Wadebridge was situated within Bridge House on the bridge. It was leased to one Grace Veale from the trustees of Wade-Bridge and in this same year postage stamps were introduced. Before 1840, coaches and carriers could charge what they wanted to deliver mail dependent on the size and distance. Having the Post Office on the bridge made good sense, as all the mail coaches and carriers would have had to pass by.

Demolition of Bridge House
A notice placed in the *Royal Cornwall Gazette* in November 1852 recorded that the tenants of two houses to be demolished on the east side of the bridge were a John Warne and Parmenas Menhenick.[7] At the Cornwall Epiphany Sessions in 1847 it was stated by Mr Molesworth that the current income for the bridge stood at twenty-eight pounds a year and that knocking down the two houses owned by the Trust would reduce this by ten pounds a year.[8] The demolition of these properties, known as Bridge House, went ahead later in 1853, allowing the bridge to be widened by three feet on either side.[9]

---

[6] Cornwall Record Office, AD2040/23.

[7] *Royal Cornwall Gazette* , 19/11/1852.

[8] *Royal Cornwall Gazette* , 08/06/1847.

[9] *Royal Cornwall Gazette*, 21/10/1853.

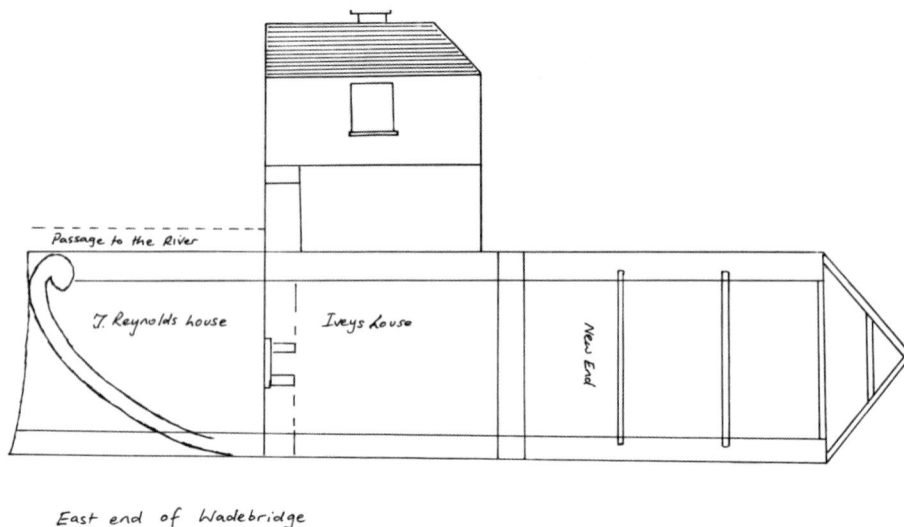

Fig 6.4 - A copy of an original sketch of Bridge House dated 1818,
Cornwall Record Office AD2040/23

Arches used as cellars

Some historians including Maclean,[10] have suggested that when the first and last arches were blocked up, they were used as cellars. The blocked first arch on the Egloshayle end of the bridge - which is still visible behind a locked door - can be located below a small flight of steps beside the downstream side of the bridge.   For many years of the twentieth century it served as a storeroom for council workmen, who kept their tools, lamps and road-signs there. Today, there is a new door barring access, but also evidence of three sets of iron gate-hangings, indicating that there were at least three previous doors and the last is still lying in the arched room among discarded rubbish. Inside this arch, on the upstream side, there is evidence of a possible doorway on the eastern side, where the stonework has a vertical joint on either side, suggesting that a door may have once existed: which could have led directly into the bottom of the property known as Bridge House.

---

[10] Maclean, J, 1873. *The Parochial and Family history of the Deanery of Trigg Minor*, **I**, 401.

St Breock Lands and Property

Although Gilbert records that the Trust was given land and property by the Prior of Bodmin, there are no records surviving other than a list of St Breock debtors during the seventeenth century, with no mention of what lands and property the Trust owned in this parish.

Porthmissen Mill, Padstow

In 1688, the Wade-Bridge trustees purchased Porthmizen (Porthmissen) Mill in the parish of Padstow from John Mills. To the author's knowledge this was the only property that the Trust held remote or detached from Wadebridge, all the other land and property being in the parishes of St Breock and Egloshayle. In 1765 the Wade-Bridge Grant (Trust) leased the mill to Richard Nance *including one Grist mill and mill house with all waters, watercourses, utensils, implements and tools, whatsoever and the appts. [appurtenances] to the said mill and mill house belonging together also with all ways passages and common use of passing to and from the said mill such have been used and occupied by the former tenant or servants there of and were here to fore in the possession of William Nott deceased and late and now of Lessee for 21 years. Yearly rent £5.*

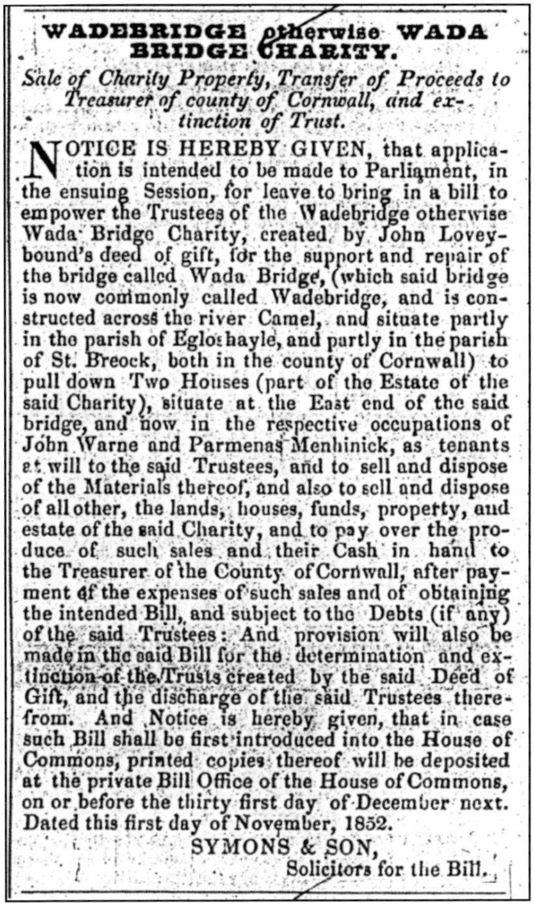

WADEBRIDGE otherwise WADA BRIDGE CHARITY.

Sale of Charity Property, Transfer of Proceeds to Treasurer of county of Cornwall, and extinction of Trust.

NOTICE IS HEREBY GIVEN, that application is intended to be made to Parliament, in the ensuing Session, for leave to bring in a bill to empower the Trustees of the Wadebridge otherwise Wada Bridge Charity, created by John Loveybound's deed of gift, for the support and repair of the bridge called Wada Bridge, (which said bridge is now commonly called Wadebridge, and is constructed across the river Camel, and situate partly in the parish of Egloshayle, and partly in the parish of St. Breock, both in the county of Cornwall) to pull down Two Houses (part of the Estate of the said Charity), situate at the East end of the said bridge, and now in the respective occupations of John Warne and Parmenas Menhinick, as tenants at will to the said Trustees, and to sell and dispose of the Materials thereof, and also to sell and dispose of all other, the lands, houses, funds, property, and estate of the said Charity, and to pay over the produce of such sales and their Cash in hand to the Treasurer of the County of Cornwall, after payment of the expenses of such sales and of obtaining the intended Bill, and subject to the Debts (if any) of the said Trustees: And provision will also be made in the said Bill for the determination and extinction of the Trusts created by the said Deed of Gift, and the discharge of the said Trustees therefrom. And Notice is hereby given, that in case such Bill shall be first introduced into the House of Commons, printed copies thereof will be deposited at the private Bill Office of the House of Commons, on or before the thirty first day of December next. Dated this first day of November, 1852.

SYMONS & SON,
Solicitors for the Bill.

Fig 6.5 - A newspaper report about the winding up of the Wada-Bridge Trust or Charity.

Porthmissen is situated west of Padstow town in the village of Trevone and today nothing survives of the former mill, although there is now a property known as Cuckoo Mill on the site. The Trust accounts shows that the mill was also known as *Cluckar Mill at Permizzen,* a name which has since been corrupted to Cuckoo Mill. Today, the northern boundary of Cuckoo Mill follows the former boundary of Porthmissen mill pond.

In December 1693, a twenty-one year lease on Porthmissen Mill was signed by William Abott, a miller from Padstow; the trustees are named as Sir John Molesworth of Pencarrow and James Kestle of Kestle, *their heirs or assignes at the Bridge House built and erected on Wade-Bridge.*[11] The rent for Porthmissen Mill was five pounds of 'lawful money of England' to be paid quarterly at the

[11] Cornwall Record Office, AD2040/1.

Bridge House. A second lease to William Abott was signed on the 25th December 1698 for Porthmissen Mill.[12]

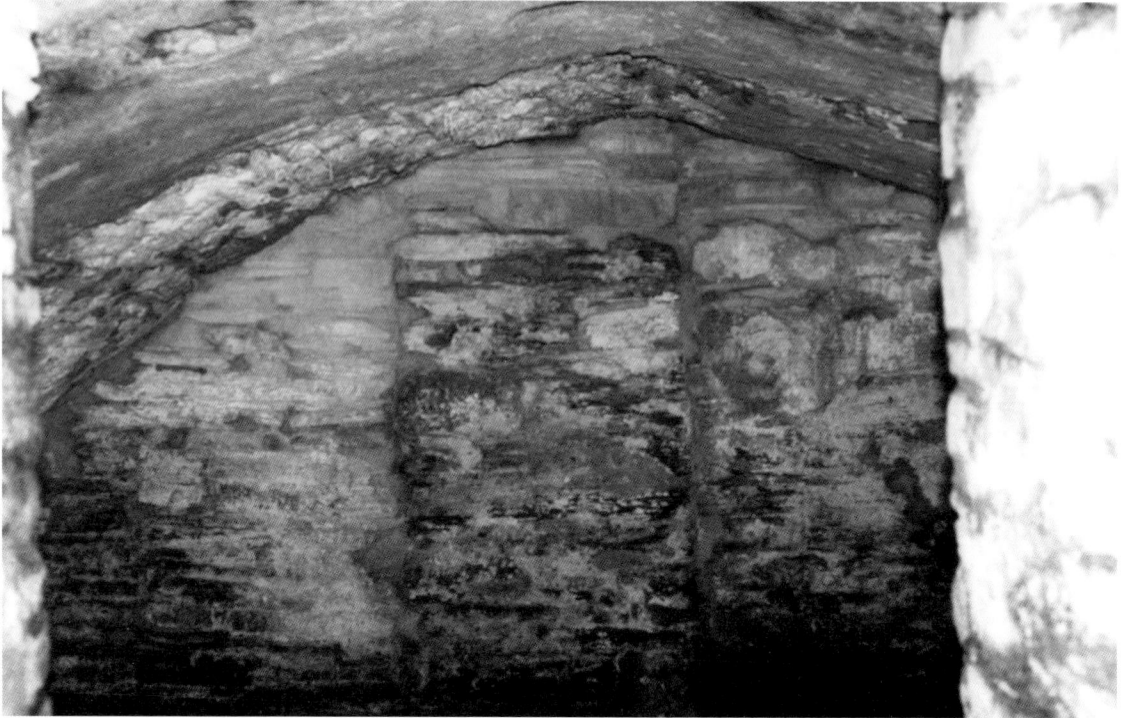

Fig 6.6 - shows arch no 1 as a cellar on the east end of Wade-Bridge, the outline of a door can be seen on the upstream side of the arch which once led into the bottom of Bridge House.

Bridge Accounts

Several of the accounts indicate that tenants of the Wade-Bridge Trust were often in arrears with their rent and hand-written notes survive demanding payment of rents, or acknowledging receipt of arrears. One such note reads:

> *The trustees of the bridge having found it very inconvenient to suffer the stock of the said bridge to lye abroade in small sums and also the continuance thereof in the same hands for above one year, without renewing their security, doe therefore order, that all debtors to the said stocke bring their several debts at the next Count day and that in future it is ordered that none of the said stock above £10 or under £5 be lent to any person, and it is likewise ordered that none of the said trustees shall take to themselves any of the said moneys on security. 1670.[13]*

In 1691, a list shows the number of persons owing money to the Trust, and another undated paper lists 'Egloshayle debtors'. In 1682 a paper names those who have paid their rent, while there are

---

[12] Cornwall Record Office, AD2040/1/2.
[13] Cornwall Record Office, DDX450/119.

also lists of Conventionary rents due for bridge lands dated 1791 and 1814. Another paper dated 1684 is a receipt for four shillings received from William Stone for twelve years high rent due to the Manor of Burneire out of a parcel of land which the Bridge Trust held. While in 1701, the trustees order one William Nott to pay five pounds rent to Richard Pascoe.

A short note written during the eighteenth century on the back of a block of Turnpike tickets for Town-End Gate, Bodmin and addressed to Mr Symons the solicitor to the Trustees reads:

> *Sir, I beg leave to inform you that my brother is from house and I am not sure he'll return time enough to attend the Gentlemen at Wadebridge as requested. You'll have the goodness to excuse the manner in which you receive this communication as I thought a day might make some difference to you and I am at a place where no paper least this can be had. I am Sir your ob.t Serv.t Wm. Chapple.[14]*

It appears that William Chapple's brother had been summoned to appear before the Trustees, probably for being in arrears with his rent.

Another single note dated 2nd October 1693 was sent to Thomas Brabant, William Hocker, Richard Marshall, William Kestle and Nicholas Parnall asking them to pay the money they owed to the bridge, i.e. arrears on the rent of property owned and leased by the Wade-Bridge Trust. It was signed Nic[holas] May and reads:

> *Neighbours*
> *The Gentlemen trustees for Wadebridge did long since command Me to call upon you for money you owe to the bridge & doe*
> *Now blame me for neglect because the money is neither payd*
> *Nor better secured, these are therefore to let you know, that*
> *You must verry speedily bring in your severall sums to me*
> *And you may have ye bonds, which if you faill to doe, you*
> *Will bee forthwith prosecuted with effect. I am your friend Nic May*

It seems that no-one paid their rent unless they were forced to and that equally, the Trust was lax in collecting it.

---

[14] Courtney Library, Royal Institution of Cornwall, Truro, ref. HP14. A small re-used account book titled General Accounts 1826 with Wade Bridge written on the spine gives details of Wade-Bridge documents that Charles Henderson recorded.

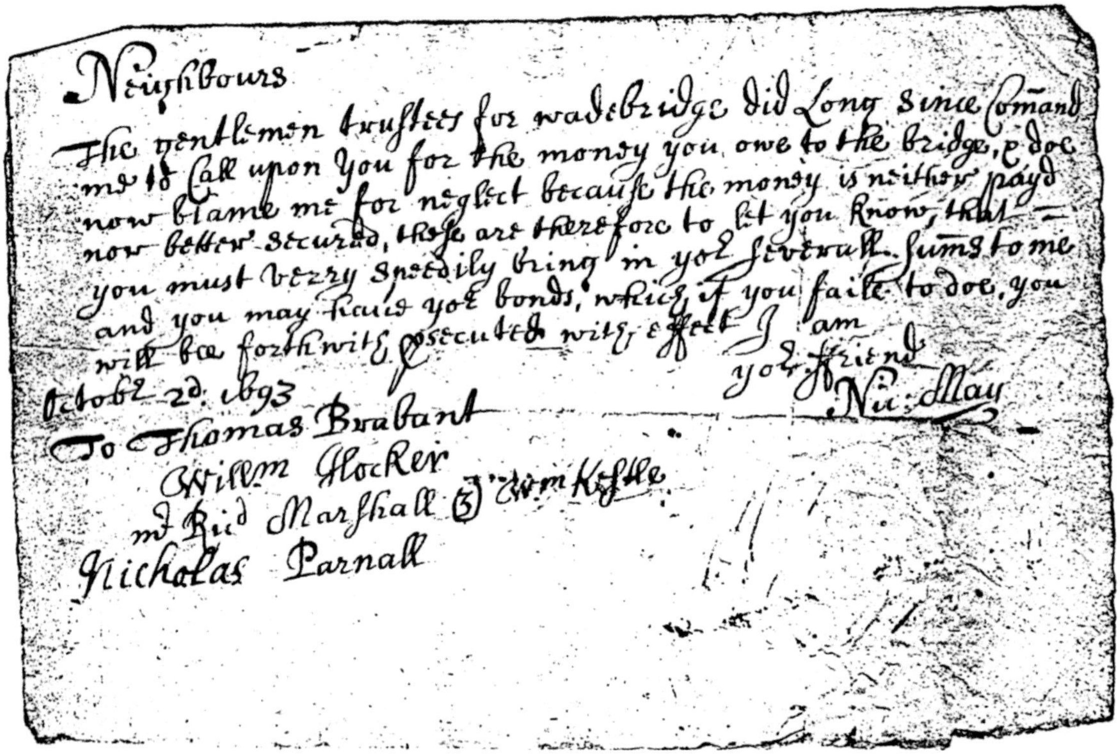

Fig 6.7 - Trustee Nic May's request to tenants of the Wade-Bridge Trust to pay their rent arrears, dated 1693. Courtesy The Royal Institution of Cornwall

Bridge Trustees and Wardens

The original trustees of the Wade-Bridge Trust are listed within the Charter of Endowment (see chapter 2); however the names of many more are contained within the numerous documents surviving in both the Cornwall Record Office and Courtney Library at Truro. A list of trustees and Bridge Wardens extracted from the many documents can be seen in an appendix to this book.

One notable trustee of Wade-Bridge is John Tregagle, recorded in Trust papers (with William Mathew, rector of St Breock) in 1678, 1695, and 1696. Elsewhere we learn that he was from Trevorder in St Breock. He appears to possibly be the son of the famous Jan Tregagle (Tregeagle) who became a legend after his death due to his harsh treatment of others. Legend states that he made a pact with the devil and that he was set a series of impossible tasks, including emptying the water from Dozmary Pool on Bodmin Moor with a holed limpet shell and weaving ropes at Roche Rock out of sand from Gwenor Cove. There were three John Tregagles recorded at Trevorder during the seventeenth century and according to Spooner, all three lives have been woven into the one legend of Jan Tregeagle. [15]

Another family called Kestle from Kestle and Pendavey in Egloshayle also appear to have stood as Trustees throughout the sixteenth, seventeenth and eighteenth centuries. It is surprising that a member of the Kestle family did not appear on the original list of Trustees of Wade-Bridge, particularly as their family arms of Kestle impaling Ravenscroft appears opposite the Lovibond arms around the western doorway of the tower at Egloshayle Church, which by tradition was built soon after the construction of the bridge, with funds and stone left over from building the bridge.[16]

In 1693, Sir John Moleworth is recorded as a trustee of the Trust, and representatives of the Molesworth family continued as trustees until the Trust was wound up in 1853. The family appear to have been the driving force behind the Trust and were influential in the widening of the bridge in 1852-53.

Fig 6.8 - The Kestle Coat of Arms, at Egloshayle Church.

Count Days and Annual Dinner

Each year, usually in November, the Wade-Bridge Trust would have their Count Day, where the accounts and bills would be settled, leases and rentals renewed or bid for and officers re-elected. These events normally took place in an inn, usually the Molesworth Arms, (formerly known as The Fox, King's Arms, or the Fountain), with an annual dinner following in the evening. Here, the Bridge Wardens would bring their accounts of money outlaid for the repair and maintenance of the bridge to be scrutinised by the Trustees. A fragment of a bill for the audit dinner of *c*1680 survives and also a lodging bill dated 1818. Receipts for drinks bought on these occasions accompany some of the surviving leases for the bridge tolls.

Pontage and Tolls

The maintenance of the bridge was funded by tolls as well as the lease of lands owned by the Trust. It is likely that a toll was routinely charged but if extra funds were required for a big repair project a further toll known as pontage might be levied. The two types of toll cannot necessarily be distinguished in documents.

---

[15] Spooner, B C, 1931. 'Tregagle, in fact or Tradition' *Journal of the Royal Institution of Cornwall*, read at the Annual Meeting 17th December 1931.

[16] Hals, W, nd (*c* 1750). *Parochial History of Cornwall*, pt 2, 111.

Pontage is a special toll occasionally levied on a bridge towards the maintenance of the structure. Although by tradition it is considered by many historians that there was always a toll on Wade-Bridge from the fifteenth century, there are no surviving documents to substantiate this. Clearly the amount that would have been collected could not have maintained the bridge alone, and it was the land that was held and rented out by the trustees that brought in the main income. According to Harrison, a toll or pontage could only be levied by either ancient custom or by royal grant at times of crisis when major repairs or maintenance was required.[17] In the case of Wade-Bridge it appears to have been through 'ancient custom'.

No documents survive that make reference to the collection of tolls at Wade-Bridge for almost two centuries after it had first been built, although this does not mean that they were not used. The earliest dated document referring to tolls is in the Bridge Wardens' Accounts for 1662, where a John Lobb is paid four pence for keeping the tolls.[18] In 1760, an Act of Parliament was passed for creating and repairing a turnpike road from Haleworthy (Hallworthy) through Camelford, to the east end of Wade-Bridge, and from the west end of Wade-Bridge to St Columb and on to Mitchell. Toll houses were built a mile either side of Wadebridge at Three Hole Cross and near Whitecross (Tollgate). Travellers having to pay a toll at each toll house for the following stretch of turnpike road may not have been too happy to pay yet another to pass over the bridge, however small it might have been. On the 25th March 1765, Bridge Trustees John Molesworth Esq., Robert Dennis and Henry Peers leased the right to collect tolls to William King for a period of seven years.[19] The agreement stated that the toll of Wade-Bridge 'shall be due and payable for coaches and other carriages passing and re-passing according to ancient custom'. As no mention of pedestrians is recorded, one can only assume that there was no toll for them. Hals[20] writing in c1750 recorded that the profit of the tolls for Wade-bridge was very small, while the Revd. William Wynne who visited Cornwall in 1755 noted that the bridge at *Wardbridge* had a small toll paid for coaches passing over the bridge.[21]

According to Lysons, the inhabitants of the two parishes of Egloshayle and St Breock were exempt from paying tolls.[22] A reference in 1765 stated that tolls were payable on passing and re-passing over the bridge, which would suggest that tolls were chargeable in both directions and therefore it is possible that tolls could have been collected at either end of the bridge.

---

[17] Harrison, D, 2004. *The Bridges of Medieval England*, 208.

[18] Cornwall Record Office, DDX450/ 166-173.

[19] Polsue, W, 1867. *A Complete Parochial History of the County of Cornwall*, **I**. 316. - This appears to be the same William King whose memorial was removed from the west end of the north aisle and was set up in the tower of Egloshayle Church. In memory of William King, who died in Wadebridge the 13th August 1775 aged 75 years and Mary King, his wife, who died at Wadebridge the 16th day November 1785 aged 75.

[20] Hals, W, nd (c 1750). *Parochial History of Cornwall*, pt 2, 111.

[21] Wynne, Revd. W, 1755. 'A Visit to Cornwall in 1755' edited by Colin Edwards, *Journal of the Royal Institution of Cornwall*, 1981, p338-349.

[22] Lysons, D, & Lysons S, 1814. *Magna Brittannia*, **III** (Cornwall), 43.

Survey of the Tolls

By the middle of the eighteenth century the tolls of Wade-Bridge were being auctioned off in a similar way to the Turnpike Trust's tolls, which guaranteed the trustees of Wade-Bridge some additional funds towards the bridge and saved them the personal responsibility for their collection. Later during the early nineteenth century these 'surveys of the tolls' or auctions were advertised in local newspapers such as the *Royal Cornwall Gazelle* or *West Briton*. The right to collect the tolls was usually auctioned at an inn in the town, and on the 25th October 1793, the auction was held in the house of Elizabeth Thomas, widow and Innkeeper at the King's Arms (later called the Molesworth Arms). There were four bidders: Joseph Robins, Thomas Geach, William Brabin and one 'Taylor'. A surviving document records each individual bid and Joseph Robins secured the job for a term of three years for a price of eight pounds.[23] On the 27th September 1796, George Borlase organised the auction of the tolls as agent for the feoffees (trustees) of Wade-Bridge. This time only three people bid, Joseph Robins, Peter Recorla and Richard Wards. Again, Joseph Robins was the highest bid, at seven pounds seven shillings, and he won the contract.

On the 1st November 1799, the lease on the tolls was won by Edward Geach of St Breock, a saddler and Thomas Geach, a watchmaker, who together paid nine pounds one shilling. The lease or contract reads:

> *'The tolls, dues, income and revenues, arising, growing, accruing and becoming due and payable of any for Wade-Bridge aforesaid and of other profits, emoluments, advantages and appurtenances whatsoever to the said bridge, for a term of three years rent. The sum of nine pounds and one shilling of lawful money of Great Britain was payable at the four most usual feast days of payment of rent in the year that is, the feast of the Birth of our Lord Christ, the feast of the Annunciation of the Blessed Virgin Mary, the feast of the Nativity and John the Baptist and the feast of St Michael the Archangel.'*

These feasts days are better known as Christmas, Lady Day, Midsummer Day and Michaelmas.[24]

Accounts of these auctions survive up until 1829, with one John Thomas winning the lease in 1808 and also on the next nine occasions until 1829. In September 1802, the auction was held at the Fountain Inn (another of the earlier names of the Molesworth Arms). In this case and several others, receipted bills for drink at the Inn are included with the lease, including one shilling four pence for Toddy and one shilling ten and half pence for beer or one shilling two pence for Grog. The price of the tolls increased as more wheeled traffic increased. It was worth fourteen pounds in 1818 and eighteen pounds eighteen shillings in 1828, although each year it became more difficult to collect.

---

[23] Cornwall Record Office, AD2040/5.
[24] Cornwall Record Office, AD2040/4.

Cessation of the Tolls

The last reference to a toll on Wade-bridge can be seen on a surviving hand written hand-bill dated 1831 and preserved in the Wadebridge Museum records. It reads:

> *Wade-Bridge Tolls. - To be let for one year from Michaelmas next, the Toll of Wade-Bridge. For which purpose a survey will be held at Wadebridge Inn in Wadebridge the seventh day of September next by 6 o'clock in the evening. For further particulars application must be made at our office. Dated 24 Aug 1831. Symons Huxmoore, Clerk to the Trustees of the Bridge.*

By the 1830s and 40s the town of Wadebridge had grown considerably and in July 1845 a traffic census on the bridge estimated that on average one thousand, six hundred and eighty persons and one hundred and seven horses passed over it daily. These numbers passing over the bridge had made it more difficult to collect a toll, especially as by this time some may have refused to pay. Many people resented having to pay a toll to cross the bridge and in 1834 the toll was ceased under the advice of counsel who found that such a toll could not be maintained and that the trustees' authority was questionable.[25]

What we do not know about the toll collection?

Documents are an invaluable source of information on the bridge, but are sometimes tantalisingly short on detail. For example, by the late eighteenth century the turnpike trusts were displaying toll boards outside toll-houses and toll-gates stating the different rates that vehicles and farmers herding animals had to pay, but at Wade-bridge there is no surviving evidence for this. There is no mention of whether pedestrians were ever charged a toll, or if there were different charges for hand carts, wagons, carriages, coaches and riders on horseback. There is no reference to herding cattle or sheep across the bridge to market, although this must of happened.

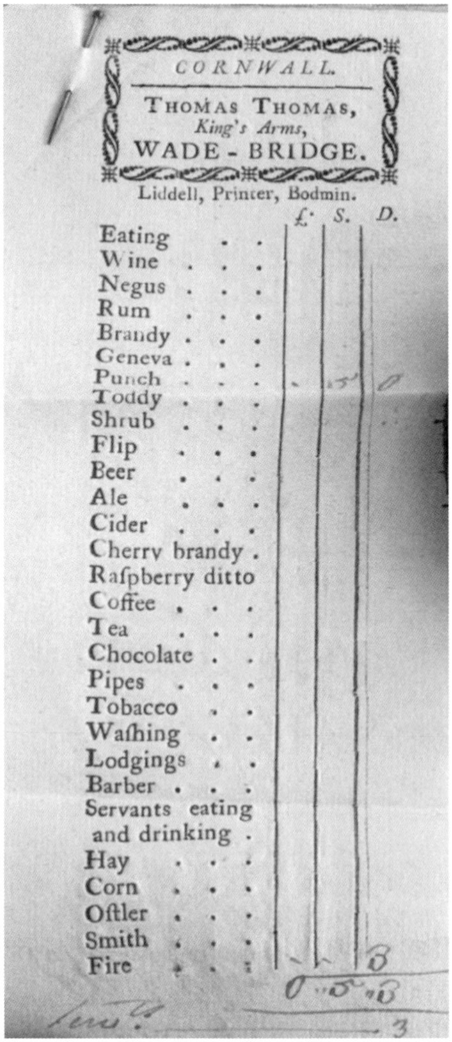

CORNWALL.
THOMAS THOMAS,
King's Arms,
WADE - BRIDGE.
Liddell, Printer, Bodmin.

	£	S.	D.
Eating			
Wine			
Negus			
Rum			
Brandy			
Geneva			
Punch			
Toddy			
Shrub			
Flip			
Beer			
Ale			
Cider			
Cherry brandy			
Rafpberry ditto			
Coffee			
Tea			
Chocolate			
Pipes			
Tobacco			
Wafhing			
Lodgings			
Barber			
Servants eating and drinking			
Hay			
Corn			
Oftler			
Smith			
Fire			

Fig 6.9 - Receipt for drinks at the King's Arms by Wade-Bridge Trustees when auctioning the lease of the tolls, © Cornwall Record Office.

[25] *The Reports of the Commissioners of Charities in England and Wales: The County of Cornwall* 1819-1837, 482.

Further questions that cannot today be answered are, was there a toll booth or toll house on the bridge?   Were the tolls collected at both ends? Was there a toll-gate or barrier across the bridge to prevent vehicles passing over without paying?   Prior to the first widening of the bridge the pedestrian refuges would have been large enough to erect a small tollbooth in, without impeding the flow of traffic, as at St Ives Bridge in Cambridgeshire where the first pedestrian refuge housed a tollbooth, and toll gates were installed across the second pair of pedestrian refuges.[26]

---

[26] Burn-Murdoch, B, 2001. *St Ives Bridge and Chapel*, 24.

7 *'paid for twenty bushels of lime'*

Bridge maintenance and repairs

Lovibond's vision of building the bridge over the Camel also included thought about its ongoing maintenance. By providing land and property in the parish of Egloshayle, to be held in trust and leased out, funds were raised for maintaining the bridge. With its piers washed by the tides twice a day, a structure of the size of Wade-Bridge requires regular repairs, and today's increasing volume of traffic causes wear and tear to the road and parapets.   Surviving records provide information about the need to replace parapets, repair piers and arches, clean vegetation from the walls and roadway, re-point masonry, repair the road surface, as well as proposals for elaborate widening schemes.

Statute of Bridges 1530

Although the foundation of a Bridge Trust in 1476 made provision for the future maintenance of the bridge, an Act of Parliament in 1530 during the reign of King Henry VIII (sometimes known as the Statute of Bridges) gave the overall responsibility of repairing bridges throughout the country to the Justices of the Peace.

The Act gave the Justices of the Peace power to keep all bridges in good repair and if a bridge was damaged or broken, it was the responsibility of the local Justice of the Peace to find who was responsible for the bridge and order them to repair it. If it was not possible to determine who was responsible the task would fall upon the people of the closest town, city or county to repair the bridge and the Justices were empowered, through the Act, to raise taxes, appoint collectors and also surveyors to assess repair needs.[1] The extent to which the Justices of the Peace needed to intervene at Wade-Bridge is not known – perhaps not often as the role of the Statute may have been required more for smaller bridges without the benefit of a Trust to raise funds for maintenance.

The Scour effect

By far the biggest threat to a bridge is the erosion of the piers that support it, as the force of the water flowing between the arches causes scouring of the piers. According to Cook, scouring occurs when obstructions such as bridge abutments and piers interfere significantly with the natural flow of a river.[2] At Wade-Bridge this effect would be enhanced by tidal flow. Scouring is more pronounced where a pier lies obliquely to the flow of water, as this creates a vortex or eddies that can undermine the piers. Rounded piers reduce this effect but pointed piers (cutwaters) reduce the scour effect most. Additional scour can be caused if the natural flow of the river is interrupted, perhaps by a tree that has fallen into it and becomes lodged between the arches of the bridge, or if the course of the river flow has been deliberately diverted, forcing the water to take a different route.

---

[1] Statute of Bridges 1530, Parliamentary Archives, 22 Henry VIII.
[2] Cook, M, 1998. *Medieval Bridges*, 51.

At Bideford Bridge on a cold frosty night in January 1968, the two end arches nearest the town collapsed without warning and caused months of chaos, with pedestrians having to be ferried across the river Torridge and all vehicles having to make a long detour while the arches were rebuilt. Although Wade-Bridge has not suffered anything quite so drastic, erosion has always been a major concern. Perhaps the event that caused the most concern about the security of the bridge was in August 1847 during the great flood, which destroyed several medieval bridges on the river Camel and its tributaries. Timber, trees and debris pounded the piers and arches of the bridge, putting enormous pressure on the structure, but the bridge survived: a credit to the medieval stonemasons that constructed it.

Bridge Wardens' Accounts[3]

Wadebridge Bridge Wardens' Accounts extend from 1660 to 1828 and record maintenance to the bridge during this time. Although the entries are brief, the accounts suggest that the fabric of the bridge was frequently being repaired and cleaned. No accounts have survived from either the fifteenth or sixteenth centuries and the first entry dated 1660 records that one pound sixteen shillings and ten pence was spent on *stones, lime etc., and cleaning of the bridge*. Two years later in 1662 the accounts are broken down and given in more detail:[4]

Drawing Stones at the quarie 7/2,
Caridge of 6 lode of stones 6s.
Workmens wages £2 6s.
Pd. for beere for the workmen 1s.
8 bushells of Lime 11s.
Making cleane the bridge 1s'
John Lobb for keeping the tolles 4d.

In the following year, 1663, the disbursements of expenditure included masons for eight days and the hire of three men and a barge, suggesting that repairs were required to the piers of the bridge.[5] In 1666, Bridge Wardens John Pettigrew, Thomas Blake, Mathew Hid and Richard Jeffery submitted their account to the trustees which included money for buying a new rope and drawing stone. By 1670, the Bridge Wardens were John Opye and James Ford of Egloshayle and Henry Hocker and Mathew Michell, gent. of St Breock. That year they received ten pounds and had paid out eight pounds sixteen shillings and nine pence in total.

---

[3] Cornwall Record Office, BridgeWardens' Accounts, DDX450/166-173.
[4] Cornwall Record Office, DDX450/111.
[5] Cornwall Record Office, DDX450/112.

Henry Hocker's account for 1670 is featured in fig 7.1 and transcribed reads:

Henry Hocker his disbusments for reparing of Wardebridge for this yeare 1670

Leaide out at the count day	0	4	0
Paid for twenty bushell of lime	1	3	4
Paid for two loades of stones	0	5	0
Paid for drauinge of a lode of stones & the caring of them to			
make the seates upone the bridge	0	2	6
Paid ffor one dayes worke to Richard Johnes			
and the use of the quarr tooles	0	1	6
Paid to John Lalby for one dayes worke	0	1	0
Paid William Wery for one dayes worke	0	1	0
Paid Phillip Horby for one dayes worke	0	1	0
For a [pece] for to make pullis for the bridge	0	2	6
Paid John Macy for a cradel and a bucket for the bridge	0	5	0
The whole summe is	2	6	10

It is unsure what the reference to seats upon the bridge means. There was certainly no room to build seats on the bridge as the roadway was less than 9ft (2.74m) and this would have caused an unnecessary restriction. Perhaps they were set back on the approaches to the bridge, in the pedestrian refuges or perhaps the term 'seat' had another meaning?

A receipt dated 1681 records one pound five shillings signed for by William Hickes in an arrangement for John Opie, Bridge Warden to be able to draw stone from Park Quarry on account for Wade-Bridge - the Bridge Wardens had been fifteen years in arrears. Three years later, in 1684, the disbursements of Sir John Molesworth and Mr Henry Hocker, Wardens, included the carriage of fifteen loads of stone from Park Quarry at Croan, Egloshayle, suggesting that the contract between Park Quarry and wardens of the bridge still continued. The disbursements of Charles Ustick gent. and John Peirce, Bridge Wardens for Wade-Bridge in 1714, included *lime for ye paving, 2 barge loads of stones, beer for the masons and stone from Park Quarry*. John Lobb was paid *for 58 days work about ye pillars of yr bridge* – three pounds, eight shillings and three pence, which suggests that some major work was required to repair the piers of the bridge at that time. Park Quarry continued to be used as the main source of stone for repairs to Wade-Bridge for well over one hundred and forty years.

Cleaning the bridge

Some of the payments in the Bridge Warden's accounts were for cleaning the bridge. This may have referred to either cleaning the roadway or removing vegetation growing in the walls and in the roadway. One must remember that for most of the bridge's history, the roadway would not have been tarmacked, but was paved or pitched with local stone, so vegetation would have grown easily between the joints and needed to be cleared frequently. The bridge was not tarmacked until the twentieth century with the advent of the motor car. In 1842, Cyrus Redding refers to a large and fine fig tree which had long flourished at the St Breock end of the bridge, the roots being fixed amongst the interstices of the stones on the sea side above an arch.[6] Though exotic and interesting, this would not benefit the structure and even today buddleia is often found growing out of some joints in the downstream masonry of the parapets and piers, and sycamore sapling trees taking root near the first arch at the Egloshayle end of the bridge. All need to be regularly removed before their roots damage the fabric of the bridge.

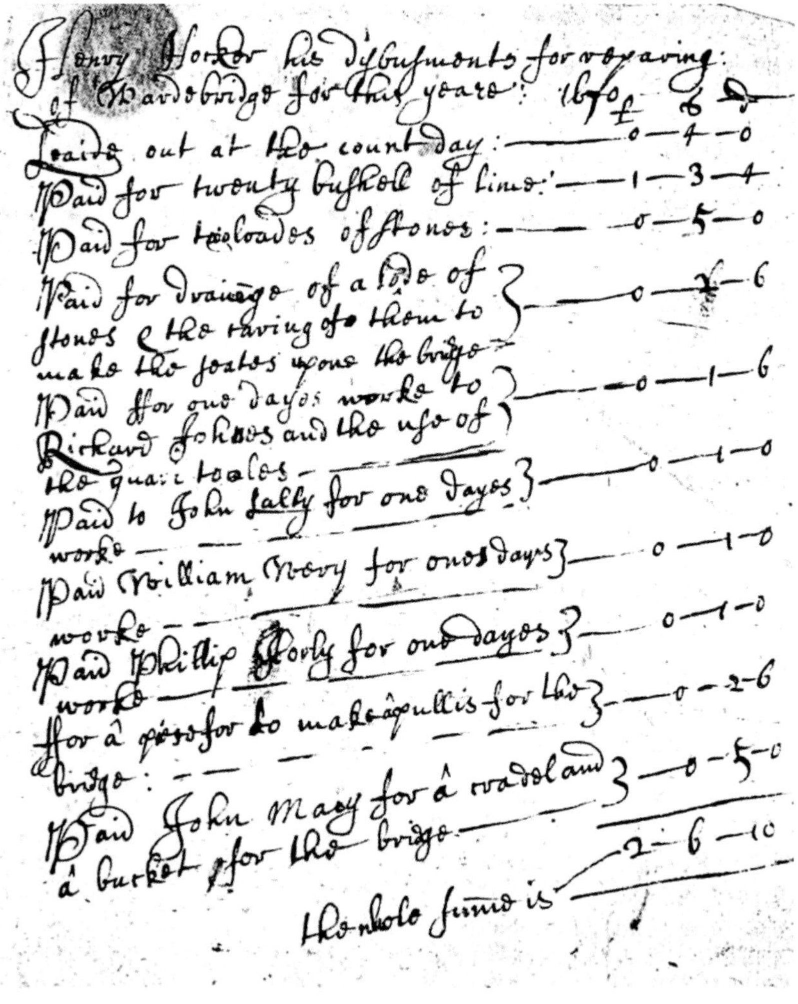

Fig 7.1 - Henry Hocker's Bridge Warden Accounts for the year 1670, courtesy the Courtney Library, Royal Institution of Cornwall, Truro.

---

[6] Redding, C, 1842. *An Illustrated Itinerary of the County of Cornwall*, 43.

Beer for the workmen

There are many entries recording payment for beer for the workmen, not only for the masons carrying out the repairs to the bridge, but also for the labourers and quarry men extracting and transporting the stone. In 1662, the disbursements or outlay by the Bridge Wardens included *'pd for beere for the workmen, 1s.'* Another entry in 1670, reads,*'stone from Park Quarry and beer for the quarrymen, beere for the masons etc. in all £2'*. This suggests many gallons of beer! In 1684 an entry reads, *'Beer to the Quarrymen as per ill costome 3s'*. Providing beer was accepted as a part of the workmens' payment and having been brewed it was also far safer to drink than water. It was usually a very weak beer or ale and the masons were not necessarily always drunk!

Park Quarry at Croan Gate

Park Quarry is mentioned by name several times in the Bridge Wardens' Accounts of 1662, 1670, 1681 and 1684. In the 1714 entry, payment is recorded for two barge-loads of stones from Park Quarry, suggesting that the stone was carried by wagon to Sladesbridge and then barged down the river to Wade-Bridge. Park Quarry or quarries are located near Croan Gate on the main A389 road to Bodmin.[7]

In 1815, the year of the Battle of Waterloo, the agreement between the Wade-Bridge Trust and the proprietors of Croan to draw stone from Park Quarry, came to an abrupt end. Letters held in the County Record Office give some suggestion that another source of stone needed to be found.[8]

After what appears to be several years since stone was drawn from Park Quarry, and after a change of landowner, a letter was written by the Reverend Richard Lyne, vicar of Little Petherick, representing the Reverend

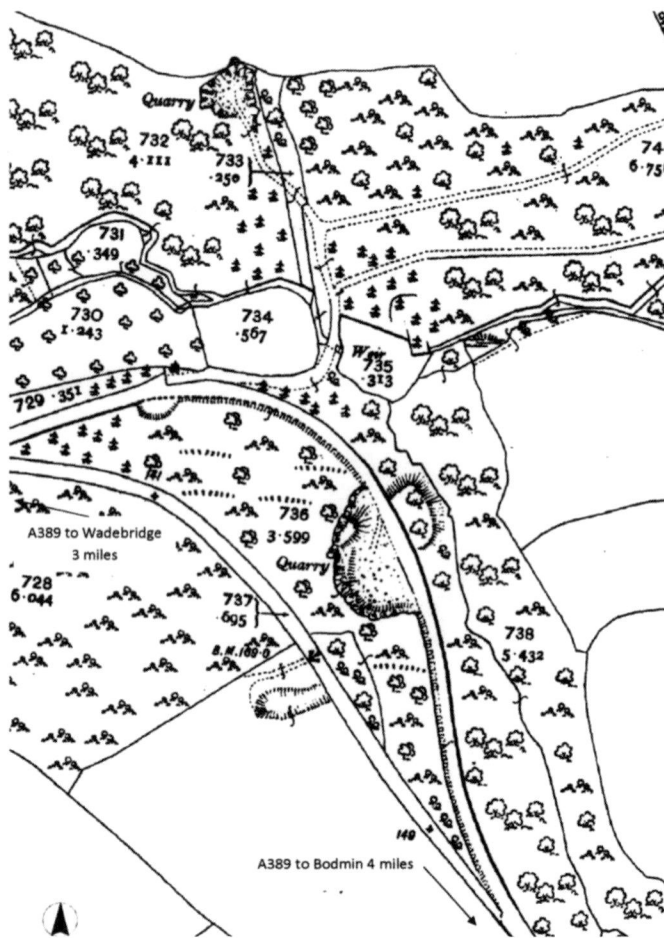

Fig 7.2 - Ordnance Survey 1907 Park Quarry, Egloshayle, © Crown Copyright.

---

[7] In 1988, the author recorded a number of stonemasons' carvings on a rock in the stone quarry, although all appear to be nineteenth century rather than seventeenth century. They consist of stonemason's tools, names and initials.

[8] Cornwall Record Office, DDX 2493 and DDX 2494.

PL. III.

Pa. 46.

Scale of 100 Yards.

To John Molesworth Esq.r this North View of WADEBRIDGE, in Cornwall, engrav'd at his expence,
is most gratefully inscribed by
Wm Borlase.

Plate 9 - Borlase's illustration of Wade-Bridge, 1758. Courtesy Andrew Eddy.

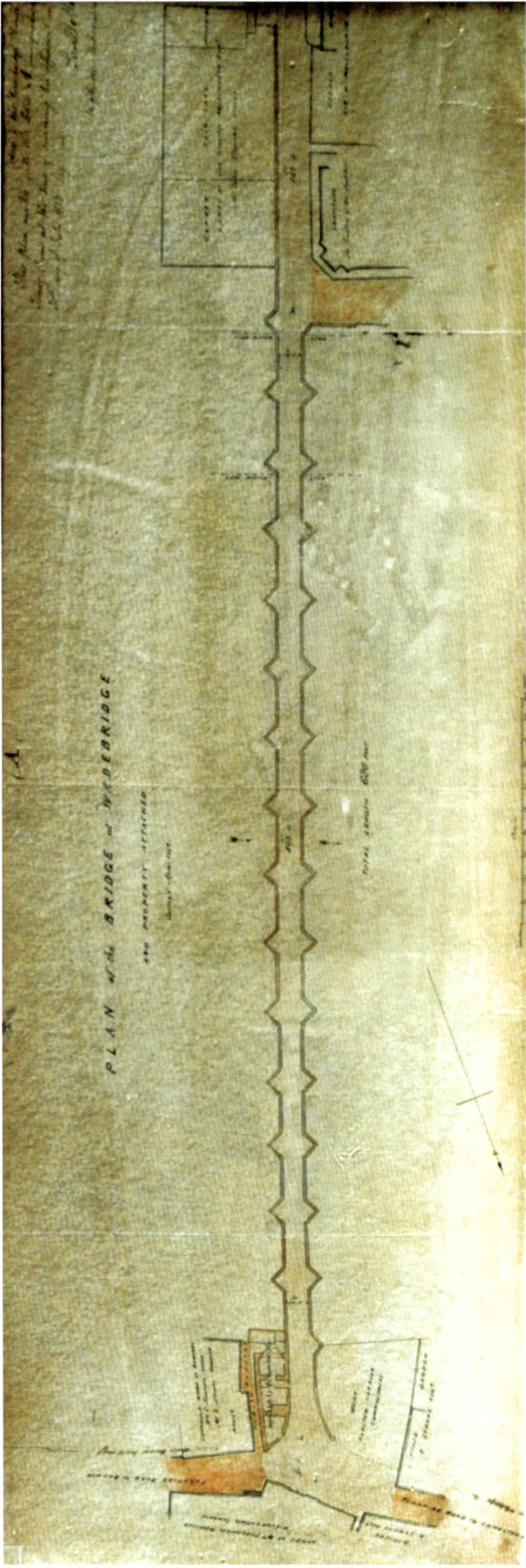

Plate 10 - The 1852 plan of Wade-Bridge commissioned to ascertain land ownership adjacent to the bridge, Courtesy Wadebridge Town Council.

Plate 11 – Reconstruction of the 1542 armed assault on Wade-Bridge, by Jane Stanley 2011.

Plate 12 – Reconstruction of the most gruesome event in the history of Wade-Bridge, part of Cuthbert Mayne's body being exhibited on the bridge, by Jane Stanley 2011.

Plate 13 – Reconstruction of Cromwell's troops holding Wade-Bridge in 1646, by Jane Stanley 2011.

The Bridge, Wadebridge.

Plate 14 – Sand barge upstream of Wade-Bridge near the entrance to the Polmorla River and the sand dock.

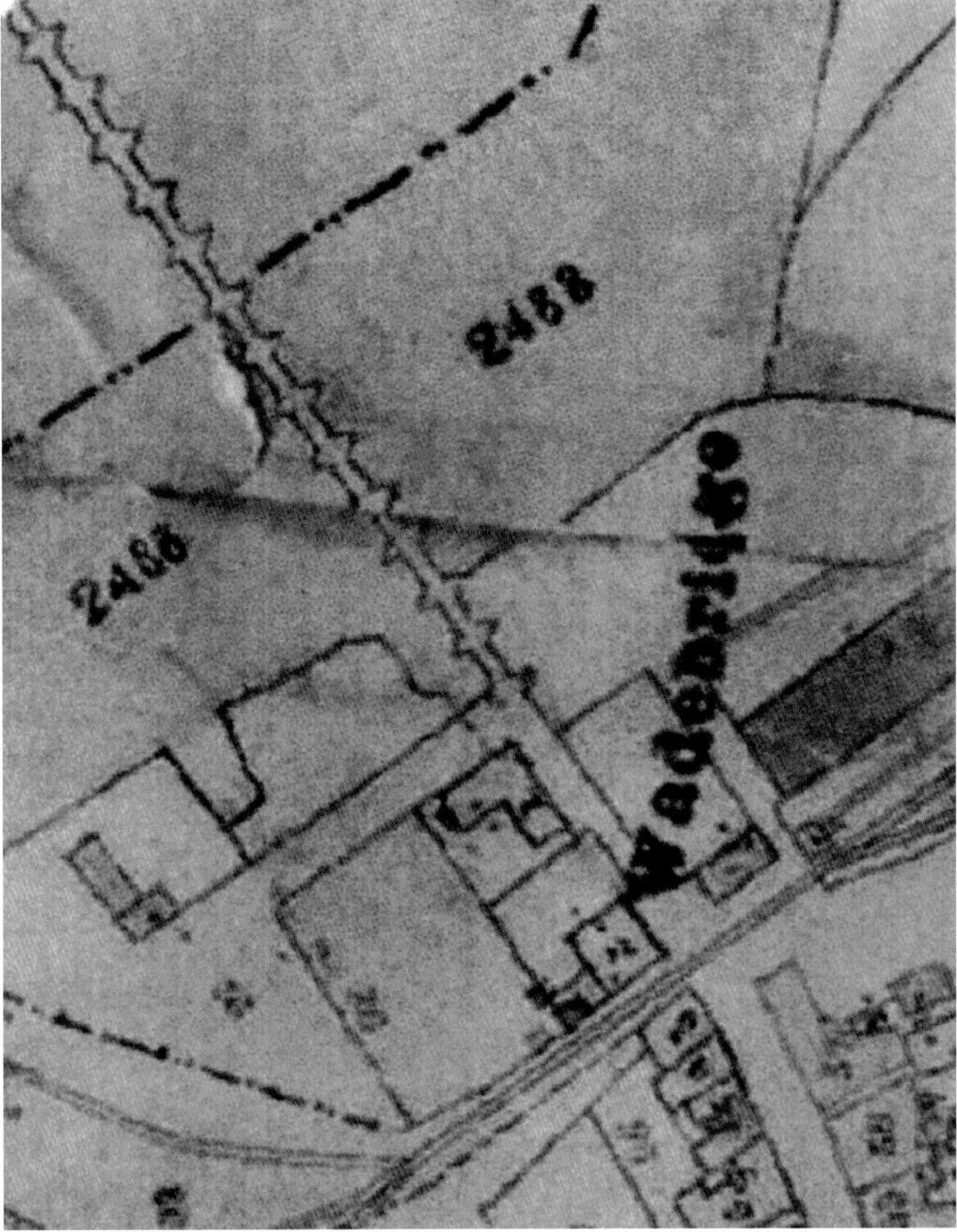

Plate 15 - A portion of the St Breock Tithe Map of 1841 which clearly shows the narrowness of the original bridge prior to widening. Courtesy Cornwall Record Office.

Plate 16a - Wade-Bridge in 1962, prior to the second widening at low tide, Courtesy May Garland.

Plate 16b – An illustrated map from the Lanhydrock Atlas in c1699 showing
Wade-Bridge, © The National Trust Photographic Library/Chris Bowden.

Prideaux-Brune, a trustee of the bridge to Reverend Tremayne of Heligan the new owner of Croan. The letter stated that there were certain repairs needed to the bridge and a request was made to draw the stone from Park Quarry at Higher Croan in Egloshayle, *according to a custom which the bridge has anciently enjoyed (though not exercised for the last twenty years) for a tribute of 3/6 per annum*. The Reverend Tremayne replied, using the back of the same letter, stating, *I will endeavour to find out the circumstances of the Wade-Bridge Trust with which I have never been made acquainted*, and politely refused the request. In a subsequent letter, after taking advice from Mr Rashleigh of Duporth, the Reverend Tremayne asked Mr Lyne to provide some evidence of the Trust's claim to draw stone from Park Quarry. In July 1815, Richard Lyne replied stating that '*a Thomas Cleve, the sexton at Egloshayle, more than 60 years of age, says, that he and his father use formerly to work at Croan under William Kirkman, and that he remembers Mr Kirkman once demanded and received from the Trustees of Wade-Bridge some years arrears (of about 3s or 3s 6d a year) for the right to draw stone from Park Quarry in Croan for use of Wade-Bridge'*. Mr Lyne went on to say that there was not a better source of stone in the neighbourhood fit for purpose and that several of the bridge piers and two of the arches were in a decrepit state. He concluded by stating that he had a number of ancient title deeds and would have them translated to see if more evidence could be found. Another reply from Reverend Tremayne again refused to accept the Trust's claim, and went on to say that '*considering the stone to be of a superior quality*' it was more valuable than for walling and he wanted to preserve the stone chiefly for his own use. In the Cornwall Record Office, amongst the Bridge Wardens' Accounts is a note written on a small piece of paper, suggesting that there was previously evidence of some form of agreement between the Bridge Trustees and the owner of Park Quarry. It is dated 1681, and reads, '*Recd. of John Opie for the liberty of drawing stones on Park for the acct. of Wade bridge, £1 5s 0d, being 15 years due signed Wm Hickes.*' It is assumed that John Opie was a steward or agent for William Kirkman the previous owner of Croan.

Croan was formerly owned by the Roscarrock family. One John Roscarrock was a founder trustee of Wade-Bridge, and Roscarrocks may therefore have started a tradition of obtaining stone from Park Quarry for repairs. The property was sold to Michael Hill, whose son was John Hill, rector of St Mabyn in 1668 and shortly afterwards to Edward Hoblyn: the Hoblyns are also mentioned as Trustees of Wade-Bridge. Later Damaris Hoblyn married Francis Kirkham and after his death and the death of all her children, Croan was bequeathed to her cousin the Reverend Henry Hawkins Tremayne of Heligan. With all these changes of owner it is easy to see how the traditional right could have been conveniently forgotten.

Barges and bargemen

Barges were often a necessity when bringing stone to the bridge site, or when work was required on the piers. The original stone for building the bridge was probably quarried from a riverside or estuary quarry and barged up the river. Barges have been used on the river Camel for hundreds of years to transport goods, as larger vessels were only able to navigate the river Camel on a high tide. Goods were often barged up to Wadebridge from vessels moored at Padstow. In August 1626, during the reign of Charles I, with the threat of war with France a maritime survey of the nation's vessels took place. On the river Camel, twenty-nine bargemen are named all from the parishes of Egloshayle and St Breock.[9] Later, barges were used to transport sea sand from the sand banks in the estuary up the river, to Wadebridge, Amble and Sladesbridge, where it was loaded onto wagons by farmers to spread on their fields as a fertilizer.

According to the late Mr George Beare, the last barges ceased to work the river just before the outbreak of the Second World War, as they were increasingly replaced by rail transport.[10] When the bridge was first widened in 1852-53, the bargemen were criticised for damaging the bridge. Mr Enys reported at the Cornwall Michaelmas Sessions in October 1853 that when passing under the bridge the bargemen were in the habit, of using an iron spike as a lever against the stone work of the arches and piers, 'when by little strength and trouble' they could get their barges through, but this was causing damage to the bridge. Today, grooves in the stonework of some of the old arches indicate that barges have consistently rubbed against the arches in the past.[11]

Re-paving the roadway of the bridge

On the 24th June 1771, during the reign of George III, a contract was signed between four trustees of Wade-Bridge, Sir John Molesworth of Pencarrow, Edmund Prideaux of Padstow, Reverend Robert Dennis, rector of St Breock, and Henry Peers, vicar of Egloshayle, with a James Carter of the borough of Lostwithiel, a paver. The agreement was that Carter *paved the bridge in a good substantial and workmanlike manner with all expedience so as to have the same completed as soon as the nature of the work will admit.* It was agreed that the trustees would supply all the materials and deliver them to the bridge. Carter was to be paid three and half pence a yard for laying the new paving. This was for the roadway or bridge-way and should not be confused with the pedestrian pavements that exist today. For a further ten shillings a year, Carter agreed to maintain the bridge paving for seven years, *to keep in good repair, uphold, sustain and maintain.* This payment was to be paid to James Carter by Sir John Molesworth on behalf of the trustees, every 24th June (Midsummer Day or Feast of John the Baptist). The agreement stipulated that if Carter received a letter from the trustees advising him that the bridge paving was damaged, he would repair it within twenty days. This contract was witnessed by Edward Fox and Trehane Symons.

Proposed elaborate widening scheme

Early in 1818, a proposal was put forward to widen the roadway above the three central arches of the bridge, to raise the height of the parapets on either side of these arches and provide some lighting. The elaborate scheme suggested extending the width of the carriageway over the three centre arches (arches, 8, 9 and 10) of the bridge from 10ft (3.05m) to 15ft (4.47m). This was to

---

[9] Gray, T, 1990 Ed. ' Early – *Stuart Mariners and Shipping – The Maritime Surveys of Devon and Cornwall 1619-35*' Devon and Cornwall Record Society. Bargemen in the parishes of Egloshayle (Egloseale and St Breock (St Breage) include Joseph Beare 55, Simon Billinge 27, Thomas Billinge 20, John Bligh 38, John Cawlinge 54, John Cocke 70, Thomas Cocke, John Corke 38, Frances Couch 40, Edward Ede 56, Humphey Grosse 34, Nathaniel Hambley 40, Jacob Hellson 56, John Hitchens 48, John Launder 40, High Lawrance 42, Richard Pearse 30, Bartholomew Phillipp 32, Stipio Preler 28, John Scott 60, Clemens Simon 42, Richard Skinner 40, James Skrout 57, Henry Sleepe 40, John Tregathen 70, John Trerubie 55, Walter Trerubie 56, Christopher Wolfe 35 and Henry Woode 24.

[10] *Sladesbridge and Wadebridge Barges*, based on an interview of Mr George Beare of Pendavey Hill, Sladesbridge and Mr W Chidgey of Wadebridge by Miss M Garland 21st August 1975.

[11] Grooves in the stone work of arch 4 made by barges rubbing against the sides of the arch can still be clearly seen.

allow wagons, carriages and coaches to pass each other on the middle of the bridge, without the need to reverse a team of horses. Sir Arscott Molesworth also offered to give the Trust the free use of stone from Dunveth Quarry. Information about this proposed scheme is found in two letters in the Cornwall Record Office, one from Sir Arscott Molesworth of Pencarrow to his cousin the Reverend William Molesworth, rector of St Breock. Both were trustees of Wade-bridge. The second is a note from Reverend Molesworth to the Trust's solicitor Richard Symons, forwarding on Sir Arscott's comments.

Fig 7.3 - This shows a watercolour sketch of the proposed widening and embellishment of Wade-Bridge in 1818. Courtesy Wadebridge Town Council.

On the topic of the lighting, Sir Arscott Molesworth stated that, *'nobody would see to keep them lyghted when dark and would be constantly broken and damaged by idle boys, whereby the clerical expense would be incurred to the Trust greatly'*. After the Trustees had discussed the project, it was decided to drop the scheme and only to raise the parapet walls.[12] The reference to proposed lighting on the bridge, suggests that either a Gas Works had already been established in the town by 1818, or more likely the lights would have been fuelled by oil. The earliest reference to a Gas Works in Wadebridge is in a trade directory dated 1852, the first gas lamp was fitted to the bridge in 1854.

There is a framed watercolour painting hanging above the main stairs on the first floor of the Wadebridge Town Hall, which depicts a similar bridge to Wade-Bridge but with a raised parapet over the central arches, decorative stone balls topping the parapet and what appears to be a lamp above the parapet on either side (fig 7.3). This appears to be the designer's impression of how the

---

[12] Cornwall Record Office, DDX450/180/1 and DDX450/180/2.

bridge would have looked had the scheme gone ahead. There is no information about the watercolour at the Town Hall, but it was certainly drawn during the early part of the nineteenth century, when the first and last arches of the bridge had already been blocked up.

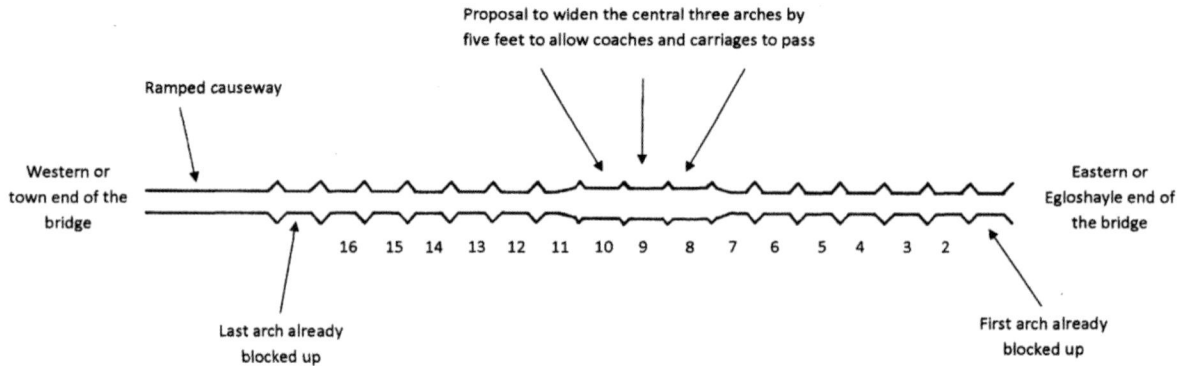

Fig 7.4 - A plan showing the 1818 proposal to widen the three central arches of Wade-Bridge.

Replacing the parapets

On Saturday March 14th 1818, local newspapers carried an advertisement inviting contractors to tender for work which included taking down and re-building the parapet walls and cleaning, pinning and pointing the piers and abutments of the bridge, according to a specification which could be viewed at Mr Symons office at Wadebridge.[13] One William Henderson, a mason from Bodmin, tendered for the work, although in the end the contract went to a local partnership, James Collins of St Breock and John Ellory of Egloshayle, masons. A contract was drawn up between the two masons and the trustees, Sir Arscott Ourry Molesworth, Bt., the Reverend Charles Prideaux-Brune, the Reverend William Molesworth of St Breock and Reverend Richard Cory, vicar of Egloshayle.[14]

The detail of the remarkably comprehensive contract gives an insight into the masons' obligations:

> 'The workmen shall and will between the first day of May now next ensuing and the first day of August then next following for the consideration here in after mentioned at their some or one of their own proper leases and charges take and pull down all the parapet walls of the said bridge at Wadebridge aforesaid and well and effectually erect, build, complete and finish new parapet walls thereon, with such materials, at such height and such thickness of walls and

[13] Royal Cornwall Gazette, 14/03/1818, 1.
[14] Cornwall Record Office, AD2040/19 - Contract to rebuild the parapet walls of Wade-Bridge in 1815.

also fully repair and point the said bridge in such a manner and form as here in it is stipulated and expressed that is to say: To take down the old parapet walls to about six inches under the present road, from the end of the bridge on the Egloshayle side on to where the parapets are somewhat higher on the Saint Breock side, to build new walls in a good and sound and neat manner of masonry called 'close hammered work' with the best of the old stones mixed with new stone to be raised from a quarry adjoining called Dunveth Quarry, to be set in good lime and sand mortar composed of one part lime and two parts sand and the walls to be built to the thickness as at present in the bottom and to be carried up so as to finish of a thickness corresponding with the width of the present moorstone coping which is to be neatly jointed and well bedded and regularly fixed throughout and to finish a full four feet high measured from the level of the road or Bridgeway to the top of the moorstone coping and to be ramped down to the old walls on the Saint Breock side as shall be directed by Mr James Chapple Surveyor or such other surveyor as the said trustees should agree.'

'To make good the deficiency of moorstone with new moorstone, which may be wrought and fixed similar to the old. To present all the gutter tiles lately fixed in the parapet walls and properly re-fix the same in the new walls and to make complete all the pitching which may be removed or damaged in consequence of erecting the new walls and all the open joints, cracks, or decayed places, or parts of the piers, Butments [abutments] from the bed of the river to the springing of the arches to be properly pinned with stones and mortar composed of Padstow Black Lime mixed with sand and well beaten together and the whole of the old walls to be newly pointed. And to provide all materials, labour, carriage, scaffolding, railing and all and every requisite whatsoever for the performing the said work and for every load of stones taken from Dunveth Quarry for the use of the said work to carry off and remove a load of rubbish out of the said quarry and perform the same in good substantial and workmanlike manner. Also some or one of them shall and will during all the time the said work is in prosecution, keep the Bridgeway so clear as not to impede or obstruct the free passage of carts, carriages, horses or other cattle, or barges thro' the arches and to prevent accidents shall rail off, or otherwise properly secure any openings when the walls are taken down.'

However, a note survives from the clerk to the Bridge Trustees to James Collins and John Ellory, dated the 24th June of that year expressing concern that the agreement was already not being fulfilled to the letter of the contract because no clerk of works was present. The note reads:

'It is expected of the Trustees of Wadebridge that one of you to be on the bridge in constant attendance upon the work and that more attention is paid to the performance of the work which the surveyor has found much fault and I hereby give you notice in the event of you failing to do so you will have failed ye contract and will be paid only for such work he hath been finished and agreeable to yr contract.'

One can only assume that in the end the contract was fulfilled and the new parapet walls completed. Today the parapet walls of the bridge are only 3ft 2ins (0.96m) high above the pavement and 3ft 6ins (1.07m) above the road level. This proposal requested the walls to be built to a height of 4ft (1.22m).

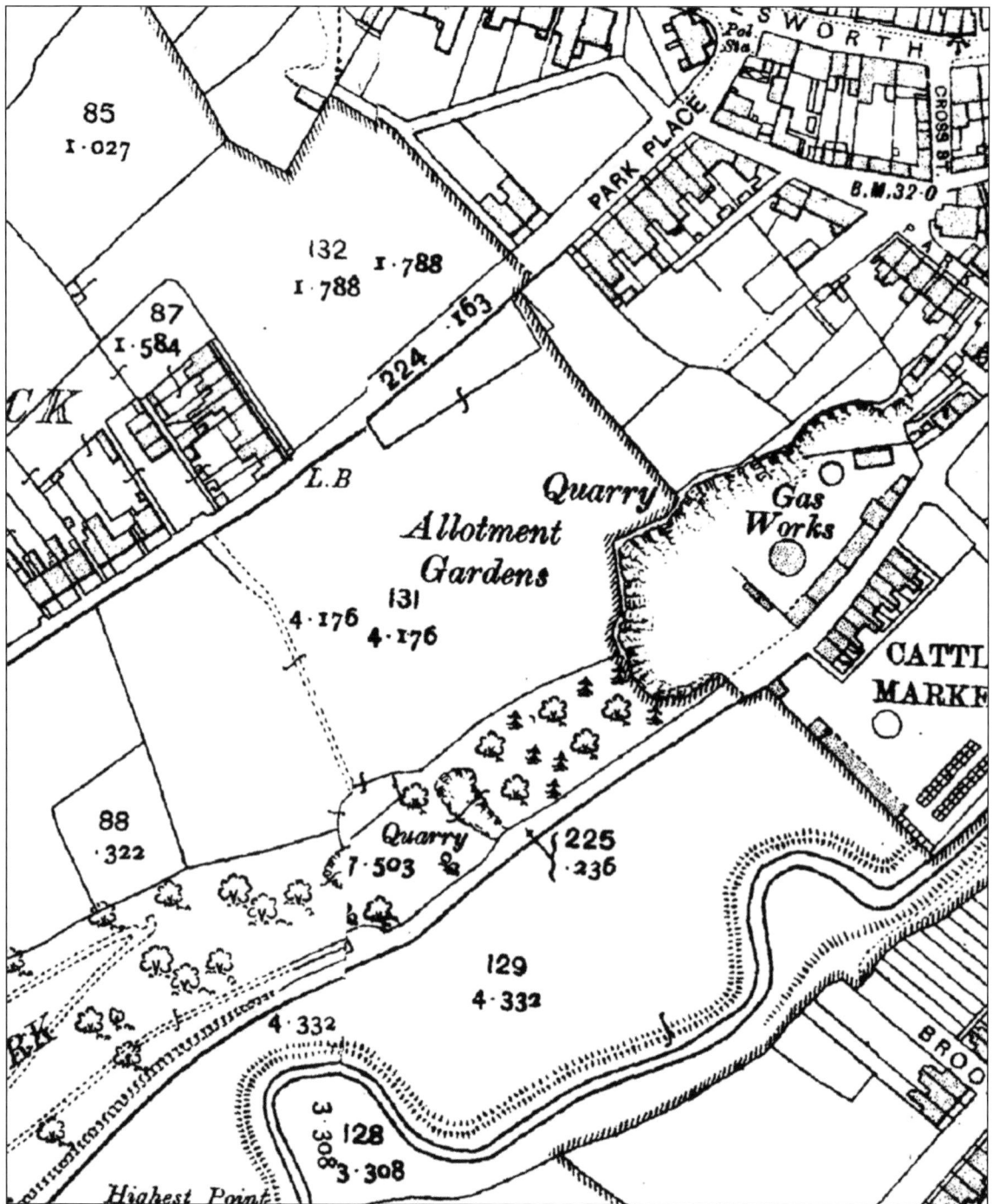

Fig 7.5 - Ordnance Survey 1907 shows the Dunveth Quarries on Polmorla Road, where the Telephone Exchange is now situated, © Crown Copyright.

The contract was to last from the 1st May 1818 to the 1st August 1819. Dunveth Quarry or quarries are on Polmorla Road, the original quarry being on the site now occupied by the Telephone Exchange and formerly the Gas Works. A second quarry is situated beside a house called Woodside and a third between Woodside and the entrance to Coronation Park. The reference to ramping down the parapet walls to the old walls at the St Breock end of the bridge is so that they could be tied into the existing causeway walls that were running down from the level of the bridge to the site of the old market house. New granite coping would have been purchased from one of the Bodmin Moor quarries, probably at St Breward; as this was before the opening of the railway it would have had to be transported by wagon.[15] The reference to gutter tiles suggests that the roadway may have been cambered in the middle to allow the water to run off, perhaps along a gutter or launder and through the bottom of the parapets. The pitching suggests that these were stones placed tight together on edge rather than on their flat. It is surprising that even in 1818, the trustees were thinking about health and safety by insisting that when parts of the parapet walls were removed, guard rails were fitted to prevent people from falling over the edge of the bridge.

Fig 7.6 - The scroll end granite coping on the Egloshayle end of the downstream parapet.

---

[15] West, J, 1991. *St Breock and Wadebridge: A Contribution to a History of Parish and Town*, 12.

An invoice for what appears to be extra work by James Collins and John Ellory reads, *'Building a circular wall as shall be directed in Egloshayle side, digging foundations, filling in the road with good pitching and scour a scrowle end, £16 15s 6d and also a wall and scrowle end at the St Breock side £1 5s 0d, in total £18 0s 6d.'* An accompanying drawing illustrates what was intended: it shows the bridge parapet on the east or Egloshayle end splayed out each side and terminated in a scroll shape complete with scroll-like coping stone.

Further re-paving of the roadway

In 1828, during the reign of William IV, the bridge was again in need of re-paving, probably due to the vast increase in traffic, carriages, coaches and wagons. The wheels of these vehicles would have caused rutting and the displacement of the paving. It would only take one stone to become dislodged, loosening the remainder, before large holes in the paving or pitching would occur. On the 7th March of that year a contract was signed between the Reverend Charles Prideaux Brune of Place, Reverend William Molesworth, rector of St Breock, Reverend Richard Cory, vicar of Egloshayle, all trustees of Wade-Bridge, with one John Haynes, Pavier, of the borough of Bodmin.[16]

The agreement or contract read as follows:

> *'That John Haynes shall take up all the pitching of the said bridge and also that part on the Egloshayle end, which belongs to the said bridge. And also form the ground as shall be directed by the said Trustees' surveyors and then pitch or pave the same with stones not to exceed nor be less in size than the pattern stones in Mr Symons office at Wadebridge aforesaid. And also that the old stones of the above pattern size shall be used in the wheel ways and the deficiency to be made good with new stones of the same size and description and shall not break or use the large stones but remove and carry off the same with all rubbish to a spot to be pointed out by Mr Symons not exceeding 300 yards from either end of the bridge – that the angles over the projection of the piers of the said bridge shall be pitched so as to carry off the water as shall be directed by the said surveyor.'*

The rate or price was to be eleven pence per yard of stone laid; the contract also mentions the re-fixing of the guard stones, which were probably some form of spur stone or kerb stone to restrict the width of vehicles entering the bridge from either end so that they would not damage the parapets. The trustees' surveyor was James Chapple, who was also the surveyor ten years earlier when the parapets were replaced. As well as re-paving the bridge, John Haynes was expected to keep the bridge-way clear and not impede or obstruct the free passage of carts, carriages, horses and other cattle. He was also responsible for removing all stone, rubbish and tools from the roadway every evening and filling any holes, for the safety of passengers by night.

---

[16] Cornwall Record Office, AD2040/20.

Lime and Lime kilns

Many of the accounts presented to the Trustees of Wade-Bridge on their Count Day record the purchase of lime. Although there were several lime kilns in Wadebridge during the nineteenth century, little is known about the sources of lime before this. Earlier forms of lime burning to create lime must have been available in the area during the medieval period for use in building the many bridges, churches and harbour walls. Isham notes that the beaches around the Camel estuary contained lime-rich sand which would have been suitable for burning to make lime.[17] This may have been the source of the material for the lime mortars. Clearly large amounts of lime would have been required to build Wade-Bridge and to maintain it over the centuries.

By the 1840s there were several lime kilns in the Wadebridge area. Limestone or sand would have been transported to the kiln by boat, where it was burned to create lime which was then mixed with water to produce lime putty. This was then mixed with sand to produce mortar for the masonry. There were kilns on Bradfords Quay and on Treguddick Quay (where the cinema now stands). According to Isham, there were a further three lime kilns to the east of the bridge, two along the river bank at the beginning of Egloshayle Road and another at Sladesbridge.[18] A sale notice for Gonvena House dated 11th April 1834 was published in the *West Briton and Cornwall Advertiser*, and apart from the actual house, there were many other buildings. These included stables around the house and below on the river, newly built cellars, wharfs, quays, coal and timber yards and a lime kiln being occupied by Mr J. D. Martyn, merchant.

---

[17] Isham, K, 2000. *Lime Kilns and Limeburners in Cornwall*, 5.
[18] Isham, K, 2000. 193.

8 'in consequence of the narrowness of the said bridge, collisions and stoppages are frequent occurrences'

The first widening

Until the mid eighteenth century, travellers, merchants and visitors to Cornwall and Wade-Bridge who came overland travelled on horseback, with pack-horses to transport their goods. Due to the poor state of the county's roads, wagons were still a rare sight in Cornwall, and roads were notoriously bad. Around the mid-eighteenth century with the introduction of the turnpike trusts the county's roads started to be improved providing a better quality road suitable for wheeled transport. In 1760, the turnpike from Hallworthy, via Camelford and Wadebridge *enroute* to St Columb and Mitchell was founded, leading to an increase in carriage and coach traffic, with more visitors and travellers over the bridge. At the same time the growth in maritime trade on the quays, also generated further traffic and together they eventually necessitated the widening of Wade-Bridge.

Gilbert when writing about Cornish bridges in 1817 stated that they were:

> 'in too many cases of insufficient width, and frequently not in unison with the line of roads that pass over them, which is a common defect throughout the island. The approach to, and departure from a bridge should always be straight, sudden curvatures and acute angles being often productive of accidents.'[1]

Blockages on the bridge

The help of the County Sessions had been sought on several occasions by the Wade-Bridge Trust to assist with both repairs and a widening scheme, but to no avail. So in the 1840s a plan was hatched to encourage two influential people to support the plea for the bridge to be widened.[2] Local timber merchant Thomas Martyn is alleged to have arranged for a wagon-load of timber to break down on the bridge on a Sunday morning, just before the Reverend William Molesworth, rector of St Breock, crossed over on his way to lunch with his nephew Sir William Molesworth of Pencarrow. The wagon completely blocked the bridge, so delaying Molesworth, while Martyn pointed out that if the bridge had been widened, he would have been able to pass by. The Reverend William Molesworth was a trustee of Wade-Bridge and his nephew Sir William Molesworth was well known in County affairs.

According to another version of this event, recorded by Donald Bray in 1983, it was even difficult for two loaded pack animals to pass on the bridge let alone two carts. Timber was often transported by ship from Norway and landed on the Egloshayle side of the river; these large baulks (trimmed tree trunks) would then be taken across the bridge to Mr Martyn's yard on the town side, making blockages and hold-ups inevitable. It is alleged that Mr Martyn offered to pay

---

[1] Gilbert, C S, 1817, *An Historical Survey of the County of Cornwall*, 396.
[2] West, J, 1991. *St Breock and Wadebridge: A Contribution to a History of Parish and Town*, 56.

half the cost of widening the bridge, but that Sir William Molesworth refused. Soon after, there was an accident on the bridge when baulks were being dragged across in a massive load drawn by six horses. The drag broke a wheel and the resultant obstruction was so effective that it blocked the bridge for a whole week. As a consequence, Sir William, who was a magistrate, is said to have missed important meetings in Truro.[3] Later, after Martyn's prank, questions were again asked at the County Sessions.

Wombwell's Caravan of Wild Beasts

Such blockages on the bridge were a regular occurrence; in July 1845 it was reported at the Cornwall Midsummer Sessions that the Wombwell's large caravan of wild beasts took an hour and a half to pass over the bridge, and that the wheels of the vehicles scraped against the parapet walls and damaged them considerably. Wombwell's was a travelling circus show or menagerie which must have included very long horse-drawn vehicles.[4] A newspaper report in October 1845 reported that: *'the traffic was very considerable and rapidly increasing; 3500 tons of coal, 6260 quarters of corn has passed over the bridge during the past year and obstructions arising to the inhabitants were a daily occurrence, averaging 6 every day. Wagons could not pass each other, although carts did, yet with great risk; and with great precaution much delay took place.'*[5]

Traffic census

During 1845, the County Sessions commissioned a traffic survey between the 14th and the 26th of July on everything that passed over the bridge. This showed that the bridge was in continuous use for thirteen days with 372 carriages, 1207 carts, 1398 horses, 280 cattle and 21,848 pedestrians passing over it. Obviously local traffic and pedestrians may have used the bridge many times in one day, but even so this figure seems surprising. The report also stated that there were 67 obstructions or blockages during this period.[6]

By this time, the urgency for widening and repairing the bridge was such that the County Sessions formed a Wade-Bridge committee, chaired by the Rev William Molesworth, to report on the possibilities for widening the structure. One concern that the County Sessions discussed was whether the County should be liable to widen the bridge, when a Bridge Trust, vested with stock to maintain the bridge, still existed. The County approached the Court of Chancery for their opinion and it was their decision that the County should be responsible for widening the bridge, while the Wade-Bridge Trust should be wound up and their funds put towards the project. The St Breock Tithe map and the 1852 plan in the town hall clearly indicate the narrowness of the bridge (see plates 10 and 15).

---

[3] Bray, D, 1983. *Stories of the North Cornish Coast*, 40-3.
[4] *Royal Cornwall Gazette*, 6th June 1838, Wombwell's circus and fair visited Truro with fourteen caravans of wild beasts, presumably a similar number of vehicles may have passed over Wade-Bridge in 1845.
[5] *West Briton & Cornwall Advertiser*, 17 October 1845.
[6] *West Briton & Cornwall Advertiser*, 17 October 1845.

In July 1846, a notice was printed on the front page of the *West Briton and Cornwall Advertiser* newspaper inviting engineers and architects to submit to the Clerk of the Peace plans, specifications and estimates for widening, altering, repairing and improving of the county bridge at Wadebridge, with due regard for efficiency and economy. The notice went on to state that any widening should consider the state of the existing piers and whether they were sufficient to support the proposed alterations.[7]

Plans to widen the bridge

At the Cornwall Epiphany Sessions in June 1847, the Reverend Molesworth reported that the committee had received six plans to widen Wade-Bridge although only two, submitted by a Mr Olver of Falmouth, appear to have been considered. One of these was for an iron parapet, which would cost not more than £300, with a further £120 for repairs and £30 for widening the eastern (Egloshayle) approach. Mr Olver's second plan was for stone parapets with a cost of £430, the repairs of the piers and the expense at the eastern approach being the same as in the previous plan. The magistrates had been at first in favour of a stone parapet; but on re-consideration opted for an iron parapet, the weight of which would be only 1 to 30, compared with that of stone, while the use of iron would gain an additional foot on the overall width. Mr Goldsworthy Gurney supported the idea of an iron parapet. Mr Molesworth stated that Trust funding for the project would consist of £150 at present in 3% stock and £146 in the hands of Mr Symons solicitor and steward to the Trustees of the Bridge Estates. He went on to say that the income of the Bridge lands was worth £28 per annum, which would be reduced by £10 if the two houses on the eastern approach (Bridge House) were pulled down.[8] The County Sessions agreed that on application to them, additional funds would be made available to assist with the bridge widening scheme.

By the Cornwall Midsummer Sessions of 1847, the idea of widening the bridge with an iron structure had been dropped in favour of a third plan by Mr Olver, to widen the bridge by three feet on either side at a cost of £800, with £500 to be provided by the county and the remainder from the sale of Trust funds and their assets. On July 16th 1847 a notice was again published in local newspapers, calling for tenders from architects and builders willing to contract for altering, widening and improving the bridge at Wadebridge, according to the plan and specifications lodged with Mr Pease, the County Bridge Surveyor.[9]

Although Wade-Bridge was saved from a cast iron parapet which would have ruined the visual character of the bridge, a similar proposal was adopted at Bideford and work started here in 1864 using cast iron and steel parapets; but by 1925, these had been replaced by reinforced concrete.

---

[7] *West Briton & Cornwall Advertiser*, 31 July 1846.

[8] *Royal Cornwall Gazette*, 8th June 1847.

[9] *West Briton & Cornwall Advertiser*, 16th July 1847.

The Great Flood

Although the go-ahead had been given to widen the bridge, unexpected events occurring even before the notice for tenders had been published caused the Wade-Bridge project to be postponed for another five years.

For on Thursday 9th July 1847, disaster struck. A massive thunderstorm with torrential rain in the Camelford and Davidstow area caused flood waters to collect in the valleys, until its pressure forced a wall of water between 12 and 18 feet above the normal level down the rivers Camel and Inny.[10] Henderson recounts that *'lower down in the valleys, it was a hot sultry afternoon with a clear sky and men working in the fields could not believe their senses when they saw the water approaching them'*, washing away everything in its path.[11] The drivers of a mineral train at Wenford Bridge drove down the line at full speed, warning everyone to leave the riverside. The engine drivers, Messrs Rosevear and Hicks, were subsequently rewarded for their quick-thinking which saved lives, livestock and property. Despite this public-spirited act, many animals were washed away including, horses, cattle, pigs, sheep and poultry. Many riverside properties were also damaged, and an array of goods could be seen floating down river: wheel-barrows, water-butts, carts, wheels, timber and planking. In the fields, whole crops were torn from the land with their soil and washed into the raging torrent. The flood water uprooted trees which were forced downstream, smashing into the piers and parapets of bridges and causing considerable damage. The first bridge to be attacked by this wall of water was Gam Bridge, followed shortly by Wenford Bridge, Pooley's Bridge and Tresarret Bridge, the latter being completely washed away. The solid medieval construction of Helland Bridge saved it from destruction, although the next bridge downstream at Dunmeer was smashed to pieces. The wooden railway bridge below Pendavey was lifted from its piers and floated down the river, though luckily men in boats managed to secure the bridge with ropes before it damaged Wade-Bridge. All the bridges on the Camel, with the exception of Helland Bridge and Wade-Bridge, were either badly damaged or lost, and on the river Inny there was a similar story, with all the bridges except Trekelland being washed away. Wade-Bridge may have survived because the flood water passed either side of the bridge as well as through its arches.

A local correspondent for the Royal Cornwall Gazette (July 16th) stated, *'the inhabitants of Wadebridge were greatly surprised by a most extraordinary rush of waters in the river Camel, bearing along trees, torn up by the roots, floating planks, and dead animals, all swept onwards with a force almost terrific, the river roaring like the sea. The bridge at Wadebridge, stood the pressure of the water better than either of these before mentioned, as a great part found its way by passing on both sides of the bridge'* - flooding the town. In the same entry it notes that, *'so deep was the stream at Wadebridge that the Inn, which stands 20 feet above its general level was flooded to the depth of a foot'*. According to the Wadebridge correspondent for the *West Briton and Cornwall Advertiser*, Wadebridge had never witnessed such a

---

[10] Henderson, C G, and Coates, H, 1972 ed. *Old Cornish Bridges and Streams*, 108-110.
[11] Henderson, C G, and Coates, H, 1972 ed. 109.

flood as this, sheep, pigs and even a horse and cart were carried through the arches of Wade-Bridge![12]

On the 29th July 1847, the County Sessions met at the Assize Hall in Bodmin to consider the state of the bridges on both the river Camel and the river Inny. Some temporary wooden foot-bridges had been constructed since the flood, but the meeting revealed that at least fourteen bridges on the two rivers had to be partially or completely re-built. Owing to this, the funding promised for the widening of Wade-Bridge was suspended, and a motion was carried to re-assess the possibility of funding the widening at the Cornwall Epiphany Sessions in 1849.

In his book *Cornish Bridges and Streams* the normally reliable Charles Henderson was in error when he stated that the bridge was widened in 1847.[13] Because of the circumstances, the widening was postponed and did not take place for another five years. It is unfortunate that since this publication, several local historians have quoted this statement in their work and it is not helped when this date is even repeated in the Listed Building documentation for the bridge. At the Michaelmas Sessions of 1851, a request was made to re-establish the Wade-Bridge Committee and widen the bridge, and in 1852, the project for widening Wade-Bridge was again debated by the County Sessions. [14]

Winding-up of the Wade-Bridge Trust.

By 1838, the tolls on the bridge had been abolished and it was therefore considered by the Wade-Bridge trustees that as any travellers could now pass over the bridge, without charge, the county should be responsible for widening and maintaining the structure. To help with organising the winding-up of the Wade-Bridge Trust, two new trustees were appointed: Sir Charles Lemon and Sir William Trelawny. Their main purpose, with the assistance of the remaining trustees, was to draw up an application to the Court of Chancery for permission to pull down the houses which were built against the bridge (Bridge House), sell off the trust's property and land, surrender all the proceeds to the county fund and dissolve the said Wade-Bridge Trust, sometimes known as the Lovibond Charity. The county would then fund the widening of the bridge and take over its future maintenance.

To assist with the application, several sworn affidavits were prepared by the trust's solicitor, Richard Symons. One of them, sworn on 30th July 1852 by Edmond Norway, a Wadebridge merchant, stated:

> *'that the said bridge at Wadebridge is in length from end to end 680 feet and is only 10 feet wide within the parapet walls so that no two carriages, or vehicles can pass each other there on and that the approaches to the said bridge are very incommodious and difficult and that by*

---

[12] *West Briton & Cornwall Advertiser*, 16th July 1847.
[13] Henderson, C G, and Coates, H, 1972 ed. 119.
[14] *West Briton & Cornwall Advertiser*, July 1851.

reason of a line of houses on each side of the road at the east end of the said bridge cannot for some distance see the same until they are close upon the entrance thereof'.

When the Wade-Bridge committee of the County Sessions had previously met on the bridge on the 9th August 1845, the width of the bridge between parapets had been measured at 9ft 8ins; however the report went on to say that between the kerb-stones it was only 8ft 10ins. This suggests that there may have been kerb-stones placed at either end of the bridge to restrict the width of vehicles and it may have been these that impeded Wombwell's caravan when it had attempted to cross the bridge during July of that year.

Norway went on to say that since 1847, when the widening of the bridge was originally proposed, trade and business in Wadebridge and the neighbourhood had greatly increased. This had led to a considerable growth in traffic crossing the bridge, in particular carriages, carts and wagons.

Norway continued:

'in consequence of the narrowness of the said bridge collisions and stoppages are frequent occurrences and the risk, or probability of such collisions and stoppages occurring is greatly increased by the abruptness and narrowness of the approaches to the said bridge and also because of the reason of the great length of said bridge. It is difficult at night for persons going on the said bridge from one end thereof to ascertain whether any carriage, cart or wagon is upon or approaching the said bridge from the other end'.[15]

A plan of the bridge was drawn up in 1852 by Henry Coom, a surveyor at Wadebridge,[16] who signed an affidavit confirming that the plan was an accurate representation of Wade-Bridge and its approaches. On Friday 6th August 1852 the petition to wind up the Wade-Bridge Trust was unopposed at the Court of Chancery and procedures began.

New plans for the bridge

The 1847 proposal to widen the bridge using Mr Olver's third plan had been adopted and in July 1852 a new contract to widen the bridge at a cost of £548 was signed between the Wade-bridge committee and contractors Nicholls, Webster and Bate.[17] The widening of the bridge was achieved by extending segmental arches out over the existing cutwaters to a distance of three feet on either side, increasing the roadway width from just less than 10ft (3.05m) to 16ft (4.9m). Prior to 1845, two arches of the bridge had already been blocked up and used as cellars or store rooms. Arch 17 on the town side of the bridge is buried under the junction with harbour road, and arch 1 can still be seen against the Egloshayle bank as a locked cellar. Therefore only fifteen arches were widened, arches 2 to 16. The new segmental arches, built out over the cutwaters were supported on blocks of moorland granite approximately 3ft 10ins (1.17m) by 11ins (0.28m), depth unknown,

15 Cornwall Record Office, DDX 450/182.
16 Cornwall Record Office, DDX 450/183.
17 *Royal Cornwall Gazette*, 2nd July 1852 and *West Briton & Cornwall Advertiser*, 2nd July 1852.

which were built horizontally into the sides of the cutwater walls to give additional support. From these, the new arches sprung across from cutwater to cutwater, supporting new parapet walls above. This reduced the surface area of each cutwater by half, and significantly altered the visual appearance of the bridge, by concealing the view of the medieval arches, and reducing the depth of the cutwaters, however by 1852, this method of bridge widening was already well established in the West Country, with similar schemes being adopted when Bideford Bridge was widened in 1796 and Barnstaple in 1835.[18] Later the Bideford Bridge adopted a cantilever construction, to widen the bridge still further.

Work commences on the first widening

By October 1852, Mr Pease the County Surveyor was able to report to the Cornwall Michaelmas Sessions that work on the bridge was well under way and that to date five arches had been widened on one side, though there was no mention of whether the building work had started downstream or upstream, or from which end of the bridge.[19] At the Cornwall Epiphany Sessions in January of the following year, he reported that although work continued, incessant rain since the last sessions meant that only nine arches on one side had been completed. However, by the Cornwall Midsummer Sessions of 1853, work was proceeding satisfactorily and only two or three arches had still to be widened to complete the work. Finally, in October 1853 at the Cornwall Michaelmas Sessions Mr Pease reported that the work to widen Wade-Bridge was complete. Additional work to have the old piers newly cased had also been undertaken, at an extra cost of £150, and iron girders had been laid across the arches to tie them together and strengthen the overall structure.[20] A full statement of accounts of the first widening of Wade-Bridge is included in appendix v.

Fig 8.1 - The four-centred arches of the 1852-53 widening supported by granite blocks and sprung out over the piers reducing the size of the cutwaters. Courtesy the Garfield Irons Collection.

[18] Whiting, F, 1997. *The Long Bridge of Bideford through the Centuries*, 9 and Cruse, J B, 1982. *The Long Bridge of Barnstaple & The Bridge Trust*, 3.
[19] *Royal Cornwall Gazette*, 22nd October 1852.
[20] *Royal Cornwall Gazette*, 21st October 1853 and *West Briton & Cornwall Advertiser*, 21st October 1853.

In October 1854, at the Cornwall Epiphany Sessions, Mr Silvanus W Jenkin, Surveyor for the eastern part of the county reported that the bridge required a fresh coating of stone over its whole length (as there was no tarmac in those days) and that the present outlets for water (drains) should be lowered as they did not work properly. Mr Jenkin suggested this would cost about £22 and that part should be borne by the contractor.[21]

The granite blocks inserted into the cutwaters to support the new arches can still be clearly seen today on the downstream side of the structure. With this method of construction, all the parapet walls, on both sides of the bridge must have been completely rebuilt, even though they had only been replaced in 1818. The only fabric of the medieval bridge surviving is likely to be in the original arches and the lower core of the piers. The cutwaters and piers were 'newly cased' in 1853 but it is probable that they had already been refaced on several occasions due to the effects of scouring. Some may have been completely rebuilt. In 1928, Henderson criticized the method used to widen the bridge stating that: *the new arches diminish the depth of the cutwaters upon which the beauty of the old bridge largely depended.'* [22]

Gas lighting

On completion of the bridge widening in 1853, a small amount of money was left over once all the accounts were settled and this was passed back to the County funds. However the following year the inhabitants of Wadebridge requested whether these funds could be used for the installation of a gas lamp on the centre of the bridge. In 1792, William Murdoch had been the first man in the country to light a house at Redruth with coal gas, while the first commercial gas works was the London & Westminster Gas Light and Coke Company, who with wooden pipes lit Westminster Bridge for the first time on New Year's Eve 1813.[23] By the 1850s, William Oatey had set up a gas works on Polmorla Road (where the Telephone Exchange now stands in the original Dunveth Quarry) with responsibility for lighting the town and in 1854 the gas works were asked to provide lighting for the bridge. At the Cornwall Michaelmas Sessions in

Fig 8.2 - The gas lamp on the centre of the upstream parapet of the Wade-Bridge.

October 1854 a motion was put forward that the interest arising from the surplus funds left over from widening of the bridge would be granted to the Wadebridge Gas Works for seven years

---

[21] *West Briton & Cornwall Advertiser*, 17th October 1854.
[22] Henderson, C G, and Coates, H, 1972 ed. 119.
[23] Henley, J. 2009 'Life before artificial light' www.guardian.co.uk (31st October).

providing that the company cause gas lights to be erected on the bridge and kept burning for such time as is required for toll bars under the Turnpike Act.

Plaque or Tablet for the bridge

At the Cornwall Epiphany Sessions in January 1854, the chairman of the Wadebridge Committee stated that he had been in contact with Mr Symons, the Bridge Trust solicitor, regarding the history of the bridge so that a tablet or plaque could be set up now that the widening had been completed. The chairman stated that the length of the inscription would depend on whether it was fixed to a central pillar set up to hold the light, or whether a slab would be carved and fixed to the bridge. However, no records exist to indicate whether a plaque, slab or tablet was ever carved and fixed to the bridge and no such plaque survives.[24]

---

[24] *West Briton & Cornwall Advertiser*, 6th June 1854.

9 *'whether any plans which may be proposed, will be calculated to endanger the security of the said county bridge'*

The impact of nineteenth century development

Increasing traffic in the Camel estuary associated with nineteenth century commercial development resulted in reclamation of mud flats and building quays out into the river on both banks below the bridge. For the bridge this involved blocking arches and an effective shortening of the structure. The river was manipulated to guide its channels towards the quays and provide a great depth of water for vessels.

First and last arches blocked

The diary of the Reverend Skinner, who visited the bridge on the 6th November 1797, recorded that Wade-Bridge consisted of sixteen arches,[1] and in 1813 Lysons when writing about the parish of St Breock, recorded the bridge with sixteen arches, but under his entry for Egloshayle quoted seventeen. The 1818 watercolour (fig 7.3) which proposes the widening of the central arches of the bridge shows that by this time only fifteen existed. Once the quays were extended out into the river beyond arch no 17 on the town side of the bridge, a track or road needed to be built so that traffic crossing over the bridge could turn down onto the quay side. Therefore all visible signs of the last arch were lost as soon as Harbour Road was constructed. Despite this, there continued to be confusion amongst historians about how many arches the bridge had.

At the time the bridge was first widened during 1852-53, two of the arches had definitely already been blocked up and had been used as cellars or store rooms, one at each end of the bridge (arches 1 and 17). By this time neither of these arches took any water, except at spring tides, and the quay side on the western side of the bridge (known as Town Quay today) had already been extended out into the river, beyond the line of arches 16 and 17.

By the 1840s, the quay sides at Wadebridge were thriving. Thomas Martyn had started a timber business on Bradfords Quay, importing baulks from as far away as Norway. Iron ore was also landed at the quay for Mr Martyn's iron foundry, while limestone and sand were brought up the river to lime kilns at both Bradfords Quay and the former Cinema site on the Polmorla River. On the west bank, between Commissioner's Quay and Town Quay, was the Copper Ore Quay, while

---

[1] Jones, R, Ed, 1985. *A West Country Tour – Diary of an Excursion through Somerset, Devon and Cornwall in 1797 by Revd. John Skinner.*

a host of different cargoes including coal and grain were landed on both sides of the river. A trade directory for 1830, records Jasper Oliver as a timber merchant and other merchants at Wadebridge included William Hawken and Neville Norway. By 1844, Thomas Martyn, Morrish Wilton and Wills & Co are all registered as merchants with Hawken & Norway in partnership. A trade directory for 1847 records that Richard Hawken was trading timber, iron, coal and guano (fertilizer), Thomas Martyn trading in timber and iron and Mrs Norway in coal, iron and general supplies.[2]

The River, Wadebridge.

Fig 9.1 – In the foreground, the quayside has been extended further out into the river, narrowing the channel to gain a greater depth of water for vessels.

---

[2] Trade Directories, *Pigots Directory of Devon and Cornwall* 1830, *Pigots and Co., National and Commercial Directory and Topography* 1844, *William's Commercial Directory on the Principal Market Towns in Cornwall* 1847, and *Slater's Directory of Cornwall* 1852-53.

Martyn's Warehouse

In January 1868, John Martyn entered into a twenty year agreement with Messrs Little, Woollcombe and Venning of Devonport, agents for the Molesworth Estate, to take a lease of a quay for building a substantial new warehouse alongside the downstream, west end side of the bridge. This required the stopping up of two arches, 15 and 16. As the bridge had been adopted by the county at the time of its first widening in 1852-53 the County Bridge Surveyor, Mr Silvanus William Jenkin, was consulted about the advisability of blocking up further arches of the structure. Mr Jenkins gave permission for Mr Martyn to go ahead and build his warehouse and according to the *West Briton* newspaper the building was in the name of Oatey & Co. or Oatey & Martyn.[3] Although permission had been granted by Mr Jenkin, complaints about the blocking up of the arches and the further encroachment on the river banks was brought to the attention of the County Sessions in 1869, leading them to request Oatey & Martyn to suspend their building pending a hearing by the Board of Trade. As it appeared that Mr Jenkin had sanctioned the new building without bringing the matter to the magistrates at the County Sessions, the Clerk of the Peace called for an independent surveyor to assess whether blocking up arches 15 and 16 would be detrimental to the ancient bridge. On 26th October 1868, the Clerk of the Peace together with the County Bridge Surveyor and several magistrates visited the bridge and found that two of the arches at the western end of the bridge had already been entirely blocked by the building of the warehouse.[4]

Stopping up arches to build

In a letter dated 2nd January 1869 to Mr H S Stokes, the Clerk of the Peace to the Epiphany County Sessions, Mr Jenkin stated that in his opinion no injury whatever would be caused to the bridge by stopping up the arches. He went on to say that no water flowed through these arches except during spring tides and that they were now behind the present line of the quay frontage. The Town Quay, Copper Ore Quay and the Commissioners' Quay had already been extended out into the river, leaving the two arches silted up. The County Justices also decided to consult Mr James Henderson, a civil engineer from Truro, about the blocking of these arches, to ascertain whether they could affect the flow of the river and create additional scouring to the remaining piers of the bridge.[5] Mr Henderson reported that the blocking of these two arches had not prejudiced the

---

[3] *West Briton & County Advertiser*, 7th Jan 1869 – 'The Alleged encroachments at Wadebridge' records Oatey & Co, *West Briton & County Advertiser*, 1st July 1869 – 'The Ore Quay at Wadebridge' records Oatey & Martyn.

[4] *West Briton & County Advertiser*, 7th Jan 1869.

[5] According to Richard Truscott, James Henderson Civil Engineer was the grandfather of Cornish Historian Charles Henderson, this may be why Henderson took such an interest in Cornish bridges.

bridge in any way, however he stated that further encroachment of the waterway might be attended with damage as a still greater scouring effect would be produced.[6]

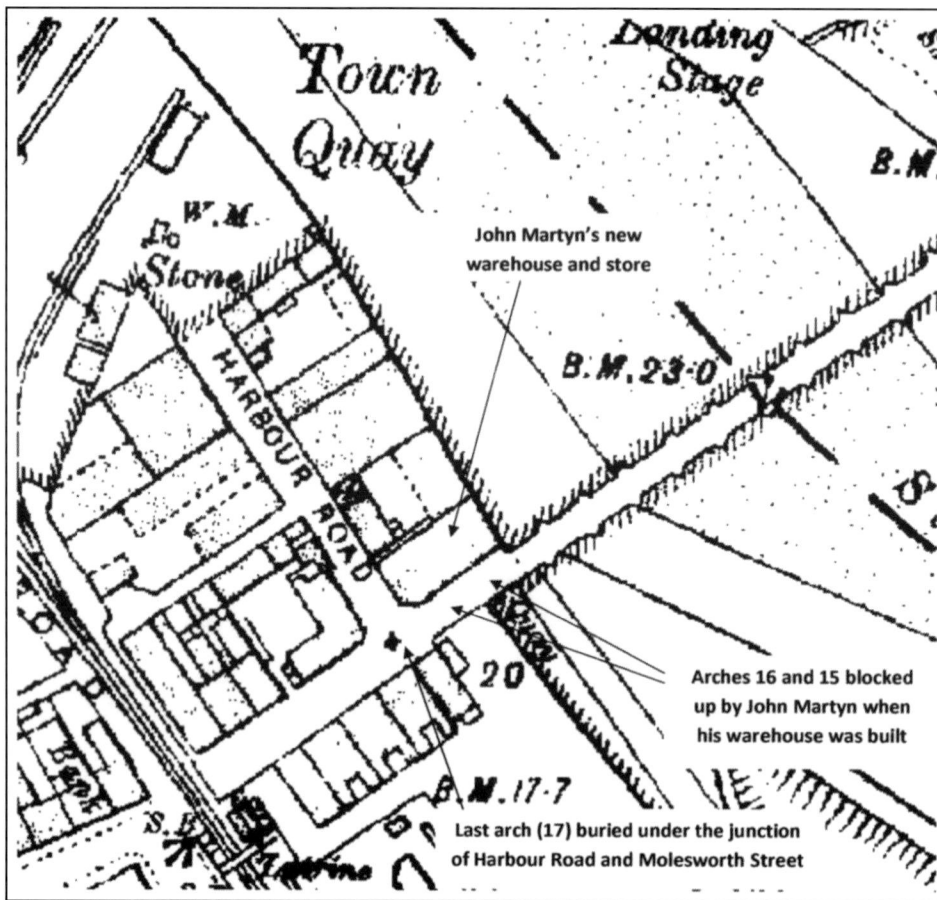

Fig 9.2 - 1907 OS map showing John Martyn's warehouse and the location of the three blocked arches, © Crown Copyright.

---

[6] Cornwall Record Office, CC3/8/5/54 - Various plans, letters and reports about the training walls in the river Camel and the proposal to enlarge the quays at Bradfords Quay and narrow the width of the river, including two copies of the Padstow Harbour Act of 1844.

It was agreed by the County Magistrates that Mr Martyn should be required to stop up the arches with solid masonry and remove the parapet at his own expense. The blocking up of the arches went ahead in 1869 and the building was continued. Mr Jenkin suggested that a certain area of land on either side of the bridge would be considered as belonging to the bridge and therefore the County and that as Mr Martyn's warehouse would be erected on their land he should pay a rent to the County.[7] This concerned the Molesworth Estate who owned the freehold, so they approached the County and were allowed to purchase the disputed strip of land against the bridge for sixty pounds. Another stipulation to the building was that no door should enter out onto the line of the bridge; the doorway was therefore set on the corner of Harbour Road, in a similar position to the Wadebridge Institute on the opposite side of the road. Plans of the warehouse in the Cornwall Record Office are dated 1871, suggesting that the building took several years to construct because of stoppages caused by the aforementioned infringements. Later, further warehouses were built along the quayside, attached to Oatey & Martyn's warehouse, including the Molesworth Stores with an impressive entrance off Harbour Road and a courtyard between them. The Oatey & Martyn warehouse later passed into the hands of George Martyn and a carved granite circular sign was placed above the entrance door that read: GEORGE MARTYN ESTAB. 1870

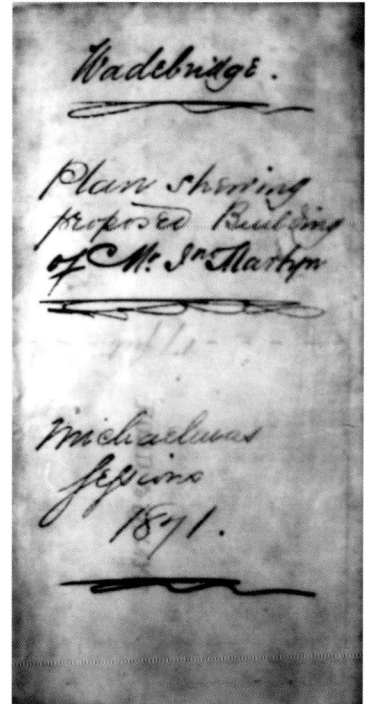

Fig 9.3 – The cover of the plan showing Mr J Martyn's proposed building.
© Cornwall Record Office.
CRO.QS/PDH/15/1

TREWEN CAMELFORD with a Cornish shield displaying the fifteen bezants. The buildings later became known as Richard Truscutt's Town Mill and eventually Cornwall Farmers Ltd, and finally finished up in the 1970s as the town's Pannier Market with a museum below before being demolished.[8]

---

[7] *West Briton & Cornish Advertiser*, 1st July 1869, 3.

[8] In the Cornish Guardian 25th January 1901, there is a reference to George Martyn & Co building new stores and seed warehouses on the town side of the river,

Fig 9.4 - An early photograph of Wade-Bridge showing arches 16 and 15 blocked on the left of the picture. Courtesy Collin Brewer.

Fig 9.5 - John Martyn's warehouse and the Molesworth Stores.

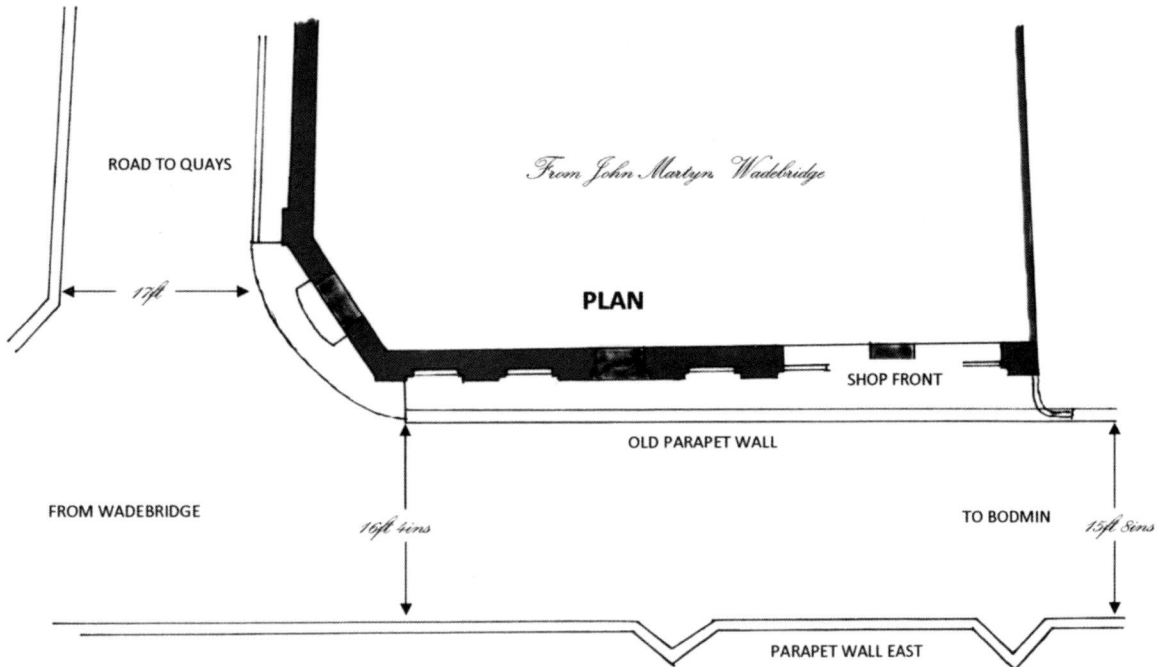

ROAD TO QUAYS

From John Martyn Wadebridge

PLAN

17ft

SHOP FRONT

OLD PARAPET WALL

FROM WADEBRIDGE

16ft 4ins

TO BODMIN

15ft 8ins

PARAPET WALL EAST

Fig 9.6 - A copy of the plan of John Martyn's warehouse dated 1871, CRO.QS/PDH/15/1

Proposed damming of the river

The town of Wadebridge has always been prone to flooding and in 1844 another proposed project to control the tidal flow of the river Camel was suggested. This involved a proposal to dam the river by installing flood or sluice gates across the river below the bridge. The effect of this would have been to regulate the height of the water upstream and prevent the incoming tide from flooding the town. Although no plans recording this proposal appear to survive, a letter from a Mr Thomas, found in the Prideaux Brune estate papers, provides some insight into the scheme.[9] Mr Thomas had been asked to give his opinion on the matter since a group from the proposed 'Rock Railway'were complaining that damming the river would affect the water level at Rock. However Mr Thomas confirmed that the scheme at Wadebridge would have no effect on Rock and that it was Wadebridge which would be disadvantaged. The letter mentions the provision of a floating harbour in the area between the sluice gates and the bridge. Neither the scheme to dam

---

[9] Cornwall Record Office, PB 6/432 - 'A letter dated 2nd March 1844, Mr Thomas' opinion as to the intended flood gates at Wadebridge'.

the river Camel at Wadebridge, nor the building of a railway to Rock ever went further than the drawing board.

Training or Guide walls

During the middle of the nineteenth century, there was no central island in the river as there is today and there were many attempts to divert the flow of water on the river Camel to ensure that the quays had a good depth of water for vessels to berth. Not only was the river silting up, but vessels were becoming larger, and there was a pressing need for an increased depth of water for longer periods, particularly as the river was tidal, thus limiting the times that vessels could access the quayside to load and unload. Because of this, the enterprising Mr Martyn built training walls in the river to divert the maximum flow of water towards his quays on the ebb tide. He placed large baulks of timber in the river to divert the flow, while the training walls were constructed from faggots of furze that were infilled with stone. His action concerned other business users of the river, particularly the agents for the Molesworth Estate who had the freehold of quays and property on the west side of the river. In a letter to the County Sessions in September 1879, the agents for the Molesworth Estate wrote:

> *'Mr J. Martyn the person referred to as the owner and occupier of a very extensive waterside premises on the north or Egloshayle side of the river, has made repeated attempts to regulate the stream on that side by means of low guide walls or baulks composed of rubble stones and faggots but his proceedings have been regarded with great jealousy by a large section of the Commissioners and not long since as will be observed from the reports of Mr W. Whitley, he was called to remove a low guide wall above the bridge on the north side, a similar wall below the bridge however still remains.'*

A plan of the river Camel dated 1843, of all the sand banks along the main navigable channel from Padstow to Wadebridge, shows that at low tide, arches 16 and 15 were already dry, that there was only a narrow channel of water flowing under arch 14, and that a sand bank blocked arches 12 and 13. The main channel of the river flowed through arches 9, 10 and 11, while arches 5, 6, 7 and 8 were blocked by silting on the upstream side of the bridge. Therefore as the ebb tide went out and at low tide, much of the water passed through the central arches, which according to the plan, led to a better depth of water on the west or town quays with less water at Bradfords Quay.[10] This may explain why Mr Martyn started to build training or guide walls in the river to

---

[10] Cornwall Record Office, OS/PDH/15/1 – 'A plan of Padstow Harbour, River and Creeks, surveyed by Henry Coom, Surveyor, Bodmin in 1843'.

rectify the problem. No doubt there were disagreements about this all the time, and by the late 1870s official complaints reached the Board of Trade.

Fig 9.7 - The remains of wooden poles set into the river bank on the north side of the upstream island that may have once supported faggots of furze for training walls prior the island walls being built in 1963.

In January 1878, it was reported at the County Sessions that training walls had been placed in the river to force the flow of water to the side arches and to provide a better depth of water on the northern quayside, while a project was under way to clear sandbanks on the south side of the bridge. This was seen as a matter of concern to Mr Jenkin the County Surveyor who considered that altering the course of the water flow could cause a greater scouring effect on the piers of the medieval bridge. It was reported that the Padstow Harbour Commissioners had spent fifteen pounds in removing the sandbanks and replacing some of the faggots of furze to prevent gravel from washing away. Two training walls had been built upstream of the bridge, one starting at the cutwater between arches 12 and 11, and another between arches 6 and 5; both walls ran diagonally to meet in a point further upstream in a similar way to the existing island. Even today

117

the stumps of faggots which may be remains of these training walls can be seen at low tide at the upstream end of the island. The Commissioners stated that there would be no danger to the bridge and that the summer flow of water may be diverted and made available for navigable purposes without causing any injury to the county bridge.

Fig 9.8 – Faggots of furze (gorse) and flat stones piled up to build guide walls at the entrance to the Polmorla River, Courtesy Joe Skinner.

Proposal to block up further arches

As well as the continuing disagreements over the diversion of water flow to the quaysides and the position and use of training walls a further and more drastic proposal was raised during 1877-78. This was to extend the northern quays out into the river which would entail blocking up another three arches on Egloshayle side of the river, arches, 2, 3 and 4. The Padstow Harbour Commissioners stated that an essential feature of their plans was to increase the quay accommodation on the northern or Egloshayle side of the bridge and that this would narrow the river bed. Furthermore their intention was to extend the line of the quay frontage all the way to the bridge (see fig 9.9). In a plan and report submitted by Mr Samuel Pollard on behalf of the Padstow Harbour Commissioners to Mr H S Stokes, Esq., Clerk of the Justices dated 23rd March

1878, it suggested that the owners of the quays at Bradfords Quay, Mr Potter of Gonvena, Mr Martyn, the Manor of Burniere, Mr Symons and the Harbour Commissioners, had already purchased parts of the river bed from the Duchy of Cornwall to allow the quays to be extended southwards into the river.

Mr Jenkin the County Surveyor referred the Harbour Commissioners to section 98 of the Padstow Harbour Act that stated that any plans to the harbour at Wadebridge that could affect the security of the bridge should be agreed by the Lord Commissioners of the Admiralty. Section 98 reads:

> *'Provided also, and be it enacted, that the Commissioners shall, on being required so to do by the Trustees of the County Bridge over the River Camel at Wadebridge, especially submit for the consideration of the Lord Commissioners of the Admiralty, or any competent person to be nominated by them for the purpose, whether any plans which may be proposed for Improvement of the said Harbour will be calculated to endanger the Security of the said County Bridge: and it shall not be lawful for the said Commissioners to carry into effect any such plans, except subject to such Directions as may be given by the Lord Commissioners of the Admiralty, or the person appointed by them in that behalf, for the Security of the said Bridge.'*

The County Surveyor stated that a great outlay in widening the bridge during 1852-53 had taken place and that the material importance of the structure should be protected. Any further encroachment of the waterway might be attended with damage as a still greater scouring effect would be produced, to the probable detriment of the whole structure and in particular to the foundations of the piers. The County Bridge Surveyor referred back to the report made by Mr James Henderson of Truro in 1869 which had stated that blocking up any further arches of the bridge would be prejudicial to the structure. The pressure on the remaining piers would be far greater due to the increased scouring effect.

In a report by Mr Nicholas Whitley for the Commissioners, he contradicted the claims by Mr Henderson quoting the volume of water flowing down the river, its velocity, and calculating the amount of water that could safely flow through each arch; taking into account the number and width of the arches he finally suggested that if the scheme went ahead the ten remaining arches could cope with the volume of water. An extract from this report gives his reasoning:

> *The basin of all the streams above Wadebridge has an area of 126 square miles, and an average annual rainfall of about 50 inches, taking 35 inches as the quantity of water carried*

off by the River, the average for the year in round numbers would be 20,000 cubic feet of water per minute passing under the bridge.

By an actual measurement of the water on the 29th March 1877, when the river was not in flood the quantity passing was 26,000 cubic feet per minute, which in the height of the summer is reduced to 12,000 cubic feet per minute.

On the 4th December 1876 after two days of the heaviest rain for the past 10 years when the river was in high flood, the quantity was 135,000 cubic feet per minute with a velocity of about 2 miles an hour only.

There are at present 13 open arches in the bridge each 18ft 9ins in width giving a total clear waterway of 243 feet. It will be seen by the map that the River above the bridge forms the actual width required for its own waterway, which in a dry time is only 100 feet, and that even after the most excessive rain and when in high flood it was only 190 feet, being still much less than the open waterway of the bridge, and that during this extraordinary flood the mean depth of the water through the arches of the bridge was only 2½ feet, while at every spring tide since the construction of the bridge the depth of water there is twice or thrice as much without doing injury to the structure.

Further, to take a practical illustration, the great mass of the water of the river coming from the granite highlands passes under a single arch at Dunmeer Bridge with a probable waterway of not more than 30 or 40 feet without damage to the bridge, it becomes an assurance that the present 243 feet of waterway at Wadebridge is greatly in excess of that required for the passing of the stream, and this moreover is confirmed by the north end of the bridge being much choked up by deposits from the river and where a very small quantity of water usually flows.

However the main issue was not about blocking up further arches but about the increased scouring effect on the bridge piers that would be caused by reducing the number of arches. Concern about this scheme increased and eventually the effect of both the training walls and the proposed extension of the quaysides were decided upon by the Board of Trade. The Board acting for the Admiralty insisted that the training walls should be adjusted to provide an equal flow of water to three arches on either side of the river. The upshot of this was that the scheme to extent the quays was rejected and the blocking of the three additional arches on the Egloshayle side of the bridge was thankfully not allowed to take place. Had this scheme been allowed to go ahead, the bridge today would have consisted of only ten open arches, 5 to 14, with three blocked on the town side and four on Egloshayle side.

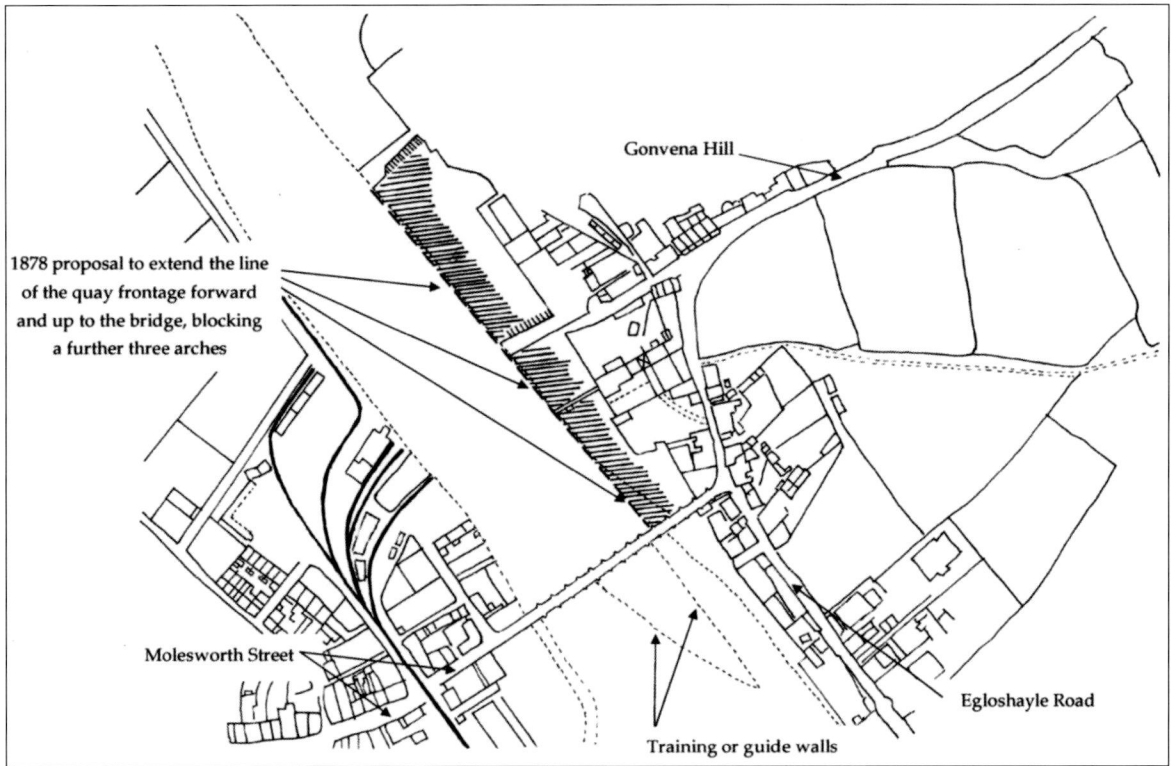

1878 proposal to extend the line of the quay frontage forward and up to the bridge, blocking a further three arches

Gonvena Hill

Molesworth Street

Egloshayle Road

Training or guide walls

Fig 9.9 - Proposal to extend quaysides further into the river with the blocking of further arches of Wade-Bridge, also showing the upstream training or guide walls.

The training walls were adjusted, as recommended by the Admiralty and later in 1881, consultants Messrs Law and Chatterton were called to report on the condition of the river bed below the bridge. The cross-section of the river bed surveyed in November 1880, compared with an earlier survey taken in May 1841, showed that by 1880, the water was equally distributed between the quays on both sides of the river whereas in 1841, most of the water was flowing on the St Breock or west bank.

The late Mr Fred Luke of Wadebridge recalled that during the early twentieth century a projection, known as the broad arrow, was built out into the river at Cliffs End.[11] Like other structures in the river this projection was built from faggots of furze (bundles of gorse) held down with large flat stones. The aim was to deflect the ebb water across to the west side of the island to deepen the channel along the town quay.   This structure was removed in about 1925.

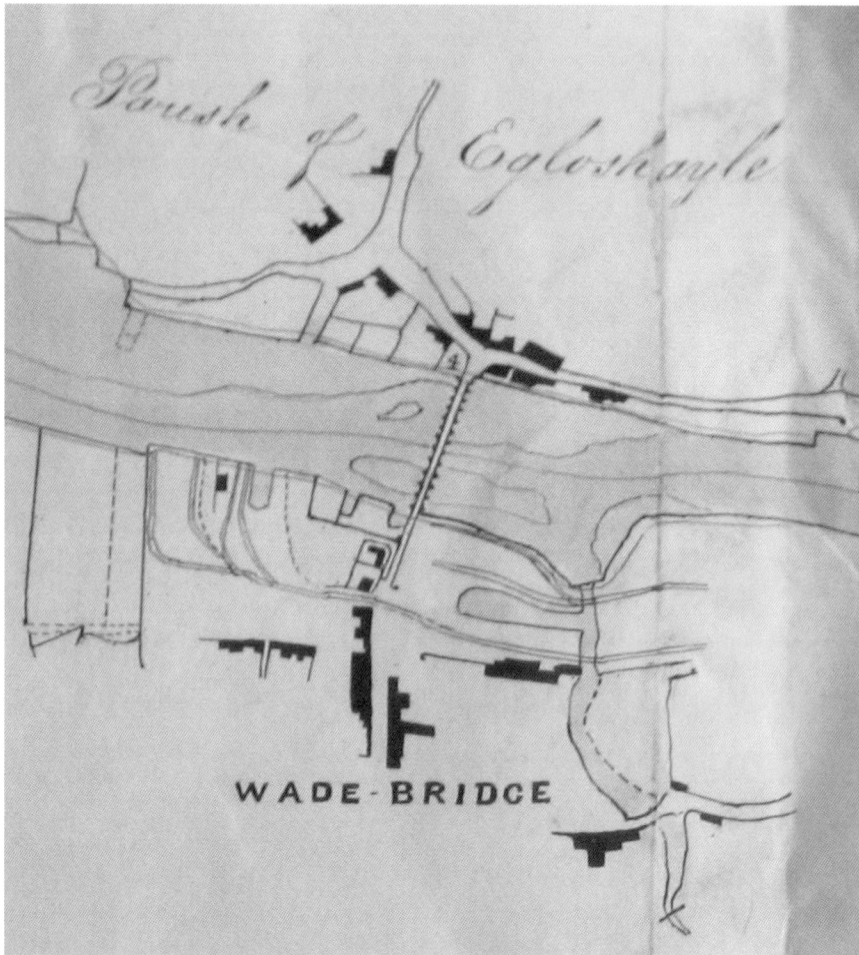

Fig 9.10 – An extract from a plan of the river Camel dated 1843, showing the position of sand banks and the river channels. © Cornwall Record Office, QS/PDH/15/1.

---

[11] Luke, F, 2006. *Reminiscences of Wadebridge and the river Camel* (compiled, edited and published by Eric Tatlow).

With its many sand banks, the river Camel has always been a difficult river to navigate, and the loss of arches has been mainly due to the silting up and subsequent narrowing of the river to maximise and maintain a high level of water at the quaysides on ebb tides. The island in the centre of the river, that started life as a sand bank, also helped to maintain and control higher water at the quays. Compared to the Camel, the two major estuary rivers in north Devon do not have such problems. At Barnstaple, the river Taw has several large sand banks between the estuary and the bridge, but the river is bigger than the Camel and does not suffer from sand banks at the bridge crossing. Bideford Bridge has retained all of its 24 arches with water still flowing through all of them, while at Barnstaple only one arch is dry out of sixteen and now used as a pedestrian subway on the eastern side of the river.

County Bridge Stones

Formerly, all county bridges in Cornwall, those that carried the main and popular routes through the county had bridge boundary stones marking the extent of the bridge and its approaches that were maintained by the county through the Justices of the Peace. These granite stones were approximately a foot square with a rounded top and each engraved with a letter 'C'. Formerly there would have been a boundary stone at each end of Wade-Bridge although neither survives today. Photographs taken during the 1950s, show that one stone was positioned near the junction of Eddystone Road and Molesworth Street close to the former railway level crossing gates. The second stone is marked on the Ordnance Survey map at Bridge End. Two bridge boundary stones also once marked Treguddick Bridge near the Cinema, one was positioned on Trevanion Road close to the Masonic Hall while the second still survives beside the Bridge on Wool public house. According to Truscott, these stones were usually placed up to three hundred feet from the abutments of the bridge.[12]

---

[12] Talk on Cornish Bridges by Richard Truscott at Camelford on 26th March 1999.

10 *'the glory of this little market town and its raison d'etre is the splendid bridge across the river Camel'*

Travellers' accounts, folklore and maps

The reports of some of the earliest visitors to Wade-Bridge were recorded in chapter 2, however the bridge was mentioned by many more travellers, travel writers and visitors. It also featured in some novels and short stories and is noted on many maps from the sixteenth century onwards. These later accounts and references are discussed here.

Up until the second widening, the bridge was still considered an important medieval structure, very long compared to its width and although widened in 1852-53, the medieval arches were still visible. Terms used to describe the bridge reflect its impact, with it being seen as handsome, fine, magnificent, splendid, noble, with arches of exquisite beauty, the most celebrated in the county, and one of the best medieval bridges in England.

Eighteenth century accounts

During 1724 Henric Kalmeter, a Swedish industrial spy who travelled to Devon and Cornwall to make a report on the state of the mining industries, recorded that 'Wadebridge was remarkable for nothing but its great stone bridge'.[1] An unknown traveller to Cornwall in 1741 stopped at *Warbrige;* but his diary fails to mention the bridge.[2] One famous visitor who travelled through Cornwall on horseback many times during the eighteenth century was the Reverend John Wesley; he would sometimes preach to open air crowds four or five times in one day. Wesley first came to Cornwall in 1743 and first preached in Wadebridge in 1748, five years later. His diaries do not mention Wadebridge by name again until he preached in the town in 1780, but on a number of his visits to the county he preached at Port Isaac and then travelled on to St Agnes, suggesting that he may have ridden his horse across the bridge several times.[3] Wesley was on a mission, preaching to the working classes, and as a result did not often record the buildings or the landscape he saw. Similarly, the famous prelate and anthropogist, Dr Richard Pococke, Bishop of Ossory and Meath in Ireland, who journeyed between Padstow and Pencarrow in 1750, only notes *'Wadbridge, which*

---

[1] Henric Kalmeter's journal which reported on the state of the mining industry was translated and published by Justin Brooke, *Journal of a visit to Cornwall, Devon and Somerset in 1724-25.*

[2] The diary of the unknown traveler was published by Todd Gray in *The Traveller's Tales* in 2000.

[3] Wesley, Reverend J, 1938. *The Journal of the Rev John Wesley,* Ed. Nehemiah Curnock, The Epworth Press, also Pearce, J, 1964. *The Wesleys in Cornwall,* D Bradford Barton, Truro.

is on the Camel'.[4] In 1755, the Reverend William Wynne recorded that there was a pretty good inn on the side of the river at *'Wardbridge which consisted of seventeen arches of moor stone and the river runs to Padstow Haven and so to the North Sea'.*[5]

By the time W G Maton visited Cornwall in 1794, the roads were much improved, the turnpike road between Hallworthy and Mitchell having been created in 1760.[6] Maton observed that *'both Wadebridge and Camelford were inconsiderable places',* but stated that *'the river Camel makes a long circuit before arriving at Wadebridge, where it is crossed by a fine bridge of 17 arches, and empties itself into Padstow harbour'.*

Clearly, for most visitors to Wadebridge in the eighteenth century, the only building of significance in the town was the famous bridge.

Fig 10.1 - A view of Wade-Bridge during the early twentieth century from downstream.

Until the turnpike was created there were no signposts nor indeed were there any 'Welcome to Wadebridge' signs and visitors enquiring about the name of the town or the bridge that they were crossing may have received an answer in a broad accent which was difficult to understand. This may explain the variations in spellings of the names of both town and bridge. The many variations are listed in appendix vii.

---

[4] *Travels through England*, 200-201.
[5] Wynne, W, 1755. 'A Visit to Cornwall in 1755', *Journal of the Royal Institution of Cornwall*, 1981.
[6] Maton, W G, 1794. *Observations on the Western Counties of England*, 259.

Nineteenth century accounts

In 1801, Britton and Brayley also thought that Wadebridge was *'an inconsiderable village'* only noted for its bridge.[7] The English Romantic landscape artist J M W Turner visited Cornwall in 1811 and his itinerary suggests that he passed over Wade-Bridge on his way to Pencarrow. Sadly he did not stop and paint the bridge. Perhaps it was low tide, or raining, or more likely he had not been commissioned.[8] Cooke's *Topographical Library* or *British Travellers Pocket County Directory* of 1813 refers to *'a handsome stone bridge at Wadebridge entitled to the travellers notice'*. Daniel Defoe, writer and journalist, most famous for his book *Robinson Crusoe*, records *'Wodbridge'* or *'Wardbridge'* on his travels through Cornwall in the 1820s, but clearly did not visit as he notes, *'a large stone bridge of 8 or thereabouts arches'*.[9] Defoe entered Cornwall on the south coast, travelled down to Mount's Bay, Penzance and St Ives and travelled up the north coast through Launceston and into Devon, presumably travelling back from St Columb Major to Bodmin, and bypassing Wade-Bridge.

A few years later, the nature of accounts changes from terse diary entries to more lyrical prose. In 1824, Hitchins writes of a *'noble bridge'*; *'it is strong, the whole building represents a magnificent and interesting spectacle. The tide regularly flows through the arches and in conjunction with the river on the island side, it enables boats and barges to convey to various places on the flux and influx of very high tides, the rapid movement of the waters is very grand'*.[10] He also states that it was the *'most celebrated bridge in the county.'* Gilbert in 1838 describes the bridge as *'an artificial ligament that fasteneth the parishes of Egloshayle to St Breock'*.[11] In 1842, Redding found *'that descending a steep hill between high banks overhung with wood, upon which stand several commodious houses, appears Wade-Bridge'*. He was interested in the old fig tree that once grew out of the stonework on the downstream side of the bridge (see chapter 7). Henry Besley wrote in his *Route Book of Cornwall: A Guide for the Stranger and Tourist* in 1853, that the town was chiefly noticeable for its fine old bridge and continued:

> *'The bridge, as originally constructed, was very narrow, only wide enough for the principal carriers of that day, the pack-horses, to pass each other by the sidings built out at intervals for the purpose, but totally inadequate for the passing of two-wheeled carriages of the present*

---

[7] Britton, J and Brayley, E W, 1801. *The Beauties of England and Wales or Delineations, topographical, historical and descriptive of Each County.*

[8] Finberg, R A, and Finberg A J, 1961. *The Life of J M W Turner.*

[9] Defoe, D, *c*1720. *A Tour thro' the whole island of Great Britain, divided into circuits or journies,* Letters of Daniel Defoe's travels through Cornwall were published by J M Dent in 1927.

[10] Hitchins, F, 1824. *The History of Cornwall,* edited by Samuel Drew and published by William Penaluna, 525-7.

[11] Gilbert, D, 1838. *The Parochial History of Cornwall, founded on the manuscripts of Mr Hals and Mr Tonkin.*

day.   To obviate this inconvenience, after many years endurance, the bridge is now undergoing enlargement, by taking down the parapets and widening it on one side'.

Fig 10.2 - A view of Wade-Bridge during the early twentieth century from upstream.

Besley must have visited the bridge in 1852, before the second side was widened. The town of Wadebridge was often dismissed by visitors as being of no interest. However White in 1855 was engaged by the town's foreign flavour:

> *'to Wadebridge – a town which has still more of a foreign aspect, write French names over the doors, and you might fancy yourself stopping to change horse at some out-of-the-way place in France, so narrow and irregular are the streets, so unaccustomed the aspect of the houses and queer little shops, while there is the same air of being left to take care of itself. The old bridge of seventeen arches across the estuary, which once had a flourishing fig tree growing from one of its piers, has been replaced by a more commodious, though less picturesque structure.'* [12]

---

[12] White, W, 1855. *A Londoner's Walk to the Land's End and a Trip to the Scilly Isles.*

White's note about the bridge again refers to its recent widening, two years previous to his visit, which had evidently ruined its medieval character. Murray's *Handbook for Travellers in Cornwall* of 1882 states that Wadebridge is a town remarkable for its bridge, '*a picturesque structure of 17 arches*', while Black's *Guide to Cornwall* of 1895 states that '*Wadebridge has a right to be proud of its antique bridge*' and notes that, '*on the flux and reflux of high tides, or after heavy rains, the river swells to a considerable extent and takes on a certain air of grandeur*'.

It is the river on a high tide that displays the bridge at its best and another author, Arthur Norway in 1897, this time a local man, described in detail a romantic and passionate view of this scene.[13]

'*I know it is my duty in this work to refrain from obtruding my personal preferences on the reader; but this makes it very difficult for me to say anything about Wadebridge, which quiet little place I look upon with eyes reserved by every Cornishman for one place only in his native duchy. Mr Penell tells me it did not impress him; but he got there at low tide. It is as the tide is flowing that I like to think of the old town with its granite bridge of many arches. For, when the first signs of the coming flood sweep round the sandy bed from out the folding of the hills, a cool salt wind runs up in advance and almost before one has felt its freshness or tasted the briny odour on ones lips, the first wavelets are lapping already round the ancient buttresses, and great flocks of ducks and geese sail by with a portentous quacking, all noisily rejoicing in the flow of dark foamy water which rushes up more impetuously every moment, cutting off the corners of the large waste banks and drowning them deeper and deeper under the rippling waves. When the tide is out, it is as if the town had lost its soul; but life and energy come back with the flowing water. A string of barges rounds the point on its way up from Padstow, and a couple of small schooners forge slowly onward underneath those hills which the sunset is dyeing rose and purple.*'

Many more travel writers and diarists describe the bridge, but most simply repeat a few basic facts. Seeing Wade-Bridge with the tide high evidently made a great deal of difference to visitors' perception of the bridge and its landscape. For example, Harper wrote, '*here is a fine bridge of 17 arches which spans the river Camel or the sands and mud that most often display themselves and are not covered until high water is reached*'.[14] Salmon as late as 1950 still praises the bridge but also refers to low tide. '*Wadebridge can never lose the prestige or noble effect of its bridge. The bridge is reckoned among the special glories of Cornwall and gives impressiveness to a spot which at low tide would otherwise*

---

[13] Norway, A H, 1897. *Highways and Byways in Devon and Cornwall*, 335.
[14] Harper, C G, 1910. *The Cornish Coast: North*, 133.

be dull'.[15] Even today, most visitors will not take a second look at the bridge in poor weather or if the tide is out, but on a bright day with the tide roaring up the river, it still has the power to inspire.

In a publication by the Cornwall Branch of the Council for the Preservation of Rural England, it is stated that, *'the glory of this little market town, and its raison d'etre is the splendid bridge across the river Camel',*[16] while in 1951, Pevsner records, *'the only structure of importance is the magnificent bridge across the river Camel, one of the best medieval bridges in England'.*[17] An undated Cornish Guide records that, *'the bridge is one of the chief objects of interest in this ancient town, a very fine structure spanning the river with many arches of exquisite beauty'.*[18]

Short Stories

At least three short stories have been written which feature the old bridge. One, which has already been noted, is *The Riverside House – a tale of Wadebridge*, published in *c*1909 by Mrs Sedding. The other two, both written by Joseph Hocking, were *Roger Trewinion* published in 1905, and *Mistress Nancy Molesworth: A tale of Adventure*, published in 1898.

Folklore

In additional to the famous legend of the foundation of woolpacks, Mrs Sedding relates to two other pieces of folklore. The first was that the roots of the old fig tree that once covered a third of the downstream walls of the old bridge during the nineteenth century grew from blood spilt by Cuthbert Mayne's execution.[19] The second is that once a year at midnight Sir Francis Drake crosses the bridge in a carriage drawn by six headless horses. Mrs Sedding recalls a story that an old inhabitant was one night rudely disturbed from her peaceful slumbers by her mother calling her to get up and look out of her window to see the said Sir Francis' carriage. *'On looking forth she saw this to be the case, for sure enough there stood a carriage in the moonlight, but without horses of any kind. Fear seized her and she quickly retired to bed, but in the morning when she looked from the window, 'the carriage was still there' and on nearer inspection found to her disgust it was nothing more or less than the old village bus that plied between Wadebridge and Bodmin, which had been left in the field the night before'.* According to Robert Hunt,[20] Sir Francis can be seen at night in a black hearse drawn by

---

[15] Salmon, A L, 1950. Ed. *Cornwall* 1st ed. 1903. 258.

[16] Anon, 1930. *Cornwall: A survey of its Coast, Moors and Valleys with suggestions for the Preservation of Amenities*, Cornwall Branch of the Council for the Preservation of Rural England, 49.

[17] Pevsner, N, 1951. *The Buildings of England: Cornwall.*

[18] Cornwall Publicity Ltd., undated. *The Cornish Guide.*

[19] Sedding, Mrs E, undated. *The Riverside House: A Tale of Wadebridge*, 32.

[20] Hunt, R, 1881. *The Drolls, Traditions and Superstitions of Old Cornwall (Popular Romance of the West of England)*, no 103, 230.

headless horses and urged along by running devils and yelping headless dogs on the road from Tavistock to Plymouth but how this legend became connected with Wade-Bridge is not known.

Wade-Bridge on old maps

Not only did early travellers to Cornwall have to deal with the terrible state of the roads and tracks, they also had to navigate their way without the maps that we take for granted. One of the earliest maps of Cornwall to show the bridge or at least the crossing over the river is Christopher Saxton's map of 1576, where he records the pass as *Wardbridge*. Saxton's map, showed no roads or tracks and only natural landmarks such as hills, rivers and streams. It was therefore of limited use to the traveller. Nevertheless, Saxton's map formed the basis for almost all the small scale maps of Cornwall produced during the following two hundred years.[21] This may be why so many maps of Cornwall including those by Web (1645), Blaeu (1648), Sanson (1654), Lea (1689), Morden (1695), Molls (1724), Kitchins (1755) and Walpoole (1784), record the bridge and town as *Wardbridge*. However, John Norden's maps drawn for his *Description of Cornwall* (completed 1610, but not published until 1728), record it as *Waad br.* and *Wade bridg,* and he depicts it as a small bridge of three arches – presumably all he could squeeze onto the space available.

It was not until cartographers started to publish larger scale maps that the bridge is clearly identified. Even then they did not always draw a representation of the actual bridge. Joel Gasgoyne's map of Cornwall published in 1699 shows the road crossing over the river, but does not depict the bridge itself; he named it *Ware bridg* alias *Wade bridg*. However, the representation of the bridge in the *Lanhydrock Atlas* is much more detailed. The three volumes of the *Lanhydrock Atlas* contain maps showing the vast estates amassed throughout Cornwall by the Robartes family of Lanhydrock during the late seventeenth century. The maps are attributed to cartographer Joel Gasgoyne and according to Holden were drawn and watercoloured on vellum between the years 1694 and 1699. They have recently been published in one volume by the National Trust and Cornwall Editions.[22] On a map titled '*A Scheme of Severall Tenements nere Ware bridg in St Breock parish*' can be seen a good representation of the arched bridge across the river. Although it is not completely accurate, having only thirteen arches shown rather than the seventeen that existed at that time, the drawing nonetheless emphasizes the length of the bridge, something that maps of a smaller scale were unable to present (see plate 16b). The map names the bridge as *Ware* or *Wade*

---

[21] Quixley, R C E, 1966. *Antique Maps of Cornwall and the Isles of Scilly.*

[22] Holden, P, Herring P, and Padel, O J, 2010. *The Lanhydrock Atlas: A complete reproduction of the 17th century Cornish Estate Maps,* 274.

bridg, and the river as the Padstow River. On the north side of the bridge a row of houses is illustrated, representing Bridgend in Egloshayle.

In 1748, the first one inch to one mile map of the whole county was surveyed and published by Cornishman Thomas Martyn. He depicted Wade-Bridge as a six arched bridge and the fact that the bridge was presented pictorially suggests that it was an important and well known structure. The first one inch scale map published by Ordnance Survey in 1813 shows the road passing over the river at 'Wade Bridge'.

Fig 10.3 – Egloshayle parish tithe map showing a plan view of Wade-Bridge,
© Cornwall Record Office.

Both the St Breock tithe map of 1841 and the Egloshayle tithe map of 1840 depict plan views of Wade-Bridge which emphasise the length and narrowness of the bridge before it was first widened. The St Breock map (plate 15) does not show the complete length of the structure as the boundary between the two parishes was the centre of the river Camel. However the Egloshayle

131

map (fig 10.3) shows the complete bridge with the outline of the cutwaters indicating the positions of the fifteen surviving arches at that time. The medieval bridge is also shown on the first large scale Ordnance Survey map of Wadebridge in 1880 (scale 1 mile : 25 inches) (chapter 4, fig 4.4), where again, the length and narrowness of the bridge is outlined, although the pointed ends of the piers (cutwaters) are not so clear. The later edition in 1907 (chapter 9, fig 9.2) rectifies this, but only shows the present thirteen arches due to the building of John Martyn's warehouse.

11 'veritable death trap'
Increased traffic and the second widening

Although the bridge was widened in 1852-53 by three feet on either side, this was only sufficient for the horse-drawn vehicles, carriages and coaches which constituted the road traffic of the time. However the introduction of steam-driven traction engines and much larger wagons at the end of the nineteenth century again put the bridge under strain.

Motor vehicles

By the turn of the century, the first motor vehicles arrived in Cornwall,[1] and their rapid growth in numbers increased the congestion on the bridge which was still only wide enough to allow two horse drawn coaches to pass. The first motor car to be registered in Cornwall was AF1, to an owner at Newlyn East, yet within a year we have a reference to a motor car in Wadebridge. In the *Cornish Guardian* in August 1901, an accident at Wadebridge was reported, between a horse-drawn trap and a motor car. Was this the first car to be seen in the town?[2] By December 1924, there were over 10,000 motor vehicles registered in the county. This must have posed an increasing strain on many of the medieval bridges in Cornwall, not just Wade-Bridge.

Dangers for children crossing the bridge

By the 1920s concerns were being voiced in the press for the safety of pedestrians walking over the bridge, and in particular of children going to school. There was a call for immediate action to provide a footpath or separate footbridge alongside the bridge. Historically, the boys' and girls' schools were separate, with the boys' school on West Hill on the western side of the bridge and the girls' school on Egloshayle Road, so many children had to cross the bridge at least twice a day. At a Wadebridge Ratepayers' meeting in March 1924, Mr E G Martyn called attention to the dangers to children crossing the bridge from the numbers of motor vehicles and he proposed that the council should take up the matter immediately.

Proposal for a footbridge

A proposal was made that the Wadebridge Council approach the county authorities to have a footbridge built outside the main bridge for pedestrians; this was seconded by Mr Ignatius Lobb and also supported by the chairman, Mr W Phillips, Mr Robert Lean and others.[3] In December

---

[1] Barham, F, 1978. *Old Cornwall in Camera: Road Vehicles*, Glasney Press, Falmouth.
[2] *Cornish Guardian*, 2nd August 1901.
[3] *Cornish Guardian*, 11th January 1924.

1924, Wadebridge Urban District Council wrote a letter to the County Surveyor, E H Colcutt, pressing for a footbridge to be erected outside the main bridge due to the increasing road traffic. When the County Council met in January 1925 and this matter was discussed, Mr Colcutt expressed concern about the *'obvious weakness of the spandrel walls, he did not consider it feasible to throw out footpaths without extending the arches, nor did he think this could be done without detracting from the fine appearance of this ancient structure'*. He also suggested that as the bridge at present was too narrow to allow two lines of traffic to pass, consideration should be given to both widening the bridge and providing footpaths.[4]

In May 1925, the County Surveyor requested a quote from Messrs David Rowell & Co. Ltd., Constructional Engineers in London for an iron footbridge. A discussion then followed about which side of the bridge would be aesthetically best for this footbridge; the County Surveyor favoured the downstream side of the bridge while Wadebridge Rural District Council preferred upstream. Agreement was finally reached to erect an iron footpath on the outside of the upstream side of the old bridge, and another request was sent to Rowell & Co. Ltd. to provide a scheme for either an iron cantilever footway or alternatively a separate footbridge outside the old bridge. Rowell & Co. Ltd. estimated that the steel and ironwork dispatched to the railway goods station would cost £439, plus another £114 to erect the steelwork and this was to be exclusive of any concrete work and repairs to masonry etc.[5] As this quote did not allow for handrails and enough protection for school children a second quote was obtained from Rowell which in total was £780 to transport and fix the footbridge.[6] By February 1926, the footbridge scheme had been shelved due to financial constraints and it was never built.[7]

Inadequate Lighting

As well as the concerns about the narrowness of the bridge, the need to widen it and provide a footpath, there were several letters to the County Surveyor requesting better lighting. On completion of the first widening in 1852-3, some surplus funds had been used to supply a gas lamp on the parapet of one of the central arches on the upstream side of the bridge. Photographs of the bridge in the 1920s suggest that at this date there was still only one lamp on the bridge, on a tall post. [8]

---

[4] County Council Minutes 16th January 1925.
[5] Letter dated 6th October 1925.
[6] Letter dated 9th November 1925.
[7] Letter dated 12th February 1926, County Surveyor to the Clerk of Wadebridge RDC.
[8] According to Kelly's directory 1926, as well as the Wadebridge Gas Works owned by Oatey & Martyn, there was also Wadebridge & District Electric Supply Co. Ltd. managed by Mr L. S. Ennor.

The Wadebridge Rural District Council requested that the County Council transfer the old Trust or Charity Funds, which had been set aside to light the bridge, to Wadebridge Rural District Council as they were now the Public Lighting Authority for the area. However the County Council resolved that this application should not be granted, that from 31st March 1927 the lighting of Wade-Bridge by the County Council be discontinued 'and that from this day also the income from the Trust funds be used for the repair and maintenance of the bridge'.[9]

Concerns about the widening and lighting of the bridge dragged on for many years with numerous letters to the press from concerned residents. Headlines such as, *'Dangers to Pedestrians'* or *'Veritable death trap'* suggested that the County Council was waiting for a fatality on the bridge in order to justify expenditure. Throughout the 1930s, many letters about the bridge were written by W E Blackwell the clerk to Wadebridge Rural District Council voicing the Council's concern.

Scheduled Ancient Monument

On the 26th November 1928, the bridge was made a Scheduled Ancient Monument by the Ministry of Works. It was the 62nd monument in the county to be given this protection. This gave the bridge a level of legal protection, which prior to this date it did not have. It required the Cornwall County Council or any other bodies working on the bridge to apply for consent before any work could be started. Charles Henderson who provided the information about the bridge to the Ministry was again critical of the way the first widening of the bridge in 1852-53 had ruined the medieval bridge by reducing the depth of the cutwaters. Henderson writes in the original scheduling information: *'In spite of the widening, the great length and comparative narrowness of the bridge have long given rise to complaints and there is talk of even more drastic widening. This could only be done by some radical alteration to the medieval structure and this should be prevented at all costs!'*[10]

Proposal to widen the bridge and create a weir

At the beginning of 1935 a local resident, Mr A F Uniacke of Hillside, Wadebridge, even drew up his own plans for an elaborate scheme to both widen the bridge and construct a dam or weir twenty yards upstream of the bridge to maintain a moderate level of water for about two miles upstream. His plans were submitted to the County Surveyor on the 29th January 1935, and copied to Wadebridge Parish Council and the *Cornish Guardian* newspaper;[11] they also featured in the town's jubilee guide for 1935. The plan suggested building out the deck of the bridge six feet on either side, either by light weight suspension or by fitting reinforced concrete bearers on top of

---

[9] County Council minutes 10/11/1926.
[10] Access to the scheduling information was provided by Ann Preston-Jones and David Hooley, English Heritage.
[11] *Cornish Guardian*, Thursday 31st January 1935.

the existing cutwaters.[12] It included building a weir or dam five feet high with sluice-gates across some of the arches and the quaysides and island levels raised with concrete to hold a higher level of water in the channels for swimming and boating facilities.[13] In his plan, Mr Uniacke shows steps leading through the parapet wall and down onto the central island, which he suggested could be a recreation area.

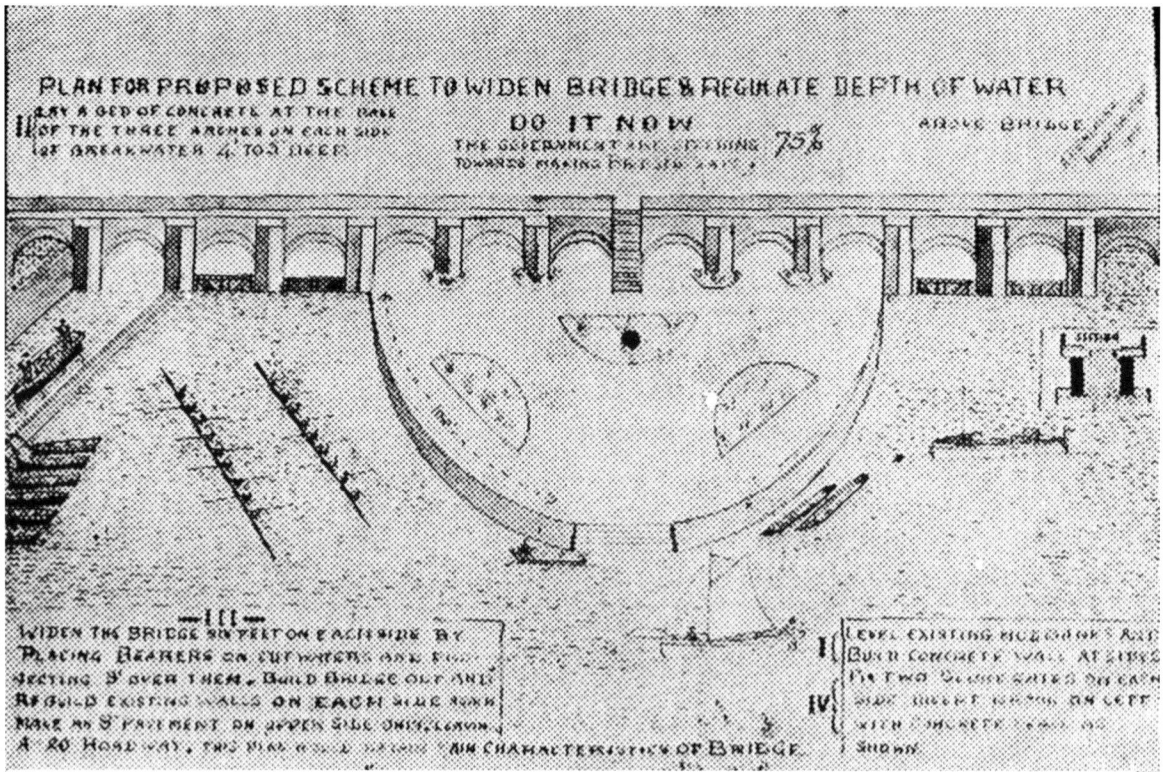

Fig 11.1 - Mr Uniacke's plan to widen Wade-Bridge, and erect sluice gates and a dam upstream.

Progressive Association of Wadebridge

Wadebridge Parish Council initially dismissed the plan out of hand, but was forced to re-consider it as public support for some of Mr Uniacke's ideas grew. A group calling itself the Progressive Association of Wadebridge was formed, probably consisting of Mr Uniacke and his supporters and lobbied the council. When the plans were reconsidered by the Parish Council, several concerns were voiced. One was that any dam or weir would have to have solid foundations and

---

[12] Letter dated 29th January 1935.
[13] *Cornish Guardian*, 24th January 1935, 7th February 1935 and 21st March 1935.

the expense of setting piles deep into the river bed would be extremely costly. A second was that the Parish Council did not own the river rights and therefore had no right to impede or restrict the movement of vessels upstream. They also noted that lock gates would need to be fitted to enable vessels to move upstream if a dam was built, and concern was also raised about the amount of silt that is washed down the river, and the enormous force of water pressure on both a dam and the old bridge. Mr Martyn for the Council stated that there were between thirty-five and forty boats using the river and that they would only be able to travel upstream on high tides, due to the dam. Several residents wrote to the editor of the *Cornish Guardian* in support of the scheme, although most remained anonymous or wrote under a pseudonym. By the end of April 1935, the Council had dismissed any idea of a dam or weir. It is clear that Mr Uniacke's was a visionary plan that took no account of the stresses and strains which would affect the bridge, the scouring effect which would be caused by blocking arches with sluice gates, or the technical, engineering or logistical problems of such a scheme. However, he did help to focus people's minds on the need to widen the bridge, and provoked much discussion at both town and county level.

In February of the same year we hear another suggestion for erecting a footbridge across from Guineaport Road to the Park at Egloshayle, this was first mooted in 1901.[14] Further elaborate schemes were mooted at this time including the possibility of building a new bridge downstream incorporating a dam and sea-gates to create a harbour or marina, an idea first proposed as early as 1840. Despite the desperate need to widen the bridge, the war years halted any chance of further progress and no serious discussion took place again until the 1950s. During the war many military vehicles used the bridge and there was a further increase in traffic.

Accidents on the bridge

In 1951, the Cornwall County Constabulary reported thirteen accidents on the bridge or at its approaches within a three year period and by their next report in 1956 another seventeen accidents had occurred.

Three options for Wade-Bridge

The County Surveyor stated that there were three options to the problems at Wade-Bridge. One was to provide a separate new bridge which would not affect the aesthetic appearance of the old one. Another was to widen the existing bridge with cantilevering as at Bideford, and the third was to widen the bridge but to keep it in character. The latter option was finally agreed as the

---

[14] *Cornish Guardian*, 23rd August 1901, also in a letter from Mrs B C Coleridge, Catesby, Wadebridge, to the County Surveyor dated 25th February 1935.

best solution. In November 1953, Mr G H Fradd the County Surveyor suggested that in the meanwhile, some measure of improvement to the eastern approach on the downstream side of the bridge could be achieved by demolishing Riverside House, widening the approach from Gonvena Hill and providing a pavement onto the bridge.[15] Despite this, however, calls to widen the bridge continued with further letters to the press, *'Bridge at Wadebridge a Scandal RDC told'*, *'Bridge must be widened, Ministry told again'* and *'Bore holes to be Sunk near Bridge – Wadebridge widening explored'*.

Fig 11.2 - Wade-Bridge viewed from upstream in 1962 just before contractors moved in.
Courtesy the Garfield Irons Collection.

Test bores to investigate the river bed

In April 1956, a contract to provide test bores in the river bed in preparation for a possible second widening of the bridge was awarded to the lowest tender George Wimpey & Co. Ltd. at a cost of £1518. The test bores confirmed the problems first encountered by Lovibond back in the fifteenth century, that on the north-east side of the bridge rock was found at a depth of 16ft 6ins (5.03m), while on the south-west bank it was at 57ft (17.4m).[16] The borings indicated alluvial sands, silts and clays over grey slate rock.[17] These results further delayed any decision to widen the bridge, with *'serious foundation difficulties at town end'* being reported. According to a report in the *Western Morning News* in 1955, the Great Western Railway had also previously drilled test bores in the

---

[15] Letter from the County Surveyor to Wadebridge & District Chamber of Commerce dated 14th November 1953.
[16] *Western Morning News*, Friday 4th May 1956.
[17] Letter 20th July 1956 from George Wimpey & Co Ltd. to Cornwall County Council.

river and between the Padstow line and the river, but they also had not hit rock until they reached 60ft (18.3m).[18]

The delay in widening the bridge was also having an impact on local utilities, with the Post Office unable to provide additional telephone cables over the bridge due to the possible widening scheme, while the Gas board only had one main on the upstream side.

A Visit by the Minister

On Saturday September 14th 1957, the *Western Morning News* reported that the Minister for the Department of Transport had been told about the problems at Wade-Bridge, while later in November 1957 representatives of the Royal Fine Art Commission, including Sir Alan Quartermaine and John Betjeman, travelled down on the night train to view the bridge. In December, the Royal Fine Art Commission proposed that the bridge should be widened and completely reconstructed.[19]

Again in January 1958 it was reported that the upstream widening was still the preferred choice as it allowed for an improved alignment with the road junctions. When the new secondary school on Gonvena Hill opened in 1957, Padstow children travelled up to Wadebridge by train each day and all had to walk across the narrow bridge to school increasing the number of children in danger. A contemporary newspaper headline announced, *'Children Cross in Danger'*.[20]

In January 1958, the County Council received a provisional estimate to remove the upstream parapet and widen the bridge to 36ft (11m) at a cost of £180,000. A further £3,250 was required for scaffolding, dams, pumps, water supply, watching, lighting and signalling. Finally, in February, a specification for the bridge was agreed between the County Council and the Royal Fine Arts Commission.

Meanwhile urgent repair and re-pointing of the bridge was required. A headline in the *Western Morning News* in 1958 announced *'Cracks in the Old Bridge at Wadebridge'*. Tenders were requested and John Garrett & Son Ltd of Truro successfully won the contract to repair and re-point the old bridge for £4,253 5s 9d. This was on the downstream side of the bridge only.

Finally, the Ministry of Transport confirmed that the bridge would be widened at a cost of £225,000 and compulsory purchase notices were issued on the 16th May 1961. These included

---

[18] *Western Morning News*, 3rd November 1955, letter to the editor from Mr Stuart Martyn of Peny Bryn, Wadebridge.
[19] Letter 31st December 1957, from the Royal Fine Art Commission to Cornwall County Council.
[20] *Western Morning News*, 31st December 1957.

land adjoining no 3 Moleworth Street, easement for the same premises, an easement for the river bed, public lavatories on the north-east side of the old bridge, part of the garden attached to W A Hawkey & Son including petrol tanks and the riparian rights owned by Sir John Molesworth St Aubyn of Pencarrow (rights leased to Wadebridge Angling Club). Throughout the second half of the year there were delays regarding ownership of the river bed and it was also reported that delays in starting were due to the technical nature of certain tenders received, reservations regarding liabilities to be borne by the tenderer and proposed structural methods which were not acceptable. By March 1962, all these issues had been resolved.

Announcement of Contract

On 27th February 1962 Mr Ernest Marples, the Minister for Transport, announced that the contract to widen Wade-Bridge had been awarded to the Cleveland Bridge and Engineering Co. Ltd., who would carry out the scheme prepared by Bridge Consulting Engineers, Messrs Posford Pavry and Partners.[21]

Contractors move in

Before the contractors could start work on widening the bridge they had to raise the level of the western upstream river bank and island by between 3 and 4 feet (0.9 and 1.2m). This was to be the main construction site, which therefore needed to be higher than the normal high tide level. At the same time the upstream parapet wall was breached in the middle of the bridge and a ramp of rubble constructed so that machinery and equipment could be driven off the bridge and on to the island. By the middle of March 1962, contractors Cleveland and consulting engineers Posford Pavry began setting up offices on the western upstream river bank close to the place where the Polmorla River enters the Camel, with further workshops on the upstream island, while work on the bridge officially started on Monday 2nd April 1962.[22]

Temporary Bailey bridge erected

Once the site offices were in place, the biggest priority was the safety of pedestrians and so a temporary footbridge was constructed against the downstream parapet of the bridge, while all the construction work and the widening of the bridge took place on the upstream side. The footbridge was a Bailey bridge, a portable prefabricated temporary steel footbridge set on tall steel piers, similar to tall scaffold towers, each pier being supported by large wooden blocks set on the river bed and downstream island and placed adjacent to the existing piers of the old bridge

---

[21] *Cornish Guardian*, 2nd March 1962.
[22] *Cornish Guardian*, 29th March 1962, 15.

(see fig 11.3).[23]   The structure was tied against the downstream parapet for additional stability. The footway was raised slightly higher than the deck of the old bridge, so creating a good viewing platform for pedestrians as the building work took place.   The downstream parapet wall was breached at the western end of the bridge at the end of the old warehouse, then Cornwall Farmers, while the east end of the footbridge continued to the edge of the garden where Riverside House had once stood.   By the end of April the Bailey bridge was completed and being used by pedestrians.[24]

A newspaper report in the *Cornish Guardian* was headlined, '*Widening the bridge will be spectacular*'. The widening of the bridge was perhaps the biggest engineering project in the town since the building of the railway in 1834 and it was certainly an incredible sight.

Fig 11.3 - The Bailey bridge erected for pedestrians while the bridge was widened upstream, Courtesy the Garfield Irons Collection.

---

[23] The Bailey bridge was designed as a temporary bridge made of fabricated steel for rapid assembly by Sir Donald Coleman Bailey (1901-85) a British Designer.
[24] *Western Morning News*, Thursday April 19th 1962 and Friday 21st April 1962.

Sequence of Construction

Construction of the new upstream section of the bridge was divided up into a number of key tasks. These included examining the foundations and drilling through the stone apron protecting each of the old piers, pile driving for each new pier, creating the new concrete sterlings and pile caps required to support the new piers, building the new piers and casting the reinforced concrete arch ribs, erecting the arch ribs from pier to pier and fitting the granite *voussoirs*. The area above and between the arches was then infilled with reinforced concrete and the new bridge deck created, while repairs to the old bridge took place at the same time. Further work included facing the piers with local stone, building the parapets and abutment walls also with local stone and resurfacing the deck of the old bridge. Many of these tasks had a set time scale, with one task overlapping another. The widening of the bridge started at the western or town end of the bridge and slowly grew eastwards towards the Egloshayle bank.

Caisson Chamber

To excavate the bridge foundations and drill through the stone apron the contractors used an air and water tight chamber called a Caisson. The chamber was open at the bottom, but sealed at the top with an air-lock. In this pressurised chamber workmen were able to work below the water line. The foundations of the old bridge could be examined and the line of stone forming a protective barrier around the old piers could be drilled through so that piles could be sunk for the new piers. Once this procedure was completed at the first arch on the town side of the bridge (arch 14), the Caisson chamber was moved eastwards to the next arch and the old pier was examined and the stone apron drilled through again. It was during this phase of the work that a man produced some wool from the

Fig 11.4 - The top section of a Caisson chamber. Courtesy the Garfield Irons Collection.

142

original foundation, although this was later considered to be a hoax.[25]

Piling begins

By July 1962, the first piles had been driven into the river bed and by September piles for nine of the twelve piers had been sunk, some to a depth of between 40 and 45 feet (12.2m to 13.7m), while those on the eastern side were driven to lesser depths where the rock bed shelved up more steeply. The piles consisted of cylindrical steel tubes, one bolted on top of another, driven into the river bed a few inches at a time with compressed air to a pressure of one ton. Once they hit bed rock a heavy metal plate with a serrated edge that could cut through into the rock was driven down through the centre of the tube. Each pile was then filled with reinforced concrete. One pile took about a day to drive in, and the target was to complete the piling for one pier each week (six piles), before moving east to start the next one. In total, seventy-two piles were required to support the new section of the bridge.[26]

Once all the piles had been sunk for one pier, another team of workmen started the construction of the concrete sterling and pile cap - the base or support for the pier. A boat shaped metal frame was placed around the piles and reinforced concrete used to form the shape of the sterling and seal the tops of the piles. On completion further steelwork was set up to form the core of the concrete pier and cast *in situ*.

The Concrete Ribs

Meanwhile a further team of contractors were casting the first of the concrete ribs; that were to form the arches, each weighing seven tons. To widen the bridge by another 20ft (6m) on its upstream side, eight reinforced concrete arch ribs had to be cast for each arch, a total of one hundred and four for the whole bridge. This was done on the upstream island nearby and was itself a major logistical problem given the limited space available with much of it already taken up with workshops and two Derrick cranes. A t tal of fourteen steel rods were slotted through holes in each rib and tensioned to a force of ten tons, giving each rib an overall force of one hundred and forty tons. These concrete ribs were cast at a rate of eight per week, the number required for one new arch.

[25] West, J, 1991. *St Breock and Wadebridge*, 55.
[26] *Cornish Guardian*, 23rd August 1962.

Fig 11.5 - Pile driving in progress,
Courtesy the Garfield Irons Collection.

Fig 11.6 - A Derrick Crane near the Egloshayle
bank, Courtesy the Garfield Irons Collection.

By September 1962, the first arches of the widened bridge were put in place, each consisting of eight concrete ribs bolted together with stainless steel rods.[27] By November all the new arches had been set in place, allowing work to continue on reconstructing the new cutwaters and stonework in character with the old bridge during the winter months.

---

[27] *Western Morning News,* Friday 21st September 1962.

Fig 11.7 - The three massive legs of a Derrick Crane seen through an arch of Wade-Bridge,
Courtesy Wadebridge Old Cornwall Society, the Roy Glasson Collection.

The outer rib of each arch was cast with slots to take the granite *voussoirs*. The contract to supply the granite for all the *voussoirs* of the arches, key stones, coping and quoins was awarded to Hanterganick Granite Co. Ltd. at St Breward, whose granite was seen as almost an exact match to the granite of the old bridge. Each arch had twenty-six granite *voussoirs*, two springer stones and a centrally placed key stone: making a total of three hundred and fifty-seven cut granite blocks for the whole bridge. All the granite blocks were fixed to the concrete with phosphor-bronze clamps and finished with mortar. Where possible the granite coping stones from the old parapet walls were re-used on the new walls, although some additional new coping stones were supplied from Hantergantick Quarry. Today most of these can be seen on the upstream Egloshayle end of the bridge.

Use of local stone

One of the main conditions of the widening scheme that the Royal Fine Arts Commission and the Ministry of Works insisted on was that the new part of the bridge must be in character with the old section.   Therefore Posford Pavry and Partners' specification included time to sample stones from a number of local quarries so that the closest possible match could be made between the old stonework and the new. Trial walls using a variety of different local stone, cement, lime and methods of pointing were constructed by masons near the railway sidings before a decision was made on the best stone to use. Air Marshall Sir John Tremayne was approached for permission to sample stone from his quarries at Crowan, which had been extensively used during the seventeenth century for repairs to the bridge.   Finally, however, stone from Blinkeywell Quarry at Helland near Bodmin, owned by Lt Col J B Peter-Hoblyn, was chosen and arrangements were made for the quarry to be re-opened to supply the stonework. [28] A local Wadebridge

Fig 11.8 - Casting the concrete arch ribs,
Courtesy the Garfield Irons Collection.

company, Messrs Sydney Jewell Ltd., won the contract to quarry and supply six hundred cubic yards of stone from the quarry.   As the quarry had been closed for many years, this involved laying a new road for access. [29]

---

[28] *Cornish Guardian*, 13th June 1963. and *Cornish Guardian*, 23rd August 1962, states that a stone quarry at Tregullan (south of Bodmin) was to be re-opened to provide stone for the bridge with the possibility of another quarry also supplying stone.
[29] *Cornish Guardian*, September 1962, 'Steel Rods will bind new concrete arches by Lovebond's bridge'.

146

Strengthening the old bridge

While work progressed with the upstream widening, repairs and strengthening work to the old bridge took place. Engineers discovered there were many voids in the old masonry and one hundred and forty tons of liquid cement were pumped into the fabric at a pressure of between twenty and twenty-five pounds per square inch, to consolidate the structure. [30] This process revealed several cracks and weaknesses in the old bridge some of which were identified when the cement poured out in unexpected places. Arch 4 on the Egloshayle side of the bridge was found to have a very bad crack and the whole arch had to be shored up with supports while remedial work took place. Once all the consolidation was completed the stonework of the old bridge was re-pointed.

Fig 11.9 - Completed concrete arch ribs ready for installation, Courtesy the Garfield Irons Collection.

---

[30] *Cornish Guardian*, 23rd August 1962 and 20th September 1962.

Fig 11.10 - Local stone used to face the piers, Courtesy Wadebridge Old Cornwall Society, Roy Glasson Collection.

During the summer and autumn of 1962, good progress was made with the construction and the Cleveland Bridge Engineering Company, reported being six weeks in advance with their work; however the winter of 1962-63 proved to be a very cold one and this led to some delays as the low temperatures prevented concrete being laid. Nevertheless, the contract never fell behind, despite some heavy rain, spring tides that flooded their workshops and having to accommodate a single flow of traffic at all times. By June 1963, enough work had been completed on the new deck to allow a free flow of traffic attending the Royal Cornwall Agricultural Show. At the height of the construction, the Cleveland Bridge Engineering Company, invited members of the South-Western Association of the Institution of Civil Engineers to visit for a tour of the construction site.[31]

On completion of the widening scheme in August 1963, a bronze plaque was fitted in the abutment wall at the town end of the new upstream section. The plaque reads: *Ministry of*

---

[31] *Western Morning News*, 29th November 1962.

Transport. This bridge was built in the 15th century, widened in 1852 and again in 1963. Consulting Engineers, Posford, Pavry and Partners. Contractors, the Cleveland Bridge and Engineering Co. Ltd.

The completed bridge had a width of 36ft (11m) from one parapet to the other, with a 6ft (1.8m) pedestrian pavement on each side of an 18ft (5.5m) carriageway. To celebrate the successful completion of the bridge widening, Cleveland Bridge and Engineering Company held an informal celebration in the Long Room at the Swan Hotel, on Friday 16th August 1963.

Ballad of the Bridge on Wool

A poem written about the history and widening of the bridge was published in the Cleveland Company's Magazine. It was also reproduced on a piece of the company's headed note paper and was signed by many of the consultants, engineers, contractors, stone masons and labourers involved in the project. The original is said to have been set into the parapet wall behind the bronze plaque, (see fig 11.15). The poem reads as follows:

In Cornwall, East of Wadebridge Town
There is a bridge of great renown
The River Camel at high tide
Laps the bank on either side.
A 'Fair' Bridge, built by Lovebond
A Vicar from a Town beyond.
Thirteen Gothic arches stand
Bedded deep in shifting sand.
On sacks of Wool they laid the piers
And these have stood five hundred years.
The old Bridge, with increasing load,
Demanded then a wider road.
And so one day Contractors came
Called 'Cleveland Bridge', a famous name.
Lofty cranes on gabbards high

Towered upwards to the sky.
Piles were driven deep below
And local people watched it grow
Some shook their heads, expressing doubt.
As ancient cracks were filled with grout.
Machines and men worked on the site.
Through summer days and in the night
Shutters, cofferdams and caissons.
Scaffolding and stone for Masons.
Welding plant, cement and sand
Covered the surrounding land
Lorries came and tipped their load.
Drains were laid along the road
Skilled engineers with planned design
Rebuild the Bridge in record time.

Fig 11.11 - *The new bridge being used prior to its completion, Courtesy Wadebridge Old Cornwall Society, the Roy Glasson Collection.*

Fig 11.12 - *Surfacing the new bridge deck and installing the pedestrian pavements, Courtesy Wadebridge Old Cornwall Society, the Roy Glasson Collection.*

Dredging the river and re-building the island

On completion of the bridge widening and removal of all of the contractor's equipment from the river banks and central island, it was agreed by the Cornwall River Board and Wadebridge Rural District Council that the central island should be reduced to its former height and much of the river bed dredged to remove the build up of silt and debris from the widening scheme. As well as reducing the level of the island both upstream and downstream, it was also decided to enlarge and build retaining walls around them, with the object of promoting better tidal flow in the channels on both sides and helping to scour the bed of the river. Employees of the Cornwall River Board also deepened the northern channel of the river.[32]

Fig 11.13 - Aerial photograph showing the length of the downstream part of the island, created to control the level of water at the quay sides. Courtesy Historic Environment, Cornwall Council.

The dredging of the river bed and the enlarging of the islands was estimated at £7000. The Cornwall River Board hired a dredger from an Ipswich firm for ten weeks and launched it into the river opposite Egloshayle Church, at the place where barges once loaded and unloaded coal and other goods (this is now the site of the rugby fields). Silt from the river bed was lifted at a

---

[32] *Cornish Guardian*, 13th June 1962, 8.

rate of two thousand tons per week and all this material was used to extent the island, both upstream and downstream.[33]

One local parishioner, Mr W S Phillips of Court Place, Egloshayle called for the shops at the west end of the bridge to be demolished, as since the bridge had been widened it formed a kink or restriction that could have been avoided.[34] The town side was still slightly restricted; however Mr P C Coleman, clerk for Wadebridge Rural District Council, stated that it was not feasible to knock down buildings on one side of Molesworth Street.

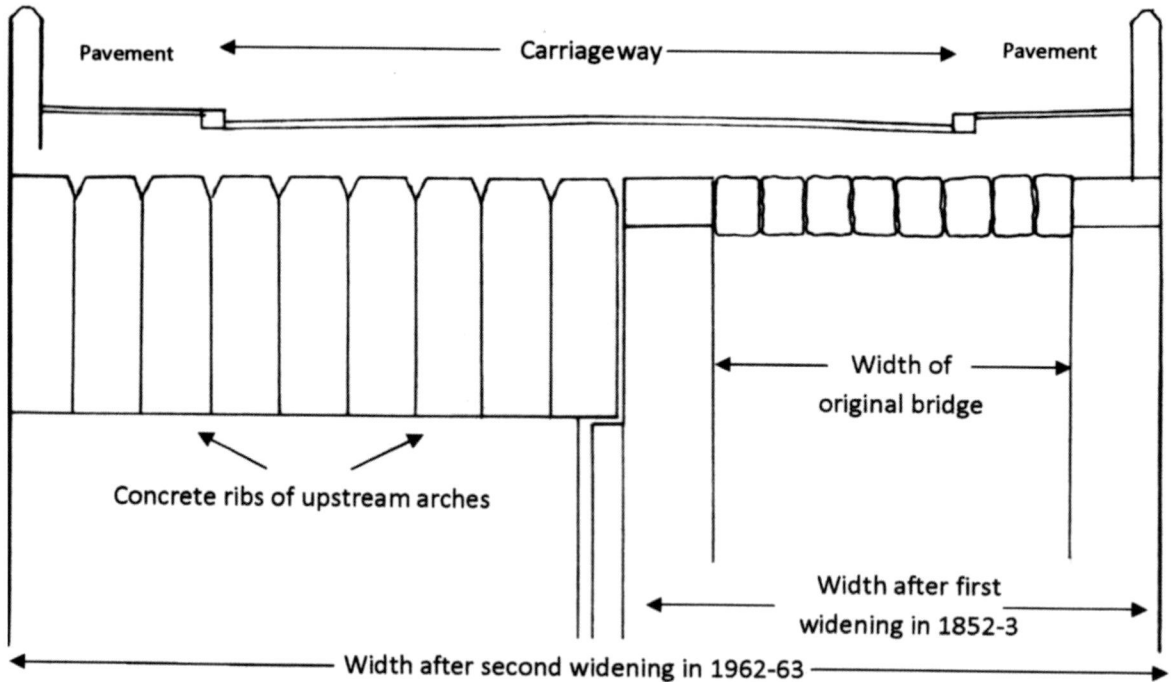

Fig 11.14 – Cross-section of Wade-Bridge showing the original width and the two widenings, based on a Cornwall County Council plan.

At the time, the widening of the bridge was seen as a great triumph and was undeniably needed. However some people, amongst them Cornish historian A L Rowse, still voiced concern. In his book, *A Cornishman Abroad*, Rowse stated that the bridge had been ruined by being doubled in size and asks: *'why couldn't they have built a second bridge for traffic the other way instead of destroying*

---

[33] *Cornish Guardian,* 22nd August 1963, 6.
[34] *Western Morning News,* 23rd July 1963 – 'Demolition of shops'.

152

something irreplaceable'. [35] On the 6th June 1969, the bridge was designated as a Listed Building and given Grade 2* listing.

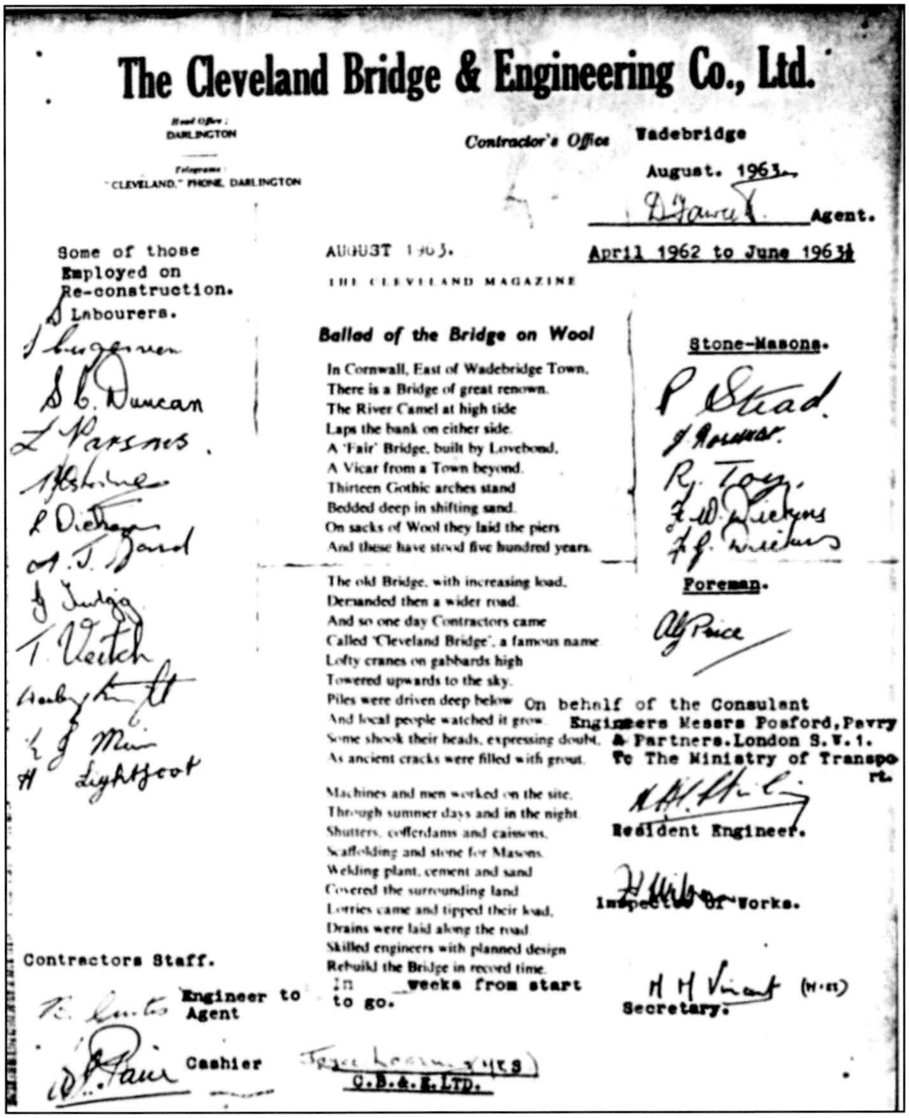

Fig 11.15 – A copy of the Ballad of the Bridge on Wool and signatures of some of those who worked on its widening.

---

[35] Rowse, A L, 1976. *A Cornishman Abroad*, 232.

12 'contain ground beneath the old piers and give added support to the whole bridge structure'

Strengthening the bridge and further repairs

Adding new to old does not always work and although the second widening of Wade-Bridge was declared to be a great success in terms of alleviating the traffic congestion, reducing the number of accidents and retaining the overall character of the medieval structure, it was later to cause unpredicted and expensive problems.

The gap between old and new

Whereas the shallow foundations of the old bridge with its medieval construction allowed for a certain amount of movement – it flexed with any movement of the riverbed - the new upstream extension to the bridge was constructed of rigid reinforced concrete, with solid foundations formed by piling down 40 to 45ft (12.2 to 13.7m) into the bedrock – with no movement. The old and new portions of the bridge were independently supported, with a small sealed expansion joint between them. The old and new structures were only joined together physically by a water proof membrane and the road deck of the bridge.

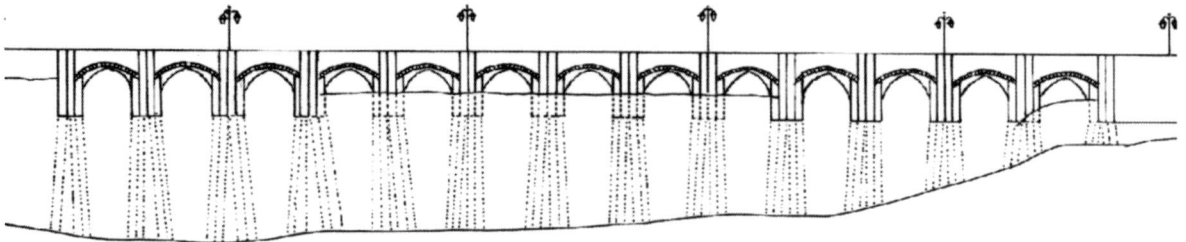

Fig 12.1 - Shows the depth of the foundations of the upstream section of the bridge, based on a 1962 Cornwall County Council bridge plan.

On completion of the second widening in 1963, bridge engineers periodically monitored the bridge for any settlement and, by the early 1970s according to Mr R L C Stephens, then the Principal Bridge Maintenance Engineer and Mr J L Carlyon Technician Bridge Maintenance Section for Cornwall County Council, a vertical movement of 2ins (5cms) and a horizontal movement of ¾in (2cms) had been recorded between the old and the new sections of the bridge. This was damaging the waterproof link '*and allowing water and salts to percolate through the segments causing severe spalling'.*[1] Spalling is caused when concrete breaks up, flakes or becomes pitted; it may be purely cosmetic or, if allowed to continue without repair, can lead to structural damage, particularly if the reinforcing bars within the concrete become exposed. A longitudinal crack up the centre of the carriageway soon became noticeable, along the line of the joint between the old bridge and the new and this required regular sealing. Tell-tale indicators were fixed into positions under the arches to monitor movement between the new and old parts of the bridge.[2]

The need to reinforce the foundations

By the early 1970s, a decision had been taken to reinforce the shallow foundations of the old part of the bridge by the Bridge Division of Cornwall County Council for which plans were drawn up in March 1972. During February 1975, tenders for reinforcing the piers of the original bridge structure were advertised and the contract was won by Wimpey Laboratories Ltd. of Hayes in Middlesex. Wimpey Laboratories provided specialist drilling teams for the piling while the remainder of the work was sub-contracted to Bovis. Bovis had responsibility for building the high level working and accommodation platforms on the islands, concreting the pile caps, construction of the cofferdams and reinstatement of the island on completion of the works. The object of the work was to *'contain ground beneath the old piers and give added support to the whole bridge structure'.*[3]

Construction Site

Wimpey Laboratories set up their site offices on the upstream side of the central island on a high level platform formed out of scaffolding, while the downstream part of the island was home to a second platform for the engineering work, which included a plant for mixing the grout that was pumped into many parts of the old bridge by a series of hoses. Access to both the accommodation platform and the engineering platform was via long ladders set up against the parapet walls of the bridge. Stone from Kestle Quarry at Sladesbridge was quarried and used to build a ramp down into the river from near the Julian Foye's furniture shop on the Egloshayle side of the river, so that all heavy equipment like diggers and cranes could access the island. The fifteen month contract was overseen by a clerk of works for Cornwall County Council.

---

[1] Stephens, R L C, and Carlyon, J L, 1994. *The History, repair and upkeep of a highway structure Scheduled as an Ancient Monument.* Proceedings of the Institute of Civil Engineers, 103 Sept. 157-162.

[2] Telltail indicators can simply be a glass plate fixed across a crack, calibrated acrylic plates or digital gauges, each to measure movement between fixed points.

[3] *Cornish Guardian*, September 18th 1975.

Fig 12.2 - Wimpey Laboratories construction site on the downstream island in 1975.

The Task

The work involved stabilising each of the old piers of the bridge by sinking 6in (15cm) diameter piles 20ft (6m) into the river bed at one foot intervals around each pier, to form a protective curtain of piles. Each of the piles was in the form of a tube, with a one inch high tensile steel bar through its centre and concrete pumped into the pile under pressure. The tops of the piles were tied together with further reinforcing bars to create a concrete starling around each of the old piers to match those around the upstream 1962-63 piers. Further horizontal holes were drilled into the walls of the piers and high tensile steel bars were grouted in and tied to the reinforcing frame of each starling. In addition a series of holes was drilled into each pier from all sides and grout was pumped in at high pressure to fill any voids in the masonry. Hundreds more holes were drilled into the walls, cutwaters, piers and deck of the old bridge; these were fitted with high tensile steel rods, grouted into place. Further grout was pumped into every hole to fill any voids in the structure, thus making the whole bridge more solid. As well as creating new reinforced starlings around the piers of the bridge, the bed of the river was concreted under the six arches of the bridge that carry the two channels of water at low tide, arches 3, 4, 5, 12, 13 and

14. These were concreted from approximately 6ft (1.83m) upstream of the bridge to 15ft (4.6m) downstream; this was to enable water to flow more easily through the arches and most importantly to reduce scouring at the base of the piers.

Cofferdams

The work to sink new piles, tie them in to each pier and cap the tops in reinforced concrete required the construction of cofferdams, especially in the main channels of the river. Work started at the western or town end and proceeded across to Egloshayle.

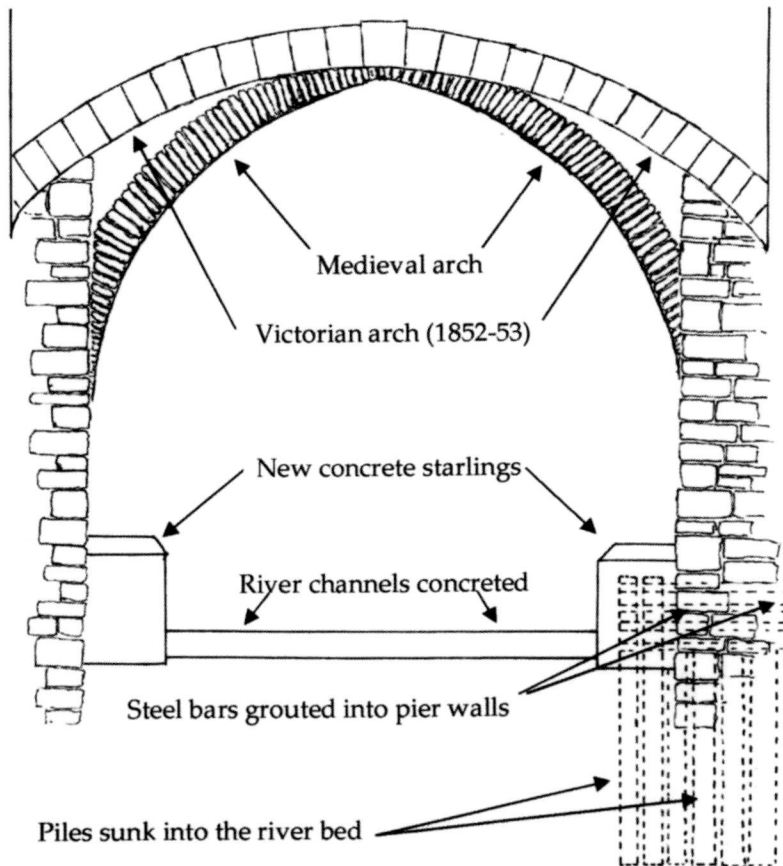

Fig12.3 - This illustration attempts to show the position of piles, steel rods, and new concrete starlings, based on a Cornwall County Council plan.

According to David Jewell, who lived locally and worked for both Wimpey Laboratories and later Bovis on the same project, the cofferdams were made out of sheet piling and were built around three piers, or two arches at a time and once the piling work had been completed, the dams would be taken down and set up around the next group of arches along the bridge. Water pumps worked constantly to ensure that the work areas behind the cofferdams remained free of water. It must have been an uncomfortable experience working within the cofferdams at high tide, when the water was at a much higher level outside. David Jewell remembers that he would have to check that the pumps were working early every morning as this was vital to the progress of the work and safety of the workers.

Fig12.4 - A cofferdam around arches 13 and 14 with pump clearing water from the work area, Courtesy David Jewell.

Exploring the foundations

In July 1975, newspaper reports again questioned whether the old bridge had really been built on packs of wool. The report went on to say that as so many large size bore holes were to be drilled into the original foundations of the old bridge, this might produce evidence, or lack of it, to confirm whether the legend was true. It was claimed that the bore holes would produce many easily identifiable samples of original foundation material.[4] However, no statement was ever forthcoming to either deny or confirm the legend of the wool packs and sadly, the pumping of liquid concrete into the foundations of the old bridge will have completely ruined any chances of inspecting the original foundations in the future.

Cost of the work

The work to the foundations of the bridge cost £425,000 with the expense being borne by the Department of the Environment, and authorised by the Ancient Monuments Division, as the bridge is both a scheduled ancient monument and a listed structure.[5]

A survey of all the arches of the bridge by the author during July 2009 revealed evidence of these repairs including parts of the cementation hoses used for pumping grout into the foundations, along with steel sheeting, cables and a scaffold pole, all partially buried in the mud on the island.

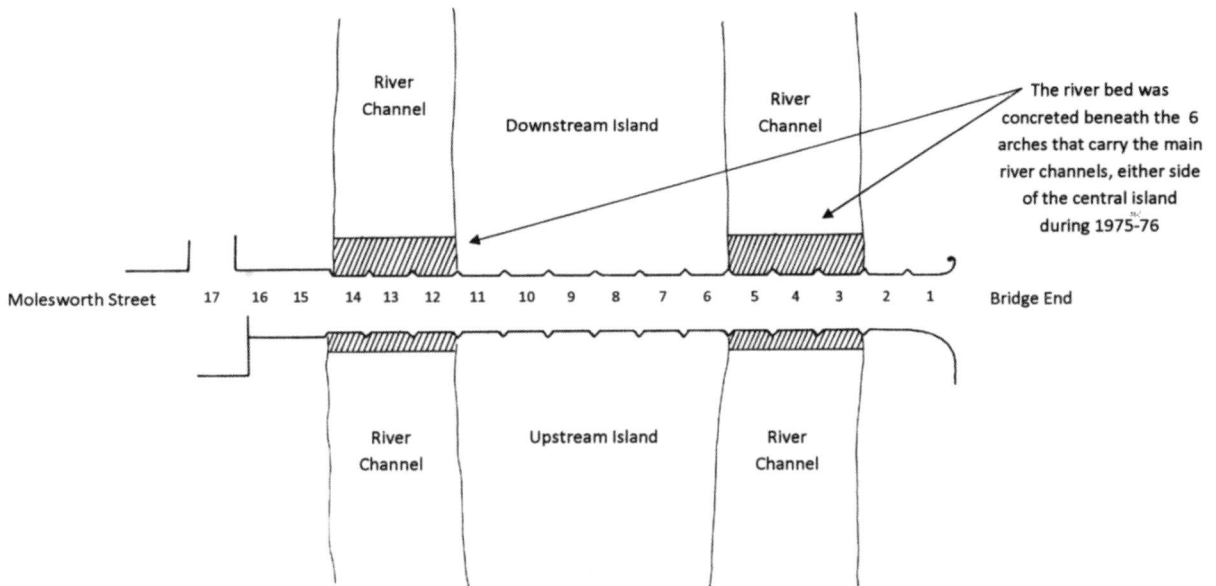

Fig 12.5 - Concreting the river bed below the arches carrying the river channels to reduce scouring.

During the 1980s, further routine monitoring of the bridge revealed that the reinforcing steel in the concrete ribs supporting the new upstream section of the bridge was seriously corroding, causing further spalling due to the penetration of water. Following this discovery more repairs

[4] *Cornish Guardian*, July 31st 1975.

[5] *Cornish Guardian*, September 11th 1975.

were undertaken during February, March and April of 1987 to cut back sections of the concrete ribs, treat the steelwork and renew areas of concrete. The repairs were carried out by Cornwall County Council's direct labour department who used 'Thorite' rapid setting concrete for their repairs.[6]

Today, if one wades under the arches and examines the eight concrete arch ribs that make up each arch of the 1962-63 widening, the extensive repairs of this period are very obvious.

Two more bridges across the Camel

After 500 years with just one bridge across the river Camel at Wadebridge, two more bridges came in quick succession during the early 1990s. The first, the Challenge footbridge, was built upstream of the old bridge in 1991, from Guineaport to the Recreation Park at Egloshayle. The second, the modern concrete bypass bridge on the downstream side of the old bridge was completed two years later in 1993. For the first time this gave both pedestrians and drivers an alternative route across the river and enabled further urgent repairs to be carried out on Wade-Bridge.

Challenge footbridge

It was in August 1901 that a suggestion to build a footbridge across the river from Guineaport to Egloshyale Road was first suggested and this was raised again in February 1935 by a Mrs Coleridge in a letter to the County Surveyor (see chapter 11). Unfortunately, with the outbreak of the Second World War, all funds were funnelled towards the war effort and a footbridge became a low priority. By 1963, the second widening of the bridge and the provision of pavements on either side of the roadway removed the dangers for children crossing the old bridge.

Nevertheless, the idea of a footbridge was raised again in the 1970s and when a popular GP and town councillor, Dr Keith Bailey, suddenly died, a fund in his memory was started. This was to go towards a new footbridge across the river to be called the 'Bailey Bridge'. However, with costs for the project spiralling upwards this project never came to fruition, and the funds collected remained in the bank. Even so the need for a footbridge persisted and the Town Council even considered purchasing a second hand British Rail footbridge. At the beginning of 1991, design engineers from CCC's bridge department showed town councillors four different designs for a

---

[6] Correspondence with John Armstrong, Bridge Department, Cornwall Council, 9th June 2011.

footbridge; a three span design found favour with the Town Council and an illustration of the proposed bridge was published in the *Cornish Guardian* newspaper.[7]

But, during the summer of 1991, Wadebridge people unexpectedly noticed work being carried out on both river banks, including the installation of concrete foundations and a concrete pier in the river. Although people began to speculate that this might have something to do with a footbridge the reason for the activity remained a secret until Wednesday 11th September, when TV personality Anneka Rice from the BBC One 'Challenge Anneka' programme arrived in the town to meet a challenge to build a footbridge across the river in four days.

Anneka's task was to persuade local companies to donate materials and labour towards construction of the bridge in record time. Of course, much of the steelwork had already been prepared, but it was still a major undertaking in such a short time. Engineers and workmen worked around the clock with flood lights through the night to complete the bridge on time.

As it had been Mrs Diane Dingle who originally wrote to Anneka, suggesting this challenge, it was only fitting that Diane and her auntie, Mrs Ada Martin, should open the bridge on the evening of Saturday 14th September. A wonderful evening of celebration included a party for the whole town.

New Bypass Bridge

Downstream, the new bypass bridge was designed by Gifford and Partners; Consultants from Southampton, with the contract to build it and the Wadebridge bypass won by Balfour Beatty, work started in October 1991. Draft plans for this route had been developed as early as 1947 and published in 1952 in Cornwall County Council's development plan.[8] It involved construction of a road from Tollgate, across the north west corner of Trevanson, to Trevilling on the opposite side of the river and was routed between the village of Bodieve and Wadebridge School playing fields to a new roundabout at Ball, where it joined the Egloshayle bypass which was constructed at the same time. To cross the river a new high level concrete bridge was constructed, set on eight slender piers.

Engineers constructing the new bypass bridge faced a problem similar to that experienced by Lovibond five hundred years earlier: - that of finding a solid foundation. Some of the piles for

---

[7] *Cornish Guardian*, February 14th 1991.

[8] Cornwall County Council, 1952. *Development Plan 1952 Report of Survey Part one – The County*, based on the Town and Country Planning Act 1947.

the new bridge were sunk to a depth of 100ft (30m) before reaching solid bedrock, however only two of the piers are in the navigable part of the river. The piling work was undertaken by a Scottish team from Balfour Beatty's sister company Stent. The official start to building the bypass was on Thursday 12th December 1991, when the Transport Minister Christopher Chope took the controls of a giant pile driving crane and sunk the first piles into the river bank of the river Camel. The 460m (1510ft) long bridge was built 14m (42ft) above the level of the spring tides, a requirement which the Padstow Harbour Commissioners insisted on, so that no vessels would be restricted. The bypass cost approximately £8.3 million, with the new bridge accounting for £4 million of the total price. The new bypass and bridge were finally opened on Thursday July 8th 1993 by the Minister for Roads and Traffic, Mr Robert Key. The opening of the new bypass certainly reduced the amount of traffic over the old bridge and June 1994 saw for the first time the long streams of traffic for the Royal Cornwall Agricultural Show following the new bypass route.

Tidal Defence Scheme

Between 1993 and 1994 the National Rivers Authority raised the levels of all the river banks upstream of the old bridge, including a higher roadside wall between the Recreation Park on Egloshayle Road and Egloshayle Church. The main impact on the old bridge was the installation of new steel sheet piling leading from the town side of the bridge across the front of Town Quay and Commissioners Quay, to secure falling masonry from the old Cornwall Farmers building, which from the 1980s had started to slip into the river directly below arch 14. The Tidal Defence Scheme cost £4.5 million and saw another major investment in the town.[9] Although the view of the old bridge was slightly affected by this work, the flooding of the town, which in the past had been a regular occurrence, was drastically reduced.

Refurbishment of the old bridge

Once the bypass bridge was opened, it gave the first real opportunity since the second widening in 1962-63 to carry out repairs as well as maintenance work on the old bridge. For many years bridge engineers had been concerned about water penetrating the fabric of the old bridge. They drew up plans to strip away the road deck of the structure and fit a waterproof membrane and new drainage which would stop the percolation of water through the old stone work and prevent corrosion of the reinforced steelwork of the upstream section. Replacing the deck also gave the opportunity for the main utilities including gas, water and telephone companies to renew and increase their services across the bridge. New telephone duct was installed beneath the downstream pavement, while new gas and water pipes were laid on the upstream side.

---

[9] *Cornish Guardian*, 3rd February1994. Shows a photograph of the piling of the quay side at Jewsons Yard.

Plate 17a - Concrete arch ribs in place to form new arches for the second widening in 1962-63, Courtesy May Garland.

Plate 17b - November 1962, the new concrete arches set in place showing the full extent of the widening, Courtesy May Garland.

Plate 18 - The construction works at Wade-Bridge taken from upstream 1962-63, Courtesy May Garland.

Plate 19a – The Challenge Bridge, Courtesy Adrian Langdon.

Plate 19b – The new Wadebridge bypass bridge, Courtesy Adrian Langdon.

Plate 20a – The banner of the Wadebridge Old Cornwall Society, Courtesy David & Carole Stark.

Plate 20b - Bollard showing the Wadebridge Crest.

Plate 20c – The Wadebridge School badge depicting the bridge.

Plate 21a – High tide at Wadebridge, August 2010.

Plate 21b – High tide under Wade-Bridge, August 2010.

Plate 22a – Martin Langdon taking levels of the bridge and causeway, January 2010.

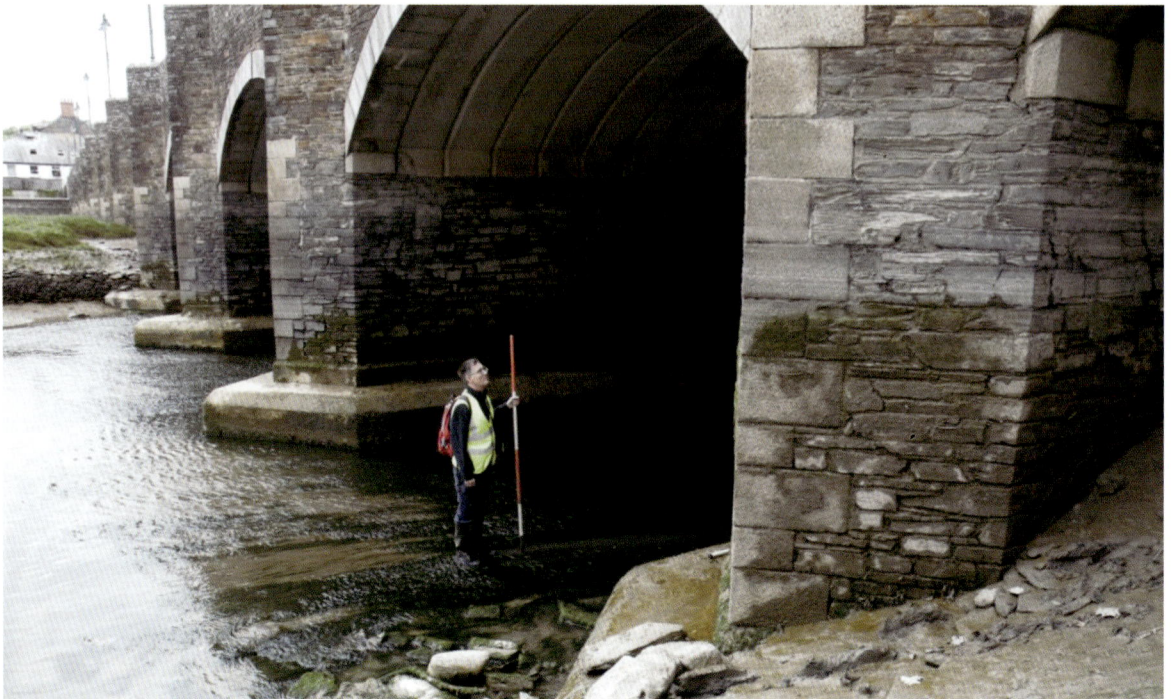

Plate 22b – The author surveying the upstream side of Wade-Bridge in 2011, Courtesy Adrian Langdon.

Plate 23 - Aerial view of the three bridges on the river Camel at Wadebridge, Courtesy Adrian Langdon.

*Plate 24a - The Cornish Gorsedh processing across Wade-Bridge in September 2005
led by piper Mervyn Davey, Courtesy Adrian Langdon.*

Plate 24b – Wade-Bridge viewed from upstream with Christmas Lights, Courtesy Adrian Langdon.

Concerns were raised in November 1993 about completely closing Wade-Bridge for renewing the bridge deck. An initial estimate suggested that the bridge could be closed for three months, or six months if open to one way traffic. The Fire brigade and other emergency services argued that closing the old bridge completely could risk life if they had to travel all around the bypass route, so it was eventually agreed that there would be single way traffic leading from Egloshayle into the town at all times during the operations. All the repairs to the bridge, which cost approximately £250,000, were paid for by the Department of Transport before handing over the control of the bridge to Cornwall County Council as part of the 'de-trunking' of the A39. The old bridge was eventually closed one way from the end of January 1994 and opened again for Easter traffic at the beginning of April.

Fig 12.6 - Refurbishment of the road deck in 1994, while allowing single track traffic.

On completion of the bypass Wadebridge, along with five other towns throughout the country which had also recently been bypassed was selected, to receive funds for a town enhancement scheme. At Wadebridge this included installing speed restriction ramps on all the approach roads into the town along with cycle paths where the width of the road was suitable. This work was completed by contractors Dean and Dyball. Local Founders, Irons Brothers Ltd. at Polmorla won a contract to provide cast iron bench ends, bollards with the Wadebridge Crest, and fingerposts. At the same time, new lamp standards were installed on the bridge, the pavements widened, brick cycle paths created and the roadway narrowed. At either end of the bridge a new cast iron sign giving a brief history of Wade-Bridge and displaying the new town Crest was installed, while further signs were set up at the entrance to the town.   The cast iron signs, lamp standards, bollards and fingerposts were all painted 'Southern Railway' green with gold, to celebrate the town's link with the railway.   Local merchandise including tee shirts and bone china mugs displaying the three bridges across the river Camel at Wadebridge was also produced to celebrate completion of the bypass bridge.

Bridge symbolism

The medieval bridge is central to the identity of the Wadebridge, its most photographed asset and was often the focal point of Victorian and Edwardian postcards of the town. According to Margaret Thompson of Wadebridge, during the First World War, Christmas cards with a photograph of the old bridge were often sent to troops overseas: an image that must have raised emotions and thoughts of whether they would ever live to return and cross the bridge again. [10]

It is not surprising to find that several organisations in Wadebridge use images of the bridge as their logos. When the Wadebridge Secondary School was opened in 1957 a school badge depicting two arches of the bridge with the Cornish shield containing fifteen bezants was adopted. This badge has been worn on the blazers of thousands of Wadebridge children for over fifty years and is still the badge of Wadebridge County Comprehensive School (plate 20c).

In 1993, Wadebridge Town Council adopted a new crest, which had been originally designed by Councillor Ben Butling in 1974 and fashioned in wood at Wadebridge Comprehensive School. This wooden Crest now hangs above the doorway into the main hall of the Town Hall. The new Wadebridge Crest is in the form of a shield which incorporates the bridge with its surviving thirteen arches across its centre, and a Ram symbolising the legend of the 'Bridge on Wool' above on the left with Lovibond's three hearts joined by a ribbon on the right, copied from the original

---

[10] The 1917 Christmas card sent from the town and district of Wadebridge featured small photographs of the town Hall, Molesworth Street and the bridge on the front, and also the county shield and motto 'one and all' with a title 'For Hope and Duty' and the soldiers name and contact details. Inside was a short message and another photograph of the bridge. On the 1918 card are two flags crossed, the White Ensign and the Union Flag, with a title 'With Every Good Wish from Wadebridge'. A message inside stated that the town looks forward to welcoming all the soldiers home and a photograph of the bridge on the opposite page.

Lovibond shield on the west doorway to the tower at Egloshayle Church. Below the bridge is depicted a swan on the river and a small Cornish shield showing the fifteen bezants.

The new Wadebridge Community Primary School has also chosen to show the bridge on its badge, which shows five arches of the bridge with an open book above being held open by a bird at each corner. Likewise the Wadebridge and District Chamber of Commerce has a logo showing five arches of the bridge with a swan in flight over the bridge. The Wadebridge Old Cornwall Society has a banner which also adopts the symbol of the medieval bridge as the central image (plate 20a).

Certain Wadebridge sports clubs have also chosen to show the bridge on their badges. Wadebridge Town Fooball Club has a similar design to the Comprehensive School – five arches, the Cornish shield with fifteen bezants, but with the addition of a pair of swans supporting the shield. The Tennis Club logo displays seven arches of the bridge with crossed tennis rackets, while the newly formed Canoe Club's badge shows seven arches with silhouettes of canoes and an oar. At least one business in the town, Merrick Solicitors, has a logo showing four arches of the bridge with shield and a tower.

Further 'bridge symbolism' in the town includes a fine ceramic mosaic by Emma Spring which depicts the bridge and the legend of the 'bridge on wool' outside the Co-op store while another image of the bridge made from terracotta tiles can be seen in the foyer of the town hall. Even the blind windows of the Co-op store alongside Lovibond Walk were designed to replicate the nearby arches of the medieval bridge.

De-scheduling part of the bridge

In January 2003, English Heritage revised the scheduling status of the bridge to reflect the fact that much of the structure is comparatively modern. The bridge has been given a new National Scheduled Monument no 15580. The protected or scheduled area was reduced to the structure of the medieval bridge and the nineteenth century widening with a 2m (6½ft) margin. The area on the town side of the bridge where there are three buried arches is not protected so as to avoid unwarranted and unnecessary constraints; the first arch on the Egloshayle side of the bridge which is converted into a cellar is within the scheduling. Although the de-scheduling of the modern (1962-63) part of the bridge has removed some legal protection, the whole bridge, including its modern structure is still protected as a Grade 2* listed building.[11]

Work on Wade-Bridge in the twenty first century

The only work to take place on the old bridge during the twenty-first century has been the installation of new lamp columns. In June 2000, scheduled monument consent was given to replace the lamp columns at each end of the bridge with new columns that would take the extra weight and wind loadings for supporting the festoon lighting system which is erected each Christmas.[12]

Cycle path under or over the bridge

Ever since the construction of the Camel Trail cycle path from Bodmin and Wenford Bridge through Wadebridge to Padstow there has been concern about the safety of cyclists crossing the busy road junction at the bottom of Molesworth Street. Many people have called for one of the old arches of the bridge to be opened up so that cyclists can ride around the river bank, cycle beneath the Wade-Bridge and continue along by Commissioners Quay on their way to Padstow. To allow for this, arch no 15, the nearest arch to the western river bank would need to be unblocked. However this apparently simple idea would in fact be difficult since arch 15 was blocked up in 1868 and when the bridge was widened in 1962-63, no new arch was formed on the upstream side.

Another solution originally put forward by North Cornwall District Council was to purchase a piece of land below the bridge on the upstream side and build a ramped pathway up to the bridge to allow pedestrians and cyclists to cross the bridge in a safer location. This would entail breaching the upstream parapet wall and installing a pedestrian crossing across the western end of the bridge. The downstream parapet was previously opened up with steps leading to the riverside, although no agreement has yet been reached to link the two ends of the cycle path at the bridge.

---

[11] Correspondence with David Hooley English Heritage, also information from the revised schedule no. 15580 for the Department for Culture, Media and Sport. The author provided some of the historical background for the revised scheduling.

[12] Scheduled Monument Consent granted on 23rd June 2000.

Present condition of the bridge

A recent visual survey of the piers and arches of the bridge by the author on the 16th May 2011 revealed further problems which will require addressing during the next few years. Some of the old piers have cracks running down through them, particularly piers 1, 2, 3 and 4. The stonework above the cutwater on the downstream pier 3 is bulging due to cracks in the walling, and the concrete starling below pier 3 has some damage. Further problems of concrete spalling can be identified in the reinforced concrete arch ribs, with corroding steelwork exposed in a few places. Additional concrete arch ribs display rust staining, indicating that the steelwork in the reinforcing is starting to corrode again. At road level, re-pointing of the parapets and granite coping is required in some parts of the structure. Although the condition of Wade-Bridge is not bad compared to some Cornish bridges, it is a structure which will always require an ongoing programme of maintenance.

Fig 12.7 - Wade-Bridge seen from downstream at low tide, Courtesy Adrian Langdon.

13 'the bridge may be regarded at the town's promenade'

A social history of Wade-Bridge

According to J H Wade, author of *Rambles in Cornwall*, 'the bridge may be regarded as the town's promenade as well as its chief ornament, for it runs like a straight and elevated causeway from shore to shore'.[1]

This idea that the bridge is a promenade is certainly true. For centuries people have lined both sides of the bridge to watch parades and processions and have used it as a viewing platform for events on the river, like regattas, swimming matches, raft races or to see visiting ships. The bridge has often been central to major activities and celebrations at Wadebridge and for people living on opposite sides of the river has been a place to meet.

Processions and parades

Although it is quite likely that the bridge was used from the very beginning of its life as a place to meet socially, or perhaps to gather before moving on elsewhere, there is no record. It was not until the beginning of the nineteenth century that the town began to grow and with the introduction of various social and religious groups, that the social link between the bridge and the inhabitants of the town first becomes apparent.

During the Victorian period and throughout the early part of the twentieth century, there was a dramatic rise in the number of social, political and religious groups; there was also a military presence with the 13th Cornwall Rifle Volunteers. The popularity of friendly and fraternity societies grew, along with abstinence or temperance movements such as the Rechabites and the Band of Hope. Most of these organisations had their own uniforms or regalia of sashes, gauntlets, aprons, badges and medals. In December 1869, the Wadebridge Total Abstinence Society and Band of Hope are noted in local newspapers, while in July 1882 a new temperance group, the Blue Ribbon Army, held their inaugural meeting in the town hall (then at Park Place) when two hundred and thirty-two persons took the ribbon and one hundred new pledges were taken. By December that year their membership had reached nearly five hundred, such was the persuasion of these organisations.[2]

---

[1] Wade, J H, 1928. *Rambles in Cornwall*, London.
[2] *Royal Cornwall Gazette*, 21st July, 22nd September, 6th October and 22nd December 1882.

168

Parades and processions by the local soldiers from the Cornwall Volunteers, the Freemasons, Forresters, Western Provident Association, Rechabites and also many church and chapel groups became a feature of life in Wadebridge and the bridge the perfect venue for their displays. Even today many local processions cross the bridge to end at Egloshayle Church for a service, or terminate at the Egloshayle Recreation Park. Parades to mark national events such as the death of a monarch, coronation or religious event often marched or processed across the bridge.

Whit Monday was often a day of processions, tea treats and local sports although in 1860, Whit Tuesday was the chosen day. After a meeting in the town, a procession of the Wadebridge branch of the Western Provident Association crossed the bridge, preceded by a band and accompanied by the 13th Cornwall Rifle Volunteers in full uniform; they then marched to Egloshayle Church, and a dinner was later held in a field at Bridge Park lent by Mr Norway.[3]

Fig 13.1 - Parade of Fire Brigades crossing Wade-Bridge from Egloshayle in 1907, Courtesy Margaret Thompson, from the Hilda Hambley Collection.

[3] *West Briton & Cornwall Advertiser*, 18th May 1860.

The field at Bridge Park is where Bridge View Estate stands now.   In July 1873 it was reported that members of the Wadebridge Band of Hope and the Independent Order of Good Templars made a 'grand demonstration'. The Templars clothed in appropriate regalia, the others bearing flags and banners and accompanied by brass bands, met at the Temperance Hall, formed a procession and perambulated the town before processing over the bridge.[4] A year later the Wadebridge Band of Hope again held their annual festival and procession, headed by a brass band, they marched from the town across the bridge and up Egloshayle Road to the parish church for a service.[5] Each time, supporters and spectators would line each side of the bridge to see the band, the procession and regalia.

Perhaps the most unusual and colourful procession to cross the bridge was on the 11th July 1907, when Wadebridge hosted a parade of the Cornish District of the National Fire Brigade Union, with sixteen fire brigades and some two hundred and thirty men, all in blue and red uniforms and wearing silver or brass helmets. Most of the brigades travelled to the town by train, although a few local brigades came by road with their engines. The parade was led by the Bodmin Brigade

Fig 13.2 - A Parade returning over Wade-Bridge after a service at Egloshayle Church in May 1910.

---

[4] *West Briton & Cornwall Advertiser*, 21st July 1873.
[5] *West Briton & Cornwall Advertiser*, 30th July 1874.

and the County Asylum brigade, both with their engines. The Lostwithiel Brigade with their steamer came next followed by the Wadebridge Volunteer Band under the direction of Mr R Elford. Behind the band came members of the remaining thirteen brigades. A report in the local newspaper stated that Wadebridge was making history, that it was a 'red-letter' day for the town, and that they could boast a spirit of enterprise and progress. Fig 13.1 shows the procession approaching Molesworth Street from the western end of the bridge.[6]

Fig 13.3 - American Troops marching across Wade-Bridge during the 'Salute the Soldier' parade on the 22nd April 1944. George Ellis Collection E8485, Courtesy The Cornwall Centre, Redruth.

The Wadebridge branch of the Ancient Order of Foresters later adopted Whit Monday for their annual parade, church service, fete and sports day. On the 20th May 1910, the *Cornish Guardian* reported that their parade left from Eddystone Road, and proceeded along The Platt, Gwendrock,

---

[6] *Cornish Guardian*, 12th July 1907, 6.

Hill Road, Trevanion Road, Polmorla Road, Park Road, Police Station, Molesworth Street, across the bridge and along Egloshayle Road to the parish church.[7]

Two days later on 22nd May 1910 another procession crossed the bridge heading for Egloshayle Church, when local organisations in the town held a memorial service following the death of King Edward VII. The rare surviving photograph of this event shows the procession on the bridge, walking down towards the level crossing on their way back from Egloshayle, (see fig 13.2).   It was led by twenty Masonic brethren from the Molesworth Lodge no.1954, followed by between forty and fifty Territorials under the command of Sergeant Instructor Grosch, with eighteen members of the Fire Brigade under the command of Captain Grant and a number of boys from both the Boy Scouts and Church Boys' brigade.

Following the First World War on 6th August 1920, there was a Comrades Church Parade, led by Wadebridge Town Band under the direction of Mr W T Lobb bandmaster. They marched from the town across the bridge and up to Egloshayle Church for a service of remembrance.[8]

In June 1924, the annual Whitsun church parade of the Wadebridge branch of the British Legion processed from the town hall, across the bridge, along Egloshayle Road to Egloshayle Church. This was led by Wadebridge Town Band, under the direction of bandmaster Mr W T Lobb, while the British Legion followed, along with Wadebridge Urban District Council, Girl Guides and Boy Scouts.[9]

Military parades took place to aid the war effort during the Second World War; one on the 22nd April 1944 saw a large combined force march across the bridge, including American troops who were based at Gonvena. The parade was part of a national 'Salute the Soldier' campaign promoted by the National Savings Committee to raise funds. The Wadebridge 'Salute the Soldier' week started on April 22nd to April 29th, with its aim to raise £150,000, the cost to equip an infantry battalion and a medical unit.   The parade assembled on Polmorla Road and marched across the bridge to the Egloshayle Recreation Ground and was led by the DCLI Band, followed by representatives from the Royal Navy, RNAS, Royal Marines, WRNS, Home Guard, Army Cadets, an American Army Band, a number of American troops with their national flag, the Women's Land Army, RAF, WAAF, local ATC, Wadebridge Town Band, Civil Defence Service, NFS, Red Cross Nurses and juniors, St John Nursing Division and Nursing Cadets and the wolf clubs. At

---

[7] *Cornish Guardian*, 20th May1910.

[8] *West Briton*, 6th August 1920.

[9] *Cornish Guardian*, 13th June 1924.

Egloshayle Recreation Ground the event was opened by Col E H W Bolitho, Lord Lieutenant of Cornwall, and there were speeches given by many senior officers and local dignitaries.[10]

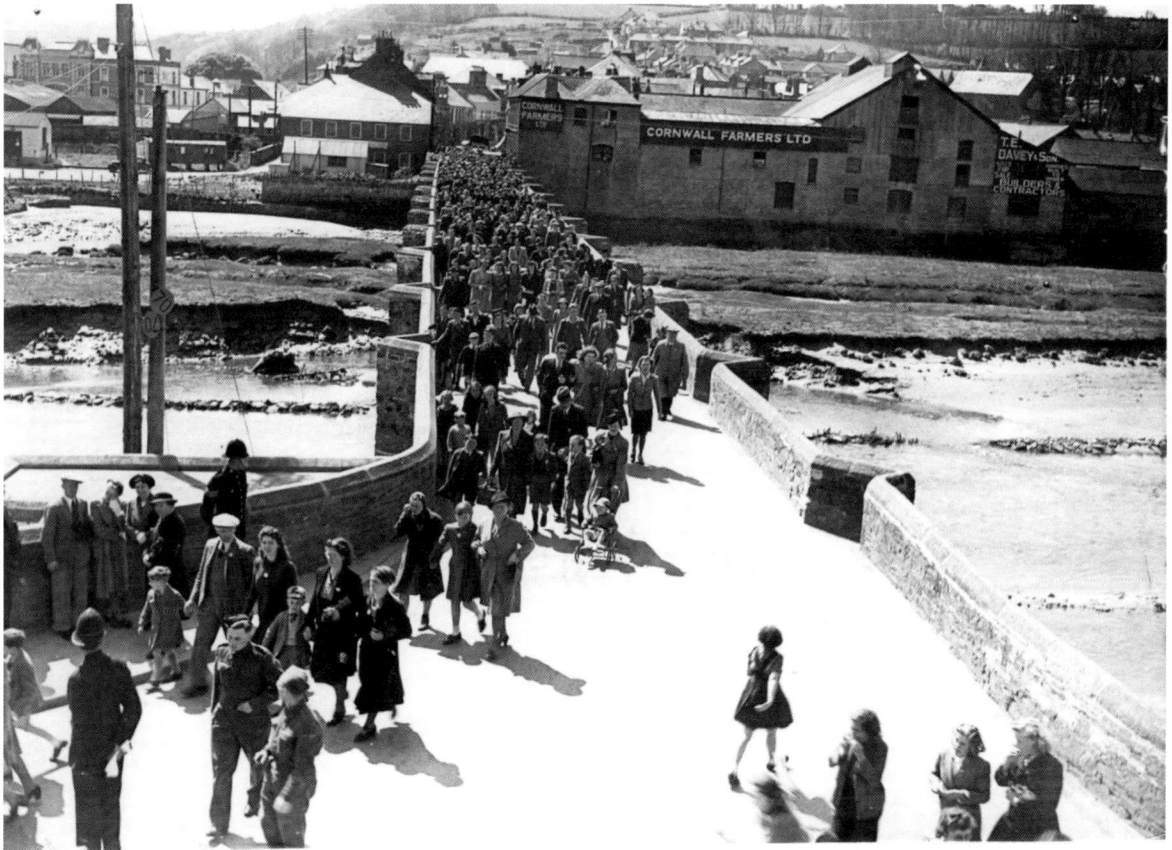

Fig 13.4 - Local people walking across Wade-Bridge behind the 'Salute the Soldier' parade on the 22nd April 1944. George Ellis Collection E8497, Courtesy The Cornwall Centre, Redruth.

Some of the most colourful processions on the bridge have included the annual Carnivals which used to cross the bridge, to terminate on the Recreation Ground at Egloshayle Road, but sadly today the Carnival only processes around the town. More recently, in September 2005, over two hundred and fifty Bards of the Cornish *Gorsedh* robed in blue processed across the bridge for their annual ceremony at the Recreation Ground, creating a ribbon of colour (plate 24a).

[10] *Cornish Guardian*, 2nd March 1944, 20th April 1944, 22nd April 1944 and the *Cornish & Devon Post*, 29th April 1944.

Throughout much of the second half of the twentieth century, one of the most common and informal processions across the bridge was that of pupils of the local boys school, walking every lunch time regardless of the weather from their school on West Hill, to the school canteen, which was at the Girls and Infants school on Egloshayle Road. This daily procession only ceased in 1992 when the boys and girls schools were amalgamated in one new school at Gonvena.

Gatherings on the bridge

In September 1907, many spectators lined both sides of the bridge to witness Donovan, a St Blazey athlete, give a demonstration of his running abilities. Donovan had taken a challenge to run a distance of a little over one and a half miles from the railway level crossing, across the bridge and up to Egloshayle Church and back, five times, making a total of nearly eight miles. He ran it in a time of just over forty seven minutes; a newspaper stated that *'his finishing sprint across the bridge with a little descent at the end was a remarkable piece of running'*.[11]

During the third week of May 1910, a large crowd of people gathered on the bridge in the evening so that they could obtain a clear and uninterrupted view of the sky. The group was amateur astronomers, who were rewarded for their patience when to their delight they witnessed Halley's Comet: a sight only seen once every seventy-six years.[12] In more recent years the bridge has again been linked with spectators looking skywards: not for a comet but to see the popular firework displays on New Years Eve. As ever, it is the bridge that is the main viewing platform.

Dangers to children

In chapter 11 we read of the large number of vehicle accidents recorded on the bridge and its approaches by the police before the bridge was widened; however there have been at least two occasions when children have fallen over the bridge and into the river below. These both occurred at the beginning of the twentieth century, but even today dangerous pranks have encouraged children and teenagers to take unnecessary risks walking on top of the parapet walls.

In *c*1900 a young girl called Gilbert fell over the side of the bridge when returning from school but was not badly hurt. However on the 4th October 1901 a little boy called Martin Burden aged about six, fell over the side of the bridge and was seriously injured. The child was coming home from school with a number of boys when he decided to climb the parapet wall beside Mr G Martyn's store. While looking down into the river a little girl accidently pushed him over into the harbour

---

[11] *Cornish Guardian* , 13th September 1907.
[12] *Cornish Guardian*, 27th May 1910, 4.

below injuring both his arm and head seriously.   He was rescued by Mr E Beare who was working nearby and waded into the river to bring the boy ashore.[13]

Visiting ships

Wadebridge was a tidal port, meaning that large vessels could only visit on the spring and high tides. These visitors were welcomed by the town, for they brought trade and sometimes provided a short-term employment opportunity on the quaysides, for local men loading and unloading their cargoes. The announcement of a ship visiting on a high tide would often attract a crowd to the quaysides and bridge. It is difficult now to comprehend how important the river Camel was to trade before the development of the town and railway in the nineteenth century; however Bartlett suggests that small ships had been getting up the river to trade at the quaysides for hundreds of years.[14] Their cargoes might include coal, nitrates, groceries, timber, rails, limestone or hardware. Early exports included corn and iron ore from neighbouring mines, later followed by granite, china clay and other minerals. The Victorian period was the busiest time for trade on the quaysides below the bridge and this in turn encouraged the development of the town.

One occasion that must have witnessed a major gathering on the bridge was the arrival of a ship from South Wales during the winter of 1833. It was not the ship that was important on this occasion, but its cargo, which was set to transform the history of the town. The cargo was the 'Camel', the first steam locomotive of the newly formed Bodmin and Wadebridge railway.

Another event that drew crowds to the bridge, quaysides and river walk was the annual visit by the Padstow Steam Lifeboat, the 'Helen Peele'. In August 1907, the lifeboat came up on the tide bedecked with flags and filled with children carrying collecting boxes for the Royal National Lifeboat Institution. On its return voyage, rockets were set off and the boat was illuminated with coloured lights.[15]

[13] *Cornish Guardian*, 4th October 1901, and the *Royal Cornwall Gazette*, 3rd. October 1901.
[14] Bartlett, J, 1996. *Ships of North Cornwall.*
[15] *Cornish Guardian*, 30th August 1907.

In March 1924, we hear of the revival of the shipping trade at Wadebridge with the arrival of three large steamers at the quaysides at one time: the SS Forester, SS Dunard and SS Emma Louise, with cargoes of coal, animal feed stuffs and manure.[16]   Even as late as 1962, the occasional large vessel visited the town.   In February of that year, the five hundred ton German trading vessel Nova with a three hundred ton cargo of farm fertilizer made a second visit to Wadebridge; on her first visit some months earlier, she had been the first ship to negotiate the Camel estuary for many years.   At the time it was hoped that the Nova's visit might herald a return of merchant trading on the Cornish river estuaries.[17]

Fig 13.5 - People lining the quaysides and Wade-Bridge to welcome home the Toria after winning the Round Britain race in 1966. Courtesy Wadebridge Old Cornwall Society.

---

[16] *Cornish Guardian*, 14th March 1924.

[17] *Cornish Guardian*, 6th February 1962, 7.

In August 1966, large crowds lined the bridge and quaysides to witness the triumphant return of the sloop-rigged centreboard trimaran Toria, from the two thousand mile Round Britain Race. The forty-two foot long trimaran was built by Derek Kelsall of the Multihull Construction Company at Trevilling Road, Wadebridge between January and May 1966 and sailed to victory by Mr Kelsall. On the 18th August spectators gathered to watch as a flotilla of small boats escorted the Toria from Padstow up the river to Wadebridge, where the skipper was welcomed by members of the town council and given an official reception at the Town Hall.[18] Eleven years later marked the building of a second popular vessel at Trevilling Road, the eighty foot passenger boat Jubilee Queen, by Brian Chapman at the Chapman & Hewitt boatyard. The boat, which cost £50,000 and was licensed to carry two hundred passengers, was launched on Saturday 2nd July 1977 amidst a large crowd of cheering onlookers.[19]

Regattas and fun on the river

Photographs and reports of Wadebridge during the Victorian period and throughout much of the twentieth century show that the river Camel - the town's most important natural asset was used far more than it is today.

Fig 13.6 - Spectators line Wade-Bridge and quaysides to watch the regatta.

---

[18] According to John Bartlett, *Ships of North Cornwall*, the Toria was renamed Gancia Girl in 1970.
[19] *Cornish Guardian*, 7th July 1977.

Regattas were a popular occasion in the town in the past. On Wednesday 29th August 1884, it was reported that the Annual Regatta at Wadebridge took place on a splendid tide and in beautiful weather. The Amazon steamer from Padstow brought a good number of people up to the town, while a special excursion train was laid on by the railway and brought a large number of people from Bodmin and surrounding district. The bridge over the Camel afforded an excellent view of the river which was occupied by several hundred people. The events included two-oared skiffs, two-oared light working boats, two-oared heavy working boats, two-oared light working boats for all comers, a scull race and a pair scull race.[20] Later in 1911, a regatta and sports day was resurrected after a lapse of several years. Again spectators lined the quaysides and the bridge to view the racing. The programme included two-oared light working boats, open sculling race, cutter rig sailing boats, centre keel punts and an open 440 yards swimming race for men. Spectators enjoyed the battle between the cutter-rigged boats *'Au Revoir'* of Wadebridge and 'White Heather' from Padstow.[21]

Separate annual swimming matches were often organised on the river, and it was reported that, *'on Saturday last* (September 1869), *spectators lined the bridge, quays, embankments and watched from the river in boats'*. The chief race was the thousand yards all comers match which was won by Dawe of Plymouth in 18 minutes 15 seconds; another match featured a local race between St Breock and Egloshayle men. There was an under 18 youths' six hundred yards; under 16s were taken upstream three hundred yards and were allowed to swim back with the tide, while the under 14s swam two hundred yards. There was also diving match'.[22]

Raft races often ended up with the participants swimming for the nearest bank. This annual event was very popular during the 1970s and 1980s but was perhaps stopped due to boisterous behaviour: sometimes the spectators on the bridge would end up wetter than those on the rafts. In July 1977, it was estimated that one thousand people lined the river banks and bridge to watch the annual raft race which was won for the third year by Johnny Beer.[23]

A more sedate race that starts at the old bridge and finishes at the Challenge Bridge is the Duck Race which is organized by the Wadebridge Scout Group. A small payment secures sponsorship of a duck; each are numbered and the sponsor of the winning duck wins a prize. In July 2010, fifteen hundred plastic ducks were launched from the parapet of the old bridge.

---

[20] *West Briton & Cornwall Advertiser*, 29th August 1884.
[21] *Cornish Guardian*, August 25th 1911.
[22] *West Briton & Cornwall Advertiser*, 9th September 1869.
[23] *Cornish Guardian*, 21st July 1977.

Fig 13.7 – Spectators at the 1974 Raft Race, note the wooden shields and flags on the lamp standards, Courtesy the Garfield Irons Collection.

Animals crossing the bridge

Before the advent of the motor car and occasionally after, local farmers living on the Egloshayle side of the bridge would herd their animals across the bridge to the market. Some residents still recall seeing flocks of sheep being led across the bridge to the cattle market in the town. Sometimes animals would escape from the market, one instance being in March 1909 when a bullock charged several persons on the Platt, knocking grocer and baker Mr William Nankivell unconscious and scattering the bread and cakes from his hand cart in all directions. The bullock then made for the bridge and after being chased into Martyn's timber yard was eventually caught. Perhaps the most unusual sight was on the 9th May 1962, during the second widening of the bridge when a herd of elephants was taken to Sir Robert Fossett's Circus and Zoo at Bodieve

179

Park. A notice in the newspaper read, *'See Fossett's mighty herd of Elephants walk from Wadebridge Station to the Circus ground, 12.30 from the station'.*[24]

Fig 13.8 - Elephants walking from the Circus site at Bodieve Park across
Wade-Bridge to the railway station, Courtesy the Garfield Irons Collection.

Decorating the Bridge

During the Victorian era and throughout much of the twentieth century the people of Wadebridge celebrated special occasions and Royal events by erecting massive evergreen arches across the entrance roads into the town or at either end of the old bridge. When the Royal Cornwall Agricultural Show first came to Wadebridge in 1895 a correspondent recorded that *'evergreen arches are springing up in all directions'*, although the report did not mention whether these were also placed on the approaches to the bridge. When the Agricultural Show again

---

[24] *Cornish Guardian*, April 19th 1962 , 3.

180

returned to the town in 1924, '*at various points seven huge arches covered with evergreens were set up and the bridge gaily decorated with hundred of bannerettes'*.

On the 12th May 1937, the town was again decorated, this time for the Coronation of King George VI and the *Cornish Guardian* reported, '*the famous old bridge which crosses the Camel calls for special mention for it has never before in its history looked so gay. Red, white and blue flags suspended from white standards fixed in the recesses of the bridge* (there being no lamp columns then) *ran the whole length of the structure on either side and huge arches erected at each end were becomingly decorated'*. An evergreen arch was also built over the main roads into the town and each arch was built by a different local builder and his men. A few weeks later the evergreen arches and decorations on the bridge were again being set up, this time because the Royal Cornwall Agricultural Show was being held at Bodieve Farm. The evergreen arches were always erected either end of the bridge rather than in the middle so that they were protected from any bad weather.

On several occasions the bridge has been decorated and lined with children and adults all waving union flags to welcome a member of the Royal family into the town. On 10th May 1927, the future King Edward VIII visited Wadebridge and was driven across the bridge in an open-top Daimler car. Prince Edward had attended the Royal Cornwall Agricultural Show at Truro the previous day and after staying the night at the Metropole Hotel in Padstow travelled through the town to visit Delabole Slate Quarry and the Lowermoor Water Treatment Works.[25] On the 11th July 1950 the town and bridge were again decorated for the arrival of King George VI, Queen Elizabeth (the Queen Mother) and Princess Margaret; this was the first time that a reigning monarch had ever officially visited Wadebridge. The royal car came down Egloshayle Road, turned onto the bridge at Bridge End and was driven slowly across the ancient bridge to a roar of welcome from those lining the route. Decorative evergreen arches were set up on Gonvena Hill, Egloshayle Road, West Hill and at Bridge End. The arch on Gonvena Hill showed a picture of the fifteenth century Bridge and swans on the river.[26] When local dignitaries were presented to the royal party outside the town hall, the Queen paused to admire the brilliantly coloured medallion on the chain of office of Mr Percy Spear, chairman of Wadebridge Parish Council, which showed a view of the old bridge.

Her majesty Queen Elizabeth II visited Wadebridge on Saturday 6th August 1977 while on her Silver Jubilee Tour. After leaving the royal ship Britannia at Falmouth she travelled through

[25] *Cornish Guardian*, 19th June 1927.

[26] *Cornish Guardian, Saltash Gazette and Cornwall County Chronicle*, 13th July 1950.

Penryn and Truro to the Royal Cornwall Agricultural Showground and later was driven down through Molesworth Street and across the bridge on her way to Bodmin.[27]

During the late 1960s some pedestrian refuges on either side of the bridge were built up with stone and used as flower borders with a miniature fir tree planted in each. Although few people may remember this, a photograph published in the *Cornish Guardian* of a snowy scene of the bridge showed the flower borders. A better idea to brighten the bridge with flowers came in the 1980s when brackets were fixed to the lamp columns to allow hanging baskets to be placed along each side of the bridge. The lamp columns, which had been erected on the bridge in 1963 were also used for fixing festive bunting or strings of lights at Christmas, and each year during the 1970s, a series of wooden shields each surmounted by three flags

Fig 13.9 - An evergreen Arch at the western end of Wade-Bridge in 1937, Courtesy Wadebridge Old Cornwall Society.

were fitted for the Royal Cornwall Agricultural Show. These can be seen in the photograph of the raft race (fig 13.7).

---

[27] *Cornish Guardian*, 4th August and 11th August 1977.

14   Conclusions

I am sure that there are further resources to be discovered with more information on the history of Wade-Bridge, but if I had continued to seek out those elusive fragments this book would never have been written. My conclusions are based on the material I have presented in this book and may need to be revised by others in the future as new material is discovered. Others may analyse the documentary evidence and present a different interpretation. This is certainly not the last word on Wade-Bridge but I hope that it provides a solid foundation for others to build on.

The bridge is the town's most precious asset, yet it is often ignored or at best taken for granted. The bridge is far more than a structure for just getting from one side of the river to the other. It gives the town of Wadebridge its name, it is an integral part of the town, it is a living bridge, part of the community, it is the town's promenade, its parade ground, viewing platform, meeting place, its history and identity.

Date of the bridge? Many historians who have written about the bridge have stated that it was built in a single year. However it is obvious that the construction of Wade-Bridge was a major project and would have taken many years. If one accepts John Lovibond is licensed to draw stone from a quarry in the manor of Penmayne in 1461, it marks the start date for building Wade-Bridge, and it is likely to have been completed by about 1476 when the Wade-Bridge Trust was set up by Lovibond, a year or so before his death, then the bridge must have taken at least 15 years to build.

Was it John or Thomas Lovibond who was responsible? All the evidence I have found leads me to conclude that the Reverend John Lovibond was the mastermind behind the building of Wade-Bridge. I have found no surviving documents recording a Thomas Lovibond. Thomas Lovibond appears to be the creation of the notoriously unreliable historian William Hals.

John Lovibond is part of the history of Wadebridge. John Lovibond is to Wadebridge what Richard Trevithick is to Camborne or William Murdoch is to Redruth. If Wadebridge was to have a special day of celebration annually (other than the Royal Cornwall Agricultural Show) perhaps it should be known as 'Lovibond Day'.

Causeway   In this work, I have identified that the bottom of Molesworth Street from the road junction with Eddystone Road to the junction with Harbour Road was originally a ramped causeway. This causeway raised the ground level from what would have been marsh and flood plain at the Platt up to the western abutment of the original bridge, a height of almost two metres.

The 'Bridge on Wool' Legend   The building of Wade-Bridge and its history is not unusual, but typical of its period, however the challenge faced by medieval builders to provide a stable foundation has put the town of Wadebridge firmly on the tourist map as the place of the 'Bridge on Wool'.   I have been unable to prove whether the bridge was built on wool sacks, but would suggest that wool could have easily been used with other natural materials in the construction of the foundations; and as a Wadebridge boy, I feel we should cherish the legend as it is part of the town's cultural identity.   Nevertheless, whether or not it was the wool that secured a firm foundation, Wade-Bridge was built with uniform width arches, a feat that eluded the builders of Bideford, Barnstaple, Exeter and Looe. Lovibond and his architect overcame the problem of building on silt and were able to precisely set each pier of the bridge.

Who financed the building of the bridge?   It is clear that neither the parishes of St Breock nor Egloshayle had the resources to build such a long and massive structure and the reason for building the bridge was not simply to link two parishes together. Here I have argued that the powerful and wealthy landowners who would have benefitted from a bridge across the river would have been the main protagonists in this venture. Chief amongst these would have been the Arundell family, perhaps aided by the Duchy and other landowners across north Cornwall. There is no evidence that their wealth necessarily came from the wool trade.

How long was the bridge and its causeway?   The length of the original bridge is recorded in the original 1852 plan of Wade-Bridge that hangs on the wall in the Wadebridge Town Hall. Although it only depicts fifteen arches since two had already been blocked up, the total length of the bridge was 503 ft (153.3m) or 680ft (207.3m) if the western ramped causeway and eastern end is included.

Where are the missing arches and when were they blocked?   The first and last arches, 1 and 17 were blocked up before the nineteenth century; the first arch still survives as a locked cellar on the Egloshayle side of the river, while arch 17 is beneath the road junction between Molesworth Street and Harbour Road.   Arches 15 and 16 were blocked up in 1868 when John Martyn's store was built. This was later Cornwall Farmers and is where the Bridal shop stands today.   There is no evidence to support the rumour that the arches of the bridge can be seen from the cellars of the shops in 1, 3, and 5 Molesworth Street: the arches of the bridge did not extend that far west, and the line of the original bridge did not come close to the front of the shops.

How does Wade-Bridge compare with other medieval bridges in Cornwall, Devon and elsewhere? Today Wade-Bridge closely resembles Barnstaple Bridge. The two are similar in length, have been widened using similar techniques and were both widened in 1962-63 by the Cleveland

Bridge Company.   Wade-Bridge is the youngest of the long bridges in Cornwall and Devon and sometimes wrongly compared with Bideford which still has twenty-four arches, a much longer structure. Today, Wade-Bridge is the only long bridge in Cornwall and Devon that still retains its pedestrian refuges, albeit much smaller in size, the bridges at Bideford, Barnstaple and Looe no longer have this feature.

Maintenance Wade-Bridge will always require a great deal of maintenance, and its recent history suggests that repairs and restoration work have taken place approximately once every ten years (as recorded in chapter 12) and is due for further repairs during the next few years.

Costs It is difficult to assess how much the original bridge would have cost, however the projects to widen, strengthen and refurnish Wade-Bridge show how costs have inflated. In 1852-53, the first widening cost £1,113; the second widening during 1962-63 cost £215,178. The strengthening work in 1975 cost £425,000, while the refurbishment in 1993 cost £250,000.   The next major work on Wade-Bridge is likely to cost several million pounds.

Appendices

I   *Glossary of terms*

Abutment - part of a pier, or wall against which an arch rests.

Agnus dei - image of the Lamb of God.

Appurtenances - minor rights and privileges.

Buckler - 'sword and buckler' a buckler is a small circular shield used with a short sword.

Causeway - a raised road across marshy ground, or shallow water.

Chantry chapel - a chapel or part of a church, where priests say a daily mass for a deceased person, or persons.

Corbel - projection of stone, or wood to support a beam, arch, parapet or moulding.

Cutwater - a pointed, or angular projection of a pier, formed to force the flow of water either side of the pier, to help prevent scouring damage.

Disbursements - expenses, total spent for goods and services, including money, time and labour.

Dragoon - infantry man armed with a carbine (light short-barrelled rifle).

Feoffee - feoffee is a word used at the end of the feudal period and during the middle ages for a trustee.

Feoffments - transfer of property that gave the new owner the right to sell land as well as the right to pass it on to his heirs.

Halbard - a weapon used between the fourteenth and sixteenth centuries consisting of a long shaft with an axe-blade, pick, and topped with a spear head.

Hereditament - any property that can be inherited.

Messuages - dwelling house with adjacent buildings and land used by a household.

Noble - medieval gold coin worth six shillings and eight pence.

Parapet - a low, or brest-high wall at the edge of a bridge.

Pedestrian refuge - the triangular recess in the parapet walls of a medieval bridge, built above the cutwaters for the protection of pedestrians against traffic.

Pontage - a toll exclusively for the maintenance of a bridge, or bridges.

Purgatory - condition or process of the purification or temporary punishment in which, it is believed, the souls of those who die in a state of grace are made ready for heaven.

Scouring - erosion of either the river bed, or piers of a bridge, by the force of water flowing by.

Seizin - possession of a freehold estate.

Spandrel - the space between the shoulder of an arch end and the rectangular moulding enclosing it, or between the shoulders of adjoining arches and the moulding.

Starling or Sterling - wedged-shaped constructions built around the base of piers to protect them from scouring.

Suit of service - having to attend the courts of their lords or superiors in time of peace and in war to follow them into military service.

Voussoir - one of the wedge-shaped stones forming an arch.

Windlasses - basket work formed from either holly or hazel branches woven to hold or support stones.

II   *Chronology of Wade and the Wade-Bridge*

1382	First mention of St Michael's chapel.
1461-2	John Lovibond licence to draw stone from the manor of Penmayne.
1468	John Lovibond still drawing stone.
1476	John Lovibond's Charter of Endowment.
1477	Death of John Lovibond.
1478	William of Worcester writes of a visit to Wade-Bridge.
1485	Hals gives date of bridge construction.
1530	The Bridge Act established, sometimes known as the Statute of Bridges.
1531	Christopher Tredeneck bequeathed 3s 4d to the store of Wade-Bridge.
1538	John Leland gave an account of the bridge.
1542	Armed assault on Wade-Bridge between John Tredeneck and George Wolcoke.
1577	A quarter of Cuthbert Mayne's body was exhibited on the bridge (and possibly his head).
1577	James Cater donates funds collected by the Blanchminster Charity for the maintenance of the bridge.
1586	Edward Arundell leaves money in his will for the repair of Wade-Bridge.
1591	St Michael's and the King's chapels granted to William Tipper and Robert Dawe.
1602	Richard Carew of Antony describes the bridge as: 'the longest, strongest and fairest that the shire can muster'.
1611	George Juell, a St Teath Helier, donates funds to Wade-Bridge.
1646	Oliver Cromwell and his troops hold Wade-Bridge.
1662	First record of stone being quarried at Park Quarry for the maintenance of Wade-Bridge.
1670	Account of Henry Hocker, Bridge Warden.
1698	Celia Fiennes crosses Wade-Bridge on a side saddle.
1714	Stone drawn from Park Quarry to repair the bridge.
1759	Act of Parliament to create a turnpike from Halworthy via Wade-Bridge to Mitchell.
1759	Borlase publishes his well known illustration of Wade-Bridge.
1771	Contract for new paving for Wade-Bridge.
1808	Revd. Warner tours Cornwall, crossing the river Camel at Rock.
1818	Tenders to renew the parapets etc.
1818	Proposed scheme to widen the central arches of the Wade-Bridge.
1828	Contract to pull down parapet walls of bridge and renew with stone from Dunveth quarry.
1838	Wadebridge Institution building completed.
1839	First lecture at the Wadebridge Institution.
1840s	Mr Martyn's timber wagon broke down on the bridge to delay the Revd. Molesworth.
1842	Cyrus Redding records a fine fig tree built into the wall of Wade-Bridge on the downstream side.

1844	Proposed damming of the river with sluice gates below Wade-Bridge.
1845	Wombwell's Caravan of wild beasts and menagerie became stuck on Wade-Bridge.
1845	First traffic census at Wade-Bridge.
1847	Great flood on the rivers Camel and Inney, and the widening of Wade-bridge postponed.
1847	Plan to widen Wade-Bridge with iron parapets.
1852	First widening of Wade-Bridge started.
1853	Wade-Bridge Trust wound up and the maintenance of the bridge transferred to the County.
1853	First widening of Wade-Bridge completed.
1854	First gas lamp fitted on Wade-Bridge.
1868	Arches 15 and 16 blocked up when John Martyn's warehouse was built.
1872	John Martyn's warehouse completed.
1877	Proposal to extend the quaysides and block up another three arches.
1878	Disagreements about the training walls in the river and the diversion of the river channels.
1901	The first motor car recorded in Wadebridge.
1907	Procession of Fire Brigades across Wade-Bridge.
1910	Parade to commemorate the death of Edward VII.
1912	Wadebridge Institution closed.
1925	Estimates received for a proposed footbridge alongside Wade-Bridge.
1928	Wade-Bridge scheduled as an Ancient Monument.
1935	Mr Uniacke's scheme to widen Wade-Bridge.
1954	Riverside House demolished at Bridge End.
1962	Second Wade-Bridge widening started.
1963	Second Wade-Bridge widening completed.
1972	Plans drawn up to stabilise foundations of the old downstream side of Wade-Bridge.
1976	Strengthening of the foundations of the downstream side of Wade-Bridge started.
1987	Repairs to the 1962-63 concrete arch ribs on the upstream side of Wade-Bridge.
1991	Challenge Bridge built by Anneka Rice and her team.
1991	Wadebridge Bypass Bridge started.
1993	Wadebridge Bypass Bridge opened.
1993	Culvert arches at right angles to the bridge discovered by British Gas at Bridge End.
1994	Refurbishment of Wade-Bridge including waterproofing the deck, and upgrading services.

III   Bridge Wardens of Wade-Bridge

This list of names has been extracted from documentary sources, but is by no means a complete list of the Bridge Wardens of Wade-Bridge. They are written as they appear in each document.

1660	William Hocker and William Pedlar.
1666	John Pettigrew, Tho. Blake, Mathew Hid and Rich Jeffery.
1670	John Opye and James Ford for Egloshayle, Henry Hocker and Mathew Michell gent. for St Breoke.
1681	Walter Reynolds and Rich. Tooker.
1684	Sir John Molesworth and Mr Henry Hocker.
1669	John Tregagle of Trevorder and Wm. Mathew, minister of St Breoke.
1686	Henry Hocker and James Kestell.
1730	John Whiteborne and Walter Wood.
1714	Charles Ustick, gentleman and John Peirce.

IV   Trustees of Wade-Bridge

This list of names has been extracted from documentary sources and is by no means a complete list of the Trustees of Wade-Bridge.   They are written as they appear in each document.

1476   Original trustees:
          Thomas Arundell Esquire. *(Sir Thomas Arundell of Lanherne, St Mawgan in Pydar).*
          Edward Courtnay Esquire *(of Boconnoc, created Earl of Devon in 1485).*
          John Carmynowe Esquire *(John Carminow of Glynn, Cardinham).*
          John Reskarack Esquire *(John Roscarrock, owner of Croan and Lamayle in Egloshayle).*
          Michael Pedyt.
          Richard Bylyon *(Richard Billing of Trevorder in St Breoke, an executor to Lovibond and also owner of Treworder in Egloshayle).*
          Thomas Bera *(Thomas Bere of Pengelly in St Breoke).*
          Thomas Lymbery *(of Padstow was steward to all the Arundell Lands in Cornwall from 1478-79).*
          Thomas Bera Junior.
          Richard Tomeow *(of St Columb Major).*
          Richard Trefry otherwise Tremer.
          Robert Loveybound.
          John Forth *(a husbandman from Egloshayle, and an executor to Lovibond).*

1586   Nich. Prydeaux *(of Prideaux Place, Padstow).*
          Tho. Castell *(Thomas Castell).*
          Chr. Collyer *(Christopher Collyer, vicar of Egloshayle 1609-1633).*
          Rad. Kestell.

1632   Nic Prideaux *(of Prideaux Place, Padstow).*
          Mw. Castell *(Matthew Castell).*
          Chr. Collyer *(Christopher Collyer, vicar of Egloshayle 1609-1633).*

1636   John Prideaux Esqr. *(of St Breoke).*
          Tho. Kestell gt. *(Thomas Kestell of Pendavey in Egloshayle).*
          Henry Hole *(vicar of Egloshayle 1634-1659).*

1651   Henry Hole clerk *(vicar of Egloshayle 1634-1659).*
          Hanniball Kestell Esq.

1667   Nich. Courtenay Esq. *(Nicholas Courtenay).*
          Wm. Mathew *(William Mathew, vicar of Egloshayle 1659-1681).*

1669   Wm. Mathew *(William Mathew, vicar of Egloshayle 1659-1681).*
          Jo. Tregagle *(John Tregagle, steward at Treworder, St Breock).*
          Ric. Gregory Craven *(Richard Gregory Craven).*

1678   John Tregagle Esq.
          William Mathew *(vicar of Egloshayle 1659-1681).*

1682   Jo. Molesworth *(Sir John Molesworth of Pencarrow).*
          Jas. Kestell *(James Kestell of Kestle).*

189

1693 Thomas Brabant.
    Willm. Hocker *(William Hocker).*
    Ricd. Marshall *(Richard Marshall).*
    Wm. Kestle *(William Kestle).*
    Nicholas Parnall.
    Nic. May *(Nicholas May, vicar of Egloshayle 1681-1708).*
    James Kestle of Kestle.
    Sir John Molesworth.

1695 Sir John Molesworth *(of Pencarrow, Egloshayle).*
    John Tregagle, *(steward at Treworder in St Breock).*
    Nathaniel Moyle *(of Pendavey, Egloshayle).*

1698 Sir John Molesworth Kt. Bt. *(of Pencarrow, Egloshayle).*
    James Kestle Esqr. *(of Kestle in Egloshayle).*

1701 Jo. Molesworth. *(John Molesworth of Pencarrow, Egloshayle).*
    Ja. Kestell. *(James Kestell).*

1705 Ja. Kestell. *(James Kestell).*

1721 Sir John Molesworth *(of Pencarrow).*
    Carolus Pole *(rector of St Breock 1720-1730).*
    Ed. Hoblyn *(Edward Hoblyn of Croan in Egloshayle).*
    Jo. Hathaway *(John Hathaway, vicar of Egloshayle 1708-1730).*

1726 Edmd. Prideaux Esqr. *(of Prideaux Place, Padstow).*
    Carolus Pole *(rector of St Breock 1720-1730).*
    Edmd. Hoblyn Esqr. *(Edward Hoblyn of Croan in Egloshayle).*
    John Hathaway, clerk *(vicar of Egloshayle 1708-1730).*

1727 Carolus Pole *(rector of St Breock 1720-1730).*
    Ed. Hoblyn *(Edward Hoblyn of Croan in Egloshayle).*
    John Hathaway, *(vicar of Egloshayle 1708-1730).*

1730 Sir John Molesworth *(of Pencarrow, Egloshayle).*
    Edward Prideaux *(of Prideaux Place, Padstow).*
    John Hoblyn.
    Wm. Ford *(William Ford, vicar of Egloshayle 1730-1731).*
    H. Lukey.

1737 Sir John Molesworth Bart. *(of Pencarrow, Egloshayle).*
    Edmd. Prideaux *(Edmund Prideaux of Prideaux Place, Padstow).*
    Robt. Brynher. *(Robert Brynher).*
    Cornelius Crawford *(vicar of Egloshayle 1733-1753).*

1765 John Molesworth Esq. *(of Pencarrow, Egloshayle).*
    Ro. Dennis clerk *(Robert Dennis).*
    Henry Peers, clerk, *(vicar of Egloshayle 1761-1793).*

1771 Sir John Molesworth Bart. *(of Pencarrow, Egloshayle).*

Edmund Prideaux *(of Prideaux Place, Padstow).*
Robert Dennis.
Henry Peers, *(vicar of Egloshayle).*

1772 Sir John Molesworth Bart. *(of Pencarrow, Egloshayle).*
James Cory *(rector of St Breock 1771-1787).*
Henry Peers *(vicar of Egloshayle 1761-1793).*

1774 Sir John Molesworth Bart. *(of Pencarrow, Egloshayle).*
James Cory *(rector of St Breock 1771-1787).*
Henry Peers, clerk *(vicar of Egloshayle 1761-1793).*

1786 Sir William Molesworth *(of Pencarrow, Egloshayle).*
Rev. James Cory *(rector of St Breock 1771-1787).*
Henry Peers *(vicar of Egloshayle 1761-1793).*

1799 Revd. Sir Harry Trelawny Bt. *(Revd. Sir Henry Trelawny Bart., vicar of Egloshayle 1793-1804).*
Revd. John Molesworth *(rector of St Breock).*

1818 Sir A O Molesworth *(of Pencarrow, Egloshayle).*
Revd. Charles Prideaux-Brune.
Revd. W. Molesworth *(rector of St Breock 1816-1831).*
Revd. Rich. Cory, *(Richard Cory, vicar of Egloshayle 1804-1833).*

1828 Sir Arscott Ourry Molesworth Bt. *(of Pencarrow, Egloshayle).*
Revd. Charles Prideaux-Brune *(of Prideaux Place, Padstow).*
Revd. William Molesworth *(rector of St Breock 1816 -1831).*
Revd. Richd. Cory, clerk *(Richard Cory, vicar of Egloshayle 1804-1833).*

1852 Sir Charles Lemon *(of Carclew House, Devoran).*
Sir William Salisbury Lewis Trelawny.
Revd. W. Molesworth *(rector of St Breock 1816-1831).*
Chas. Prideaux *(Charles Prideaux-Brune of Prideaux Place, Padstow).*
Sir William Molesworth *(of Pencarrow, Egloshayle).*
Revd. Thos. Stackhouse Carlyon *(Rev Thomas Stackhouse Carlyon, vicar of Egloshayle 1833-1849)*

1853 The Wade-Bridge Trust was dissolved.

V   The statement of accounts for the widening of Wade-Bridge 1853

(Reported in the Royal Cornwall Gazette on Friday 21st October 1853)

In addition to the contract, the committee have thought it right from certain indications of weakness, to have the old piers newly cased throughout, at an extra expense of about £150, and iron girders have also been laid across the arches but the committee are glad to say that not only has every charge been met by the sale of the Trust Lands, but that a balance of £244 18s. will now be handed to the treasurer of the County.

To balance of rent in Mr Symon's hand	£651 4s 5d
Proceeds of sale of property	£950
Amount of sale of stock	£317 0s 4d
Two and a half years' dividends	£25 4s 7d
Total	**£1357 19s 4d**
By Nichols and Co., for Casing piers	£189 10s
Chancery charges	£151 2s 2d
Parliamentary charges	£231 2s 2d
Clerk of the works	£67 10s
Expenses on sale of property and stock etc.	£44 12s 3d
Messrs. Coodes' bill	£15 10s 4d
Surveyors amount	£33 12s
Contractors' account	£587 12s 5d
Total	**£1113 1s 4d**
Left in balance	£244 18s

VI   Cost of the second widening 1963

Total price of contract	£215,178

VII   *Place-names, Wade and Wadebridge*

1360	*Wade in decenn' de Poughton*	Assize Plea Rolls, (National Archives)
1382	*Capella de Wade*	Episcopal Register of Thomas Stayndope
1423	*Wade*	Feet of Fines, (National Archives)
1476	*Wada Bridge*	Charter of Endowment
1478	*Wade-brygge*	William of Worcester
1576	*Wadebryge*	William Carnsew Diary, JRIC 33, Bokelly Diary
1577	*Wade brydge*	Blanchminster Charity Records
1577	*Wadbridge*	Sentence of Cuthbert Mayne
1582	*Wade-brig*	*The Briefe Historie* (McEloy)
1584	*Waade bridg*	John Norden's map of Cornwall
1646	*Warebridge*	Moderate Intelligencer 1645
1670	*Wardebridge*	Accounts of Bridge Wardens
1675	*Warbridge*	John Ogilby's map
c1694	*Ware bridg*	*Lanhydrock Atlas* by Joel Gasgoine
1698	*Waybridge*	Celia Fiennes
1699	*Wade bridg*	Map of the County of Cornwall by Joel Gasgoine
1741	*Warbrige*	*Diary of an unknown traveller* (Todd Gray)
1750	*Wad bridge*	Dr Richard Pococke's itinerary
1755	*Wardbridge*	Revd. William Wynne's itinerary
1724-6	*Wod bridge*	Daniel Defoe
ND	*Wydebrygge*	Devon County Record Office 74/9/2/2

BIBLIOGRAPHY

I   *Primary Sources*

Cornwall Record Office - Documents relating to Wade-Bridge.

DDX.450/181   John Loveybound's Charter of Endowment, creating the Bridge Trust in 1476.

DDX450/85   Porthmizen Mill, near Padstow. Accounts and receipts for rent and land tax, 1688-1751.

DDX450/86   Plan of Porthmizen Mill, n.d. c.1820-1830.

DDX450/87/1, 2   Letters to Mr Symons, Wadebridge, from Jn. Old concerning Porthmizen Lease 1845.

Trust papers, Rents and rent accounts.

DDX450/100   Receipt paid by Wm. Stone, high rent due to Manor of Burneire out of parcel of land which he holds of the bridge, 1682.

DDX450/101   Order by Trustees to Wm. Nott to pay Rich. Pascoe £5 for rent, 1701.

DDX450/102   Summary of rents received (names only) 1706.

DDX450/103   Accounts of rent due to Wade-Bridge, 1750-1751.

DDX450/04   Receipt for land tax for the Bridge land in Egloshayle churchtown paid by Wm. Rundell, 1751.

DDX450/05   Rough rental of Conventionary and Rack tenants, n.d. c.1750.

DDX450/106   Survey of Wadebridge lands with summary of leases for lives and rents, c.1775.

DDX450/107   Rental of Wadebridge lands, 1795.

DDX450/108   Rental of Conventionary and Rack tenants, 1791.

DDX450/109   List of Coventionary rents due for bridge lands 1814.

Bridge Wardens Accounts

DDX450/110   Account of Wm. Hocker and Wm. Pedlar, Bridge Wardens, 1660.

DDX450/111   Disbursements towards repair of bridge, 1663.

DDX450/112   Disbursements for the bridge, 1663.

DDX450/113   Account of Jn. Pettigrew, Thos. Blake, Mathew Hidern and Rich Jeffery, 1666.

DDX450/114   Bridge Account, 1667.

DDX450/115	Account of Jn. Tregagle of Trevorder Esq. and Wm. Mathews, minister of Egloshayle, Bridge Wardens, 1669.
DDX450/116	Jas. Ford's disbursements for the bridge, 1670.
DDX450/117	Jn. Opye and Mr Michell's disbursements for the bridge, 1670.
DDX450/118	Summary of Bridge Wardens' expenses, 1670.
DDX450/119	Account of Jn. Opye and Jas. Ford (Egloshayle) and Hen. Hocker and Mathew Michell (St Breock) Bridge Wardens, 1670, with a note requesting for those in debt to the Trust to pay up.
DDX450/120	Account for repairs to bridge, 1673.
DDX450/121	Part only of Hen. Hocker's disbursements for the bridge, 1674.
DDX450/122	Mr Hocker's account, 1675.
DDX450/123	Disbursements of Jn. Hocker towards repairing the bridge, 1678.
DDX450/124	Disbursements of Bridge Wardens for loads of stone, 1679.
DDX450/125	Receipts by W. Hicks for £1 5s 0d rent from John Opie for 15 years drawing stones for bridge, 1681.
DDX450/126	Disbursements of Walter Reynard and Rich. Tooker, 1681.
DDX450/127	Disbursements about Wade-Bridge, 1682.
DDX450/128	Disbursements of Wm. Pridham for repairs to bridge, 1682.
DDX450/129	Bridge Wardens' Account, with list of rents received, 1682.
DDX450/130	Accounts of Hen. Hocker and Jn. Burrowes, 1682-1683.
DDX450/131	Accounts of Sir Jn. Molesworth and Hen. Hocker, 1684.
DDX450/132	Accounts of Hen. Hocker and Jas. Kestell, 1686.
DDX450/133	Accounts of Jn. Mynard and Thos. Blake, 1689.
DDX450/134	Account of Peter Blake to Eliz. Robins *'for the Bridge'*, 1690.
DDX450/135	Disbursements Nich Lukey and Walter Reynard, n.d. 17th cent. endorsed: list of St Breock debtors.
DDX450/136	Peter Blake's disbursements for the bridge, n.d. 17th cent.
DDX450/137	Phil Payne and M. Mitchell's disbursements for the bridge, n.d. 17th cent. endorsed: list of Egloshayle debtors.
DDX450/138	Bill and receipt of Nich Ellyott for lime etc. for the bridge, supplied to Tregagell, n.d. 17th cent.
DDX450/139/1-5	Bridge Wardens Accounts (unnamed) n.d. 17th cent.

DDX450/140	Receipt by Edw. Hoblyn for 10s paid by Bridge Trustees for rent for drawing stones in Park quarry, 1701.
DDX450/141	Chas. Ustick and Jn. Peirce's account, 1714-1719.
DDX450/142	Account for mason's work, 1718-1719.
DDX450/143	Wm. Lobb's bill for work done about the bridge, 1719.
DDX450/144	Account of Jn. Hodges and Peter Rescorla, 1728-1728.
DDX450/145	Account of Jn. Hodges and Peter Rescorla, 1728-1729, with account of money due to the bridge account, 1701, 1721-1730.
DDX450/146	Account of Jn. Whiteborne and Walter Wood, 1730.
DDX450/147	Account of Jn. Whiteborne and Walter Wood, 1731.
DDX450/148	Bridge Wardens' disbursements (not named), 1733.
DDX450/149	Bridge Wardens' disbursements (not named), 1734.
DDX450/150	John Whiteborne's disbursements about Wade Bridge, 1740.
DDX450/151	Account of mason's work on bridge, 1744.
DDX450/152	Bridge Wardens' Account, 1744.
DDX450/153	Draft Bridge Wardens' Accounts 1745-1746.
DDX450/154	Mason's bill for work on bridge, 1745-1748.
DDX450/155	Cover only of Wade-Bridge Accounts, 1750-1751.
DDX450/156	Account of Geo. Borlase with Trustees of Bridge, 1790-1799.
DDX450/157	Account of Geo. Borlase with Trustees of Bridge, 1812-1814.

Bonds

DDX450/158 -165	Eight bonds dating between 1636 and 1695.
DDX450/166	Wm. Stone's receipt for 20 shillings paid by Nich Opie, 'Upon Account of Wade-Bridge', 1678.
DDX450/167	Memorandum of gift of Edw. Arundell, 1586.
DDX450/168	Writ to Francis Grigg to distrain Penalegan Richards to appear at Pawton Manor Court to answer Henry Hall, clerk and Hanniball Kestell, Esq. 1651.
DDX450/169	Fragment only of bill? for audit dinner, n.d. *c.*1680.

DDX450/170	List of persons to appear, with account of money due, 1691.
DDX450/171	Memorandum that Francis Grigg owes for 6 years', use of £2 10s 0d. also of bond of Rich. Brabant, Jn. and Wm. Woolcock of debt to Bridge Trustees, n.d. 17th. cent.
DDX450/172	Receipt of Jn. Kestell for £1 1s 2d paid by Chris. Hull towards his debt due to Wade-Bridge 1705.
DDX450/173	Lodging bill, Wadebridge 1818.

Leases

DDX450/174 -179	Six leases relating to Wade-Bridge Trust property in Egloshayle Churchtown.

General

DDX450/180/1, 2	Part of letters from ? of St Breock to Rich. Symons re: Wade-Bridge, enclosing part of Sir Arscott's letter re: necessary repairs, widening centre of bridge etc.
DDX450/181	Translation of grant of 21st Oct. 1476.
DDX450/182	Chancery Case (unopposed): brief for petitioners on behalf of Wadebridge Charity Trustees. Sir Wm. Molesworth of Pencarrow, Sir Chas. Lemon of Carclew, Sir W. Lewis Salisbury Trelawny of Harewood. Recites: grant of Jn. Loveybond (as above).
DDX450/183	Draft petition in Chancery concerning repairs to bridge 1852.
DDX450/184	Abstract of title of Trustees of the Bridge to the Trust estate in Egloshayle and Padstow, 1836-1853.
DDX364/20	Demolition of Riverside House, Wadebridge , 1954.

Official

AU3/8/5/54	Padstow Harbour Commissioners re: County Surveyor and Training walls at Wadebridge. 1878.
QS/PDH/15/1	Plans and sections: Padstow harbour and creek's, improvements of the harbour and wharf at Wadebridge, including book of reference 1843.

Churchwarden A/Cs. St Breock

DDP19/5/1	fo.13v. contd. 'for standing at St Mychaells chapell at ye fere (fair) 11d, 1566.
	fo.15. William Well hath taken of the parish of St Michael Chapell for the term of 7 years yelding and paying therefore yearly/ to rent to the church wardens on behalf of the parish, 1565.
	fo.17. Item rec for a standing in St Mychaells chapell haye 2d. Item rec of M Vyell for 3 years rent for St Mychaell chapell due before this a/c 12s., 1556.
	fo.20. Standing in St Michaels Chapel haye 4d. for M. Vyell for St Mich. Chapell rent 6s., 1568.
	fo 21. For a standing in St Mychaells chapel haye 6d., 1569.

fo 22. Care of halt thowsyn 500 of helying stone to St Mychaells ch apel & the bringing of gar ? to the cherche. 8d. for the helyer for helying of St Mychaells chapel 2s., 1569.

fo 25. Rec. of Master Vyell for S Mich Chapel rent 2yrs. 12s., 1571.

fo 26v . M. Vyell St Mich. Chapel 6s., 1572.

fo 34v . For the store howse at the bryge 2yrs. rent 12s., 1575.

fo 38. John Martyn hath taken of par. St Michael Chapel per term of 7yrs. paying 18s. p.a., 1576.

John Martyn for rent St Michael Chapel 18s., 1578.

Blanchminster Charity Records, Edited by R. R. Goulding

Stockwardens Account Book for Stratton 1557 - 1581.

Item payde to James Cater for the collecyon for Wade brydge ijs. vjd. (2s. 6d.), p69, 1577.

Leases

DDCF904 -909   Six leases on a dwelling house known as *The Chapple* near Wade-Bridge, dated between 1758 and 1826.

New accession to Cornwall Record Office by Macmillians Solicitors, Wadebridge in May 2010

AD2040/1/1	Lease of Porthmisson Mills, Padstow from Wade-Bridge Trustees to William Abott, miller, dated 25th December 1693.
AD2040/1/2	Lease of Porthmisson Mills, Padstow from Wade-Bridge Trustees to William Abott, miller, dated 25th December 1698.
AD2040/2	Lease of Bridge Lands, Bridge House on Wade-Bridge built by Humphrey Sink deceased on the east side of Wade-Bridge, dated 30th November 1786.
AD2040/3	Conditions of survey (auction) for leasing Chings (Chirsy) House and premises in Egloshayle Churchtown, including a list of bidders.
AD2040/4 -17	Fourteen leases of the Wade-Bridge Tolls including bidders, dated between 1799 and 1829.
AD2040/18	Article of Agreement to pave the bridge, between the Trustees and one James Carter of the borough of Lostwithiel, dated 24th June 1771.
AD2040/19	Contract to repair Wade-Bridge, replace parapets, re-point piers etc. by James Collins of St Breock and John Ellory of Egloshayle, Masons, dated 30th April 1818.
AD2040/20	Contract for re-paving the bridge by John Haynes of the borough of Bodmin on 7th March 1828.

AD2040/21	Specification of repairs proposed to be done on Wade-Bridge dated 15th October 1818, report by James Chapple, Trust surveyor, also Jas. Collins and John Ellory's tender to do the work, dated 21st March 1818.
AD2040/22	Letter to Mr W Symons, Solicitor, Wadebridge from Mr Oliver Rouce at Tetcott, Devon.
AD2040/23	A plan of Wadebridge, 1818.
PB6/432	Letter from a Mr Thomas dated 2nd March 1844 regarding building flood gates at Wadebridge to dam the river.

Probate Records

AP/J/154/ 1-4	Will of George Juell, St Teath, Hellier, 1612 (microfiche) Left 5s. for the maintenance of Wade-Bridge.

National Archives, Kew

SC6/821/11	John Lovibond, license to draw stone from Penmayne, Ministers' Accounts, 1st & 2nd Edward IV, 1461-3.
C66/1382/m24	Sale to William Tipper and Robert Dawe, the chapels at either side of Wade-Bridge, Calendar of Patent Rolls 34th Elizabeth, part 4 m24, 1591.
C1/59/309	Chancery Records, Six Clerks Office, John, son of John Raskarrek v John Forde, executor of John Lovibond, clerk, executor of Thomas Rowe chaplin: Detention of deeds to Land at Lamaill, Cornwall.
STAC 2/18	Court of Star Chamber, Riotous Assault on Wade-Bridge, Tredeneck v Wolcoke, 1542-3.
STAC 2/18/3	Court of Star Chamber, Riotous Assault on Wade-Bridge, Tredeneck v Wolcoke, 1542-3.
STAC 2/18/5	Court of Star Chamber, Riotous Assault on Wade-Bridge, Tredeneck v Wolcoke, 1542-3.
STAC 2/31/11	Court of Star Chamber, Riotous Assault on Wade-Bridge, Tredeneck v Wolcoke, 1542-3.
STAC 2/18/22	Court of Star Chamber, Riotous Assault on Wade-Bridge, Tredeneck v Wolcoke, 1542-3.
STAC 2/18/255	Court of Star Chamber, Riotous Assault on Wade-Bridge, Tredeneck v Wolcoke, 1542-3.
REQ 3/20	Court of Requests: Miscellanea, Geo Wolcock v John Tredeneck, et al (bill), 1542-3.
E112 07/200	Bills & Answers Etc. Elizabeth I. Reference to selling St Michael's Chapel to William Tipper and Robert Dawe, membranes 1 and 8, 1542-43.
SP 12/118 f.105	Domestic State Papers Elizabeth I. Examination of Cuthbert Maine prior to his execution. Gale document number MC4304187867.
SP 12/118 f.106	Names of Papists indicted with Cuthbert Mayne. Gale document number MC4304187868

Stoate, T. L.   1985 *Cornwall Subsidies in the reign of Henry VIII 1524 and 1543 and the benevolence of 1545.* Almondsbury, Bristol.

Stoate, T. L.   1987 *The Cornwall Military Survey 1522 with loan Books and Tinners Muster Roll c1535.*, Almondsbury, Bristol.

British Library - Civil War Documents

Moderate Intelligencer (1645), London, England. March 5th 1646, 17th-18th century Burley Newspaper Collection. Gale document number Z2001391349.

Kingdomes Weekly Intelligencer, London, England. March 2nd 1646 to March 10th 1646, 17th-18th century Burley Newspaper Collection. Gale document number Z2001381805.

Perfect Diurnall of some Passages in Parliament, London, England, March 9th 1646, 17th-18th century Burley Newspaper Collection. Gale document number Z2000099815.

II   *Newspaper references*

Royal Cornwall Gazette, 14th March 1818 - Requests for Tenders to re-build the parapet walls.

West Briton & Cornwall Advertiser, 3rd January 1845- report of the Cornwall Epiphany Sessions.

West Briton & Cornwall Advertiser, 4th July 1845 - report of the Cornwall Midsummer Sessions.

West Briton & Cornwall Advertiser, 17th October 1845 - report of the Cornwall Michaelmas Sessions.

West Briton & Cornwall Advertiser, 9th January 1846 - report of the Cornwall Epiphany Sessions.

West Briton & Cornwall Advertiser, 3rd July 1846 - report of the Cornwall Midsummer Sessions, 'Two plans to widen Wade-Bridge.

West Briton & Cornwall Advertiser, 31st July 1845 - 'To engineers and Architects' invitation to submit plans for the widening of Wade-Bridge.

West Briton & Cornwall Advertiser, 23rd October 1846 - report of the Cornwall Michaelmas Sessions, Two further plans to widen Wade-Bridge.

West Briton & Cornwall Advertiser, 5th January 1847 - report of the Cornwall Epiphany Sessions, Consideration of plans.

Royal Cornwall Gazette, 8th January 1847 - report of the Cornwall Epiphany Sessions, six plans submitted.

Royal Cornwall Gazette, 9th April 1847 - report of the Cornwall Easter Sessions, tenders for first widening.

West Briton & Cornwall Advertiser, 2nd July 1847 - report of the Cornwall Midsummer Sessions, Iron Bridge rejected.

West Briton & Cornwall Advertiser, 16th July 1847 - Request for tenders for widening Wade-Bridge.

West Briton & Cornwall Advertiser, 16th July 1847 - 'Thunder Storm and Destructive Flood'.

Royal Cornwall Gazette, 6th August 1847 - report of Cornwall Adjorned Sessions – widening suspended until the Epiphany Sessions 1849.

West Briton & Cornwall Advertiser, 9th January 1852 - report of the Cornwall Epiphany Sessions.

West Briton & Cornwall Advertiser, 2nd July 1852 - report of the Cornwall Midsummer Sessions, Contract to Messrs. Nicholls, Webster and Bate.

West Briton & Cornwall Advertiser, 22nd October 1852 - report of the Cornwall Michaelmas Sessions.

Royal Cornwall Gazette, 19th November 1852 - Public Notice advertising sale of Trust Property.

West Briton & Cornwall Advertiser, 7th January 1853 - report of the Cornwall Epiphany Sessions, Progress report on first widening.

Royal Cornwall Gazette, 7th January 1853 – report of the Cornwall Epiphany Sessions, incessant rains, nine arches completed on one side.

Royal Cornwall Gazette, 22nd April 1853, Public Notice, asking if anyone has a claim on the Wade-Bridge Trust.

West Briton & Cornwall Advertiser, 1st July 1853 - report of the Cornwall Midsummer Sessions, Progress report on first widening.

West Briton & Cornwall Advertiser, 21st July 1853 - report of the Cornwall Midsummer Sessions, first widening completed, accounts reported.

Royal Cornwall Gazette, 21st October 1853 - report of the Cornwall Michaelmas Sessions, First widening completed, accounts presented.

West Briton & Cornwall Advertiser, 21st October 1853 - report of the Cornwall Michaelmas Sessions.

Royal Cornwall Gazette, 11th November 1853 - Letter to the Editor requesting tablet with inscription on the history of the Wade-Bridge and provision of a gas lamp for the bridge.

Royal Cornwall Gazette, 25th November 1853 - Letter to the Editor.

Royal Cornwall Gazette, 9th December 1853 - Letter to the Editor.

Royal Cornwall Gazette, 23th December 1853 - Letter to the Editor.

West Briton & Cornwall Advertiser, 6th January 1854 - report of the Cornwall Epiphany Sessions, Discussion about Tablet or Inscription and gas lamp for the bridge.

Royal Cornwall Gazette, 6th January 1854 - report of the Cornwall Epiphany Sessions, Discussion about Tablet or Inscription and gas lamp for the bridge.

West Briton & Cornwall Advertiser, 20th October 1854 - report of the Cornwall Michaelmas Sessions.

Royal Cornwall Gazette, 5th January 1855 - Interest from Wadebridge Fund to be paid to Wadebridge Gas Light Co.

West Briton & Cornwall Advertiser, 17th October 1856 - report of the Cornwall Michaelmas Sessions.

West Briton & Cornwall Advertiser, 21st October 1869 - The Encroachment on the County Property at Wadebridge.

Royal Cornwall Gazette, 9th April 1880 - report of the Cornwall Easter Sessions, 'The Obstruction of the river at Wadebridge'.

Western Morning News & Mercury, 5th January 1925 - Ancient Bridges, Survivals in the West, A Plea for Preservation by Charles G Henderson.

Cornish Guardian, 20th February 1925 - The bridge at Wadebridge by Old boy, B.C.S.

Cornish Guardian, 26th January 1928 - The building of Wadebridge by Charles Henderson.

Western Morning News & Mercury, 23rd May 1928 - 'Veritable death Trap' Waiting for fatality in order to justify expenditure.

Cornish Guardian, 21st March 1935 - Wadebridge dam scheme: Question to be reconsidered, some difficulties suggested.

Cornish Guardian, 14th March 1935 - Wadebridge Improvements Schemes.

Cornish Guardian, 21st January 1935 - Wadebridge 15th Century Bridge, some suggestions for improvement.

Cornish Guardian, 24th January 1935 - Proposed dam at Wadebridge.

Cornish Guardian, 31st January 1935 - Fifteenth century bridge: A proposed improvement at Wadebridge.

Cornish Guardian, 7th February 1935 - Wadebridge swimming pool: Scheme turned down by parish council.

Cornish Guardian, 28th February 1935 - Improving Wadebridge bridge.

Cornish Guardian, 28th March 1935 - Letters to the editor, Wadebridge Jubilee suggestions.

Cornish Guardian, 18th April 1935 - Wadebridge Parish Council: The Dam across the river.

Cornish Guardian, 2nd May 1935 - County Highways Meeting.

Western Morning News, 11th October 1952 - 'Council approves method of widening bridge'.

Western Morning News, 13th October 1952 - 'Widening of bridge at Wadebridge' Letter from Wadebridge Old Cornwall Society.

Western Morning News, 15th October 1952 - Two photographs of cars passing on Wade-Bridge.

Western Morning News, 30th April 1954 - 'Wider Bridge better than Bypass'.

Western Morning News, 14th May 1955 - Bridge at Wadebridge, A Scandal RDC told'.

Western Morning News, 11th June 1955 - 'Bridge must be widened, Ministry told again'.

Cornish Guardian, 3rd November 1955 - 'Was it built on Rock or on Wool? Lovibond's bridge at Wadebridge and modern needs'.

Western Morning News, 9th November 1955 - 'Bridge ought to be wider'.

Western Morning News, 10th December 1955 - 'Bore holes to be sunk near bridge, Wadebridge widening explored'.

Western Morning News, 14th April 1956 - 'Bridge widening'.

Western Morning News, 4th May 1956 -Photograph of trial borings into the river downstream.

Western Morning News, 3rd October 1956 - 17 accidents on or at approaches to bridge.

Western Morning News, 10th November 1956 – 'Rural Council against new bridge over Camel'.

Western Morning News, 26th November 1956 - Letters regarding proposal for footbridge.

Western Morning News, 29th November 1956 - New bridge 300ft downstream.

Western Morning News, 9th April 1957 - 'Another request for footbridge'.

Western Morning News, 13th April 1957 - 'Ministry Reply on Bridge plan still awaited – RDC criticism over delay'.

Western Morning News, 11th May 1957- ' Bridge widening plan, safety comes first'.

Western Morning News, 14th September 1957 - 'Minister hears about problem at Wadebridge'.

Western Morning News, 31st December 1957 - 'Children cross in danger'.

Western Morning News, 15th February 1958 - 'Bridge Widening'.

Western Morning News, 10th May 1958 - 'Cracks in the old bridge at Wadebridge'.

Western Morning News, 31st May 1958 - Repairs and re-pointing of the bridge.

Western Morning News, 16th October 1958 - Photograph of scaffolding on bridge for re-pointing.

Western Morning News, 13th November 1958 - Photograph of re-pointing.

Western Morning News, 15th October 1960 - 'Bridge widening will start in June next year'.

Western Morning News, 29th March 1961- 'Start agreed on bridge widening'.

Western Morning News, 13th May 1961 - 'Ancient bridge widening may start in June'.

Western Morning News, 10th June 1961 - Bridge widening scheme delay criticised – Council disappointment'.

Western Morning News, 29th July 1961 - 'Bridge scheme delay not deliberate'.

Western Morning News, 8th November 1961 - 'Reply to MP on bridge criticism'.

Cornish Guardian, 25th January 1962 - No progress on Widening scheme for Wadebridge: Lack of action by Ministry of Transport – concern over delays.

Cornish Guardian, 6th February 1962 - 500 ton ship's second visit to Wadebridge, negotiating the Camel estuary.

Western Morning News, 10th February 1962 - 'Problems of Bridge work solved'.

Cornish Guardian, 15th February 1962 - News of plan to widen bridge over the river Camel: Ministry's letter to Wadebridge Rural Council.

Western Morning News, 16th March 1962 - 'Work to start on bridge at Wadebridge'.

Western Morning News, 23rd March 1962 - 'Wadebridge Bridge mystery solved'.

Cornish Guardian, 1st March 1962 - Contract Awarded for widening bridge over the river Camel: Wadebridge scheme will take about 15 months to complete.

Cornish Guardian, 15th March 1962 - Widening the bridge will be spectacular: Firm's work plan to be based on what is found in river bed at Wadebridge.

Cornish Guardian, 29th March 1962 - Search for stone to match old section of bridge: Work starts at Wadebridge on new structure beside the old.

Cornish Guardian, 5th April 1962 - Matching old and new stones, Letter to the editor by the Revd. B B Clarke of Padstow.

Western Morning News, 19th April 1962 - Photograph of builders laying deck of Bailey Bridge for pedestrians.

Cornish Guardian, 23rd April 1962 - Bridge-widening, two weeks ahead of scheme: despite high tides on river Camel.

Cornish Guardian, 23rd April 1962 - Three contracts keep Granite Quarries busy at St Breward: London and Wadebridge schemes mean overtime at Hantergantick.

Western Morning News, 27th April 1962 - 'Wadebridge Plan, temporary footpath completed'.

Cornish Guardian, 13th June 1962 - 'Bridge-Widening ahead of Contract time'.

Cornish Guardian, 12th July 1962 - 'Major Operation' in progress at Wadebridge.

Western Morning News, 17th July 1962 - 'First piles of Bridge sunk into river bed, Wadebridge scheme begins'.

Cornish Guardian, 23rd August 1962 - 'Bridge-Widening two weeks ahead of schedule'.

Cornish Guardian, 20th September 1962 - 'Piles for new piers of bridge, driven 40ft into river bed: Wadebridge work, ahead of schedule, will take another year'.

Western Morning News, 21st September 1962 -'First new bridge arches in place'.

Cornish Guardian, 8th November 1962 - Steel Rods will bind new concrete arches by Lovibond bridge: Pile driving completed in widening operation at Wadebridge.

Western Morning News, 29th November 1962 - Photograph showing new concrete arches.

Cornish Guardian, 6th December 1962 - Good weather aids bridge widening.

Cornish Guardian, 7th February 1963 - Work on bridge widening should be finished before Autumn: Wadebridge scheme on schedule despite weather.

Cornish Guardian, 18th April 1963 - Proposed bridge plaque criticised by Wadebridge RDC: Ministry asked to change wording.

Western Morning News, 11th May 1963 - Two photographs showing new parapets being built.

Western Morning News, 2nd August 1963 – 'Bridge is six weeks ahead of schedule'.

Cornish Guardian, 8th August 1963 – 'Bridge widening nearly complete, Easter Traffic Flow at Wadebridge'.

Western Morning News, 17th August 1963 – 'Widening of Old Bridge completed'.

Cornish Guardian, 22nd August 1963 – Rebuilding the island at Wadebridge: To get stronger tidal flow on either side of the bridge.

Cornish Guardian, 22nd August 1963 – 'Bridge widening scheme complete'.

Wadebridge Post, 24th August 1963 – 'Bridge widening is complete'.

Cornish Guardian, 20th February 1969 – Photograph of Wade-Bridge in the snow showing the pedestrian refuges with flower borders.

III Secondary Sources

Anon, 1881. *A Picturesque guide to North Cornwall*, Cater, Westgate Street, Launceston.

Anon, 1884. *A Guide to North Cornwall*, Cornish and Devon Printing Company, Launceston.

Anon, 1935. *Wadebridge Jubilee Souvenir*, Progress Association.

Anon, 1962. *Town Hall and Community Centre, re-opening ceremony pamphlet*, Wadebridge Parish Council.

Beresford, M, 1988. *New towns of the Middle Ages*, 2nd. Ed. Alan Sutton Publishing.

Black, A, & Black, C, 1864. *Black's Guide to the Duchy of Cornwall*, Adam & Charles Black, Edinburgh.

Bartlett, J, 1996. *Ships of North Cornwall*, Tabb House, Padstow.

Bartlett, M, 2004. 'A Bridge Story', *North Cornwall Advertiser*, April issue, Wadebridge.

Blackwall, A, 1985. *Historic Bridges of Shropshire*, Shropshire Libraries and the Highway and Transport Department, Shropshire County Council.

Beresford, M, 1988. *New towns of the Middle Ages*, Sutton Publishing Ltd.

Besley, H, c1852. *The Route Book of Cornwall: A Guide for the Stranger and Tourist*, Directory Office, Exeter.

Bond, T, 1823. *East and West Looe*, J. Nichols & Son, London.

Borlase, W, 1758. *The Natural History of Cornwall*.

Bray, D, 1983. *Stories of the North Cornish Coast*, Dyllansow Truran, Redruth.

Britton, J, and Brayley, E W, 1801. *The Beauties of England and Wales, or Delineations topographical, historical and descriptive of each county.*

Browne, A L, 1904. *Corporation Chronicles*, being some account of the Ancient Corporations of East Looe and of West Looe, J Smith, Plymouth.

Burn-Murdoch, R, 2001. *St Ives Bridge and Chapel*, The Friends of Norris Museum.

Carew, R, 1602. *Survey of Cornwall*, Ed. F. F. Halliday 1953, A. Melrose Ltd. London.

Coates, M, 1963. *Cornwall in the great Civil War and Interregum 1642-1660*, D Bradford Barton Ltd., Truro.

Cook, M, 1998. *Medieval Bridges*, Shire Publications, Risborough.

Cooke, G A, 1805. *Topography of Great Britain: British Traveller's Directory and travelling companion*, London.

Cruse, J B, 1982. *The Long Bridge of Barnstaple*, Aycliffe Press Ltd., Barnstaple.

Dudley, D, 1954. 'The demolition of Riverside House, Wadebridge' *Devon and Cornwall Notes and Queries*, XXVI.

Duffy, E, 1992. *The Stripping of the Altars*, Yale University Press, Newhaven and London.

Dunkin, E H W, 1882. *Monumental Brasses of Cornwall*, Spottiswoode & Co., London.

Edwards, C, 1981. Ed. 'A Visit to Cornwall in 1755 by William Wynne', *Journal of the Royal Institution of Cornwall*, NS **VIII** pt4. 338-349.

Fiennes, C, 1698. *Through England on a Side Saddle: in the time of William and Mary*, Tour - Lands End to Winchester.

Folliott-Stokes, A G, 1928. *The Cornish Coast and Moors*, Stanley Paul & Co. Ltd., London.

Fox, H S A and Padel, O J, 2000. *The Cornish Lands of the Arundells of Lanherne, Fourteenth to Sixteenth centuries*, Devon & Cornwall Record Society.

Gilbert, C S, 1817. *An Historical Survey of the county of Cornwall*, J. Congdon, Plymouth.

Gray, T, 1990. Ed. *Early Stuart Mariners and Shipping*, Devon and Cornwall Record Society.

Gray, T, 2000. Ed. *Cornwall: The Traveller's Tales*, The Mint Press, Exeter.

Hals, W, 1736. *Parochial History of Cornwall*.

Halliday, F E, 1953. *The Survey of Cornwall*, Andrew Melrose, London.

Hatcher, J, 1970. *Rural Economy and Society in the Duchy of Cornwall 1300-1500*, Cambridge University Press.

Harris, R, 1933. *Up the Camel River*, The After Glow essays no.1, University of London.

Harrison, D, 2007. *The Bridges of Medieval England: Transport and Society 400-1800*, Oxford University Press, Oxford.

Henderson, C G, and Coates, H, 1972. Ed. *Old Cornish Bridges and Streams*, Bradford Barton, Truro.

Henderson, C G, 1924. Original mss of *The Ancient Bridges of Cornwall*, with some remarks upon the rivers, streams and ancient roads compiled from original sources. Courtney Library, Royal Institution of Cornwall.

Henderson, C G, 1963 Ed. *Essays in Cornish History*, A. L. Rowse and M. I Henderson Eds., Clarendon Press, Oxford.

Henderson, C G, 1928. Notes on Wade-Bridge (in an old account book with Wade Bridge and HP14 on its spine). Transcriptions of documents on Wade-Bridge, Courtney Library, Royal Institution of Cornwall.

Henderson, C G, and Jervoise, E, 1938. *Old Devon Bridges*, A Wheaton & Company, Exeter.

Herring, P, 1993. *An Archaeological Evaluation of St Michael's Mount*, Cornwall Archaeological Unit, Cornwall County Council.

Hingeston-Randolph, Rev. F C, Ed. 1901. *The Register of Thomas de Brantygham, Bishop of Exeter* (AD1370-1394) William Pollard, Exeter.

Hingeston-Randolph, Rev. F C, Ed. 1901. *The Register of Walter de Stapledone*, Bishop *of Exeter (AD1307-1326)* William Pollard, Exeter.

Holden, P, Herring, P, and Padel, O J, 2010. *The Lanhydrock Atlas: A complete reproduction of the 17th century Cornish Estate Maps*, Cornwall Editions and The National Trust.

Hoyle, R, 1983. *Old Wadebridge*, Westward Press, Wadebridge.

Hoyle, R, 1993. *Death on the Camel*, Gemini Productions, Burlawn, Wadebridge.

Hunt, R, 1903. *Popular Romances of the west of England or Drolls, Traditions and Superstitions of Cornwall*.

Langdon, A G, 2000. 'Notes on John Lovebond', *North Cornwall Advertiser*, October issue, Wadebridge.

Langley, M, and Small, E, 1984. *Estuary and River Ferries of South West England*, Waine Research Publication.

Leland, J, 1535-39. Leland's Itinerary published in *Parochial history of Cornwall* by Joseph Polsue., **IV**, Lake, Truro.

Lorigan, C, 2009. *Connections: Aspects of the History of North Cornwall*, Pengelly Press.

Luke, F, 2006. *Reminiscence of Wadebridge and the river Camel 1914 to 1945*, Eric Tatlow Ed. Wadebridge.

Lysons, D, & Lysons, S, 1814. *Magna Brittannia, Cornwall*, **III**, T. Cadell & W. Davies, London.

Maclean, Sir J, 1873-79. *The Parochial and Family of the Deanery of Trigg Minor*, **I, II, III**, Nicols & Son, London.

Mattingly, J, 2005. *Looking at Cornish Churches*, Tor Mark Press.

Mc Elroy, R A, 1929. *Blessed Cuthbert Mayne*, Sands and Co. London.

Murdoch, R B, 1988. *St Ives Bridge and chapel*, The Friends of the Norris Museum.

Murray, J, 1859. *Handbook for travellers in Devon and Cornwall*.

North, C, 2001. 'The Will and Inventory of Edward Arundell of Treveliew and Lanherne, 1539-1586', *Journal of the Royal Institution of Cornwall*, Truro.

Norway, A H, 1897. *Highways and Byways in Devon and Cornwall*, Macmillan & Co. Ltd., London.

Oliver, B W, 1938. 'The Long Bridge of Barnstaple', *Transactions of the Devonshire Association*, **LXX**, 193-197, pt. 1.

Oliver, B W, 1946. 'The Long Bridge of Barnstaple', *Transactions of the Devonshire Association*, **LXXIII**, 177-188, pt. 2.

Padel, O J, 1985. *Cornish Place-name Elements*, English Place-name Society, **VI-LVII**.

Padel, O J, 1988. *A Popular Dictionary of Cornish Place-Names*, Alison Hodge, Penzance.

Pearse, R, 1963. *The Ports and Harbours of Cornwall*, H. E. Warne Ltd., St Austell.

Peter, T, 1906. *A Compendium of the History and Geography of Cornwall*, Netherton & Worth, Truro.

Peter, T, 1909. *A Short History of Cornwall*, The Scholastic Trading Co. Ltd., Bristol.

Penaluna, W, 1848. *An Historical Survey of the County of Cornwall, vol. 1*, Helston.

Pierce, P, 2001. *Old London Bridge: The story of the Longest Inhabited Bridge in Europe*, Review, London.

Polsue, J, 1867-72. *The Parochial history of Cornwall*, **I, II, III, IV**, Lake, Truro.

Pevsner, N, 1951. *The Buildings of England: Cornwall*, Penguin Books, Harmondsworth.

Redding, C, 1842. *An Illustrated Itinerary of the County of Cornwall*, How & Parsons, London.

Rowse, A L, 1969. *Tudor Cornwall*, 2nd. Ed. Macmillian & Co. Ltd., London.

Rowse, A L, 1976. *A Cornishman Abroad*, Jonathan Cape, London.

Sedding, Mrs E, undated. *The Riverside House - A tale of Wadebridge*, Western Morning News, Plymouth.

Shepherd, P, 1980. *Historic Towns of Cornwall*, Cornwall Committee for Rescue Archaeology.

Stockdale, F W L, 1824. *Excursions in the County of Cornwall*, reprint 1972, D Bradford Barton Ltd. Truro.

Truscott, R P, 2005. *The Historic Bridges of Cornwall: The Ancient Monuments*, mss Courtney Library, Royal Institution of Cornwall, Truro.

Walker, J W, 1931. *A History of Maidenhead*, 2nd. Ed. The St Catherine Press, London.

Warner, Revd. R, 1809. *A Tour through Cornwall in the Autumn of 1808*, Wilkie and Robinson, London.

West, Revd. J, 1991. *St Breock and Wadebridge - A Contribution to a History of a Cornish Parish*, Dyllansow Truran, Redruth.

Westwood, J, 1992. *Albion: A Guide to Legendary Britain*, Grafton, Hammersmith, London.

White, W, 1855. *A Londoner's walk to the Land's End and trip to the Scilly Isles*, London, Chapman and Hall.

Whiting, F E, 1997. *The Long Bridge of Bideford - through the centuries*, with additions by P. Christie 3rd Ed. Bideford Bridge Trust.

Whelan, H, 1984. *Snow on the hedges - A life of Cuthbert Mayne*, Fowler Wright Books Ltd.

Wilkinson, J J, 1874. Ed. *Receipts and Expenses in the building of Bodmin Church*, AD *1469-72*, Camden Society.

Worcester, W, 1478. William of Worcester's Itinerary published in *Parochial history of Cornwall* by Joseph Polsue, IV, 93-112, Joseph Lake, Truro.